Pr̶ ̶ ̶ ̶ ̶ .or *Britain etc.*

'Entertaining and eye-popping facts leap out of Mark Easton's elegant hand-book on who we are. Social research blends with social history in this charming and erudite portrait of modern Britain' Polly Toynbee

'Easton doesn't go in for easy clichés . . . Setting each topic in its historical context, from Britain's obsession with bobbies on the beat to the resurgence of cheese-making, Easton looks beyond all the pomp and circumstance to offer a highly readable insight into a complex nation' *Financial Times*

'An eminently readable exposition of some of the things we take for granted every day. Mark Easton tells us something of who we are by looking at the ways we got here' Mark Radcliffe

Britain etc.

The Way We Live and How We Got There

MARK EASTON

**SIMON &
SCHUSTER**

London · New York · Sydney · Toronto · New Delhi

A CBS COMPANY

First published in Great Britain by Simon & Schuster UK Ltd, 2012
This paperback edition published 2013
A CBS COMPANY

Simon & Schuster UK Ltd
1st Floor
222 Gray's Inn Road
London
WC1X 8HB

www.simonandschuster.co.uk

Simon & Schuster Australia, Sydney
Simon & Schuster India, New Delhi

A CIP catalogue record for this book is available from the British Library

ISBN 978-1-84983-302-8

Typeset in Minion by M Rules
Printed and bound by CPI Group (UK) Ltd, Croydon, CR0 4YY

To Antonia

CONTENTS

Acknowledgements 1

Introduction 3

A is for Alcohol 7

B is for Bobbies 17

C is for Cheese 25

D is for Dogs 33

E is for Error 43

F is for Family 53

G is for Grass 63

H is for Happiness 77

I is for Immigration 89

J is for Justice 105

K is for Knives 115

L is for Learning 121

M is for Murder 133

N is for Numbers 145

O is for Opium 155

P is for Poverty 169

Q is for Queen 181

R is for Regions 191

S is for Silly Hats 205

T is for Toilet 213

U is for Umbrella 223

V is for Vegetables 231

W is for www 241

X is for XXXX 253

Y is for Youth 267

Z is for Zzzz 281

Further Reading 293

Index 310

ACKNOWLEDGEMENTS

This book grew in the crannies. It has been an interstitial project, squeezed into the tiny spaces between my (full-time) job and my (full-time) family. So, it simply could not have been written without the support and forbearance of my colleagues, my children and, above all, my wife.

Particular thanks go to Andrew Gordon who planted the seed, Jo Whitford who helped harvest and box the crop and Mike Jones who steered the cart to market. I am hugely grateful to Mike O'Connor, Malcolm Balen, John Kampfner, John Humphrys, Brian Higgs, among many others, who gave sane advice and welcome encouragement along the way. I must also mention my late father, Stephen Easton, whose genius as a bookman guided me even in his last days.

My children – Flora, Eliza, Annis and Ed – deserve recognition for generously putting up with my alphabetical obsessions as well as denial of access to the home computer. But greatest thanks go to my wife Antonia who was ally, advisor and inspiration. She helped me find the space to write and, just as importantly, told me when it was time to stop.

INTRODUCTION

As I write, Britain is trying to make sense of an extraordinary few years. Institutional scandals have rocked the pillars of our state: Parliament, the City, police and press. The country appears determined almost to purge itself, digging around in the alluvial mud of its recent history to unearth individual wrongdoers and establishment failure.

At the same time, Britain is reflecting on what's been called the glorious summer of 2012. People had expected the Queen's Diamond Jubilee and the London Olympics to present to the watching world a nostalgic retrospective of an ancient island people, resounding to the echoes of past glories while revealing the flaws of a declining nation, the whole sorry affair conducted in the rain.

They were right about the rain. But far from exposing mediocrity and incompetence, the summer's events portrayed a confident and successful country; a land of wonderful contradictions, simultaneously contemplative and daft, self-deprecating and clever, organised and whimsical, controlled and rebellious.

This is not a bad time, then, to consider contemporary Britain: what kind of place is it? Since first joining my local paper in 1978, I have attempted to answer that question by peering through a standard lens – the familiar perspective of daily news and current affairs.

But so often this blinkered view confounds rather than clarifies. The picture is neither wide enough nor detailed enough to grasp the real story. As the electronics salesman might put it, we need a 3D HD 55" plasma screen and we are watching on a 12" cathode ray tube telly. So, in thinking how to write this book, I sought inspiration from two pioneering British lens-masters who made it possible for people to see the world in new and wonderful ways.

The first I found at a Palo Alto ranch in June 1878, a wild-bearded man in a wide-brimmed hat. Under a bright Californian sky, crowds watched as Eadweard Muybridge took a series of photographs that, for the first time, revealed the mysteries of equine motion. The speed of a galloping horse was too fast for the naked eye to see precisely how the animal moved. Only by slowing the action down to a series of stop-motion frames, captured by a line of triggered cameras, was Muybridge able to answer the much-debated question as to whether all four hooves were ever airborne at the same time. (Answer: yes, but tucked under, not outstretched as many artists had assumed.)

The second of my photographic guides I discovered in his garden three decades later, behind a suburban home in north London. Percy Smith was working on a film that also allowed people to see the world in a new way. When *The Birth of a Flower* was shown to British cinemagoers in 1910, it is reported the audience broke into riotous applause. Smith's use of time-lapse photography achieved the opposite of Muybridge, accelerating the action of days into a few seconds. Plants bloomed before astonished eyes: hyacinths, lilies and roses. One journalist described the result as 'the highest achievement yet obtained in the combined efforts of science, art and enterprise'.

What would contemporary Britain look like through Muybridge's or Smith's lenses? Instead of just hyacinths or horses, I resolved to apply their techniques to numerous and varied aspects of British life: the time-lapse sweep through history and the stop-motion analysis of the crucial detail.

The alphabet would structure my journey but serendipity and curiosity would decide direction. The idea was not to stick to well-worn paths but to search for a better understanding of Britain wherever impulse led. So, yes, A was for alcohol – a stiff whisky to start me off. But my wandering inspired me to examine my homeland's relationship with foreigners and computers and vegetables and drugs and dogs and youth and silly hats and beggars and toilets and cheese, and more.

Some subjects may appear almost frivolous, but each strand of the national fabric I chose to follow revealed something unexpected, fascinating and profound. At times, the detail prompted me to laugh aloud; at others almost to despair. When woven together, the threads formed a coherent canvas, a portrait of contemporary Britain simultaneously inspiring and troubling. In the background, a weather-beaten landscape shaped by the glacial and seismic forces of history; in the foreground, a diverse crowd moving, eating, kissing, arguing, laughing, working, drinking, worrying, studying and wearing silly hats.

After more than thirty years chronicling Britain's story for newspapers, radio and television, I thought I had a handle on what the place is like. But my travels have allowed me, as Eadweard and Percy promised, to see the country in a new way, to go beyond the standard-lens view of news and current affairs. It is a picture of Britain etc.

A IS FOR ALCOHOL

When I first arrived in Fleet Street in the early 1980s as a starry-eyed young radio journalist, my initiation began with a colleague leading me to the pub. It was barely opening time as we walked into the King and Keys. There, amid the smoky gloom, I was introduced to one of the newspaper world's most celebrated figures, the editor of the *Daily Telegraph*, Bill Deedes. The great man sized me up. 'You will have a malt whisky, dear boy,' he said. I started to splutter something about how it was only eleven in the morning, but he quickly closed the discussion by adding, 'a large one.'

It would be years before I fully understood the gesture: I was being blooded for an industry where alcohol was as much a part of the process as ink and paper. But it was also an indication of something apparently incredible: that Britain's drink problems should not be blamed on drink.

In those days every Fleet Street title had its pub: the *Telegraph* occupied the King and Keys; the now defunct *News of the World* drank at 'The Tip' (The Tipperary); the *Daily Express* was resident at 'The Poppins' (The Popinjay); the *Mirror* pub was known as 'The Stab In the Back' (The White Hart). Drinking was ritual and tribal. Tales of drunken fights and indiscretions were sewn into the colourful tapestry of Grub Street legend, inebriated misadventures to be reverentially recounted and embellished. Pickled hacks could be found propping up many of the bars, victims treated with the respect of war veterans.

Newspaper people drank around the clock; magistrates had been persuaded to adjust local licensing hours so that city workers could enjoy a glass or two of ale at any time of the day or night. The social wreckage from alcohol was strewn all over Fleet Street – broken marriages, stunted careers and inflamed livers. The British press were pioneers of 24-hour opening and regarded themselves as experts on its potential consequences years before the 2001 General Election, when Tony Blair wooed young voters with a promise on a beer mat: 'cdnt give a XXXX 4 lst ordrs? Vote labour on thrsdy 4 xtra time.'

By that point, of course, the Fleet Street presses had been dismantled, staff had scattered across the capital and a sandwich in front of a computer terminal had replaced the once traditional liquid lunch. Small wonder, perhaps, that journalists were so sceptical about Labour's idea to introduce a family-friendly cafe-style drinking culture to Britain.

The government's argument was that our obvious problems with alcohol stemmed, in part, from outdated and austere licensing laws. Ministers pointed to southern Europe where a relaxed attitude resulted, it was said, in a more mature relationship with drink. Instead of booze being consumed between strict opening and closing times behind frosted glass, they proposed new light-touch legislation promoting freedom, choice and 'the further development within communities of our rich culture of live music, dancing and theatre'.

Almost without exception, the press thought the idea was bonkers. Far from replacing drunkenness and social disorder with community dance and drama, they predicted 24-hour opening would mean 24-hour mayhem. Our towns and city centres, already resembling war zones on Friday and Saturday nights, would become permanent no-go areas.

Britain's relationship with alcohol, critics argued, was built upon a northern European beer-drinking tradition entirely at odds with the habits of the wine-sipping south. Just look at what happens, it was pointed out, when UK tourists arrive in Spain, France and Italy to experience their foreign ways. Entire television series had been commissioned solely to document the shameful alcohol-soaked fallout from this culture clash. The conclusion was obvious: it might be fine for Rome but it could never work in Romford.

There is, though, a huge hole in this argument – the common but mistaken belief that alcohol *causes* violence. Indeed, experts argue that it is this misconception, the assumption that drinking is responsible for aggression and antisocial behaviour, that is the true root of our problems.

Early evidence that boozy Britain's lager louts and bingeing yobs might not be the monstrous creations of the evil drink can be traced to flower-strewn California in 1969. Two social scientists at UCLA, Craig MacAndrew and Robert Edgerton, were looking at how people from different cultures react when they drink. They argued that, if alcohol itself is responsible for drunken behaviour, there should be little variation between cultures. To their surprise, they discovered wide differences. In some societies drinking made people passive; in others they became aggressive. What was more, if the cultural belief was that alcohol made people less inhibited they did indeed become noisy and extrovert. If the cultural belief was that drinking made you quiet and depressed, drinkers reacted that way instead.

MacAndrew and Edgerton's book, *Drunken Comportment*, introduced readers to the Urubu Indians of Brazil – ferocious head-hunters when sober, but partial to a song and a dance with their enemies when drunk. Then there was the morose and sombre Aritama tribe of northern Colombia, who grew more so on rum, their favourite drink. 'All conversation stops,' the authors found, 'and gloominess sets in.'

The conclusion was that the way people behave when drunk is determined 'not by alcohol's toxic assault upon the seat of moral judgement', but by how their society responds to drunkenness. The book closes with a homily: 'Since societies, like individuals, get the sorts of drunken comportment that they allow, they deserve what they get.' Britain's drink problems, it was suggested, were not the fault of drink but of Britain.

Drunken Comportment inspired dozens of sociologists and anthropologists to get legless with different tribes and cultures around the world. Scientists who went boozing with the Bolivian Camba found that they regularly consume huge quantities of almost pure alcohol to the point of falling over. The tribe successfully demonstrated to the research team that they have absolutely no concept of moderate or responsible drinking. And yet alcoholism and antisocial or violent behaviour are completely unknown to them.

Another intrepid team of academics headed for Cuba, where traditional standards of behaviour require drinkers to down large amounts of alcohol but hold their own in fast-flowing conversations. The researchers hung about in Cuban bars and recorded how customers rarely slurred their speech or fell off their chairs despite being very drunk.

Research demonstrated that it was a similar story at Danish dinner parties, Georgian ritual feasts, the drinking contests of Laos and (until the Europeans arrived) the cactus-wine ceremonies of the Papago of Mexico. In all these situations, people drank until they were completely plastered, but in none was there the kind of violence and antisocial behaviour familiar to the residents of a British market town on a Friday night.

The link between alcohol and aggression did not exist in the majority of societies investigated. Behaviour varied even within contemporary Western culture. One piece of research observed what happened when northern European tourists went drinking in a southern European setting. At one restaurant table, a

Scandinavian would be drinking a bottle of wine; at the next, a Spaniard or an Italian would consume an identical bottle. In most cases, the experts noted a striking difference: the northern visitors showed classic signs of intoxication, while the locals seemed unaffected.

Scientists attempted to replicate these field observations in the laboratory. In the early 1970s, psychologists at Washington State University somehow managed to recruit young male under-graduates for a series of experiments involving free alcohol. On arrival in a simulated bar room in the basement of the department, half the eager guinea pigs were given what they thought was vodka and tonic while the rest were told they were drinking only tonic water. What they didn't know was that the half of those who thought they were drinking vodka received only tonic, and the half of those who were told they had a glass of tonic were actually drinking alcohol. The concentrations and quantities of alcohol served were at the brink of what people may detect, so that even the most experienced drinker would be unlikely to spot any deception.

The students were then put through a series of tests to meas-ure how drunk they felt and observe their behaviour. Subjects who drank tonic water but thought it was alcohol showed most of the 'classic' symptoms of intoxication, while those who drank alcohol but thought it was tonic water did not. Similar results were later recorded in tests for aggression and sexual arousal.

The evidence was compelling. The way people behave when they are drunk is largely determined by the way their society expects them to behave. It is less a chemical and more a cultural phenomenon.

The startling idea that there is nothing inevitable about the link between drink and disorder reached Britain in the mid-1990s and began to filter into Whitehall thinking. The Home Office Drugs Prevention Office advised ministers that, while most violent crime was committed by people who are drunk, 'there is room to argue that this is a culturally mediated effect rather than a necessary effect of alcohol.'

This finding probably raised no more than an eyebrow among the few Members of Parliament who read the report, but it should have posed profound questions for policy. What was it about British culture that caused drunks to become aggressive and unpleasant while their counterparts in other countries just fell asleep?

Social scientists had been pondering the same question and came up with a theory. Alcohol, it was suggested, gives drinkers a time out from normal sober behaviour, permission to behave in ways that would otherwise be unacceptable. There are still social limits on how and how far a drunk may stray, but these limits vary between cultures. In some societies, notably in northern Europe and North America, alcohol is imbued with a malevolent power to lead people into sin. Its effects are often likened to possession by evil spirits, echoing the 'demon drink' warnings of the nineteenth-century temperance preachers.

Anthropologists draw a distinction between what they call temperance and non-temperance cultures, suggesting a link between people's behaviour and their belief that alcohol contains some dark diabolical force. In 1889, the English journalist George Sims, an advocate of the temperance movement, wrote about the appalling living conditions that drove the poor to alcohol. 'The drink dulls every sense of shame,' he said, 'and reduces them to the level of brutes.' A century later, heavy metal rocker Ozzy Osbourne recorded these lyrics on his album *No Rest For The Wicked*:

I'll watch you lose control,
Consume your very soul.
I'll introduce myself today,
I'm the demon alcohol.

In Britain, a country that has long questioned the moral status of alcohol, drinking has traditionally taken place in enclosed bars, with opaque windows and solid doors often adorned with details of the strict licence operating within. Cross the threshold and the rules change. In southern Europe, drink enjoys a very different status – unremarkable and morally neutral. Bars are open and drinking is highly visible, spilling into and merging with everyday life. As one academic study of drinking habits in Madrid put it, 'the consumption of alcohol is [as] integrated into common behaviours as sleeping or eating.'

Britain's relationship with booze has been described as an 'intoxication culture': while controlling alcohol more strictly, we are more accepting of drunkenness. Although the UK courts operate on the principle that drunkenness is no excuse for criminal behaviour, even more fundamental to the common law tradition is that there must be criminal intent as well as a criminal act. If it can be argued that intoxication affected the capacity of the accused to form criminal intent, judges may rule that being drunk reduced the crime.

For instance, a 2005 Court of Appeal judgment against a murder conviction stated, 'if the defendant ... claims to be so intoxicated that he is experiencing hallucinations and imagines that he is fighting giant snakes then he can be guilty only of manslaughter.'

The Canadian Supreme Court wrestled with a similar issue in the 1990s when considering a sexual assault in which the 65-year-old victim was in a wheelchair and the 72-year-old perpetrator was blind drunk. The judges emerged with the concept of drunken automatism, ruling that extreme drunkenness could be a defence. Such was the political furore that followed, however, that Parliament passed a new law declaring intoxicated violence to be a breach of the standard of reasonable care that Canadians owe each other.

A Home Office research study in 2003 concluded that, for many young Britons, fighting while drunk was seen to be an inevitable fact of life. The report quotes a young woman saying: 'I have a drink and I just want to fight anyone.' A young man agrees:

'It is part of the way of life. It is part of our heritage. Like football matches, you always get a fight at the end.' Another says: 'Everybody does it, it is the way the world is.'

But is it? Are Britain's booze habits so engrained within our psyche that it is hopeless to imagine we could ever import a culture of family-friendly cafe-style drinking? Indeed, might our troublesome lager-lout habits spread to infect other countries? That was certainly the view of the Oxford-based Social Issues Research Centre (SIRC), which in 2000 presented a detailed report to the European Commission warning that economic and political convergence would almost certainly result in 'a shift towards the negative beliefs and expectations associated with problematic drinking'. The report pointed out that, in some parts of Europe, it was already happening.

In Spain, for example, young local males were found to have adopted the antisocial behaviour of beer-swilling British holidaymakers. Italian youth were also said to be adopting 'alien' drinking patterns. It was not as simple as wine versus lager, the report was quick to point out. 'This has nothing to do with any intrinsic properties of the beverages themselves – beer, for example, may be associated with disorderly behaviour in some cultures or subcultures and with benign sociability in others.'

The European Commissioners were urged to introduce immediate and continuous monitoring of shifts and changes in mainstream European drinking habits. Cultural convergence, they were warned, had 'not been accompanied by an adoption of the more harmonious behaviour and attitudes associated with wine-drinking cultures'. In other words, it appeared that Britain's bad behaviour was spreading south rather than cafe culture moving north. The real danger was that government responses would make matters much worse.

Professor Dwight Heath, an American anthropologist and one of the foremost experts on alcohol's place within different cultures, has been railing against the 'myths' that have underpinned social policy for decades – not least the common view that the way to reduce problematic alcohol-induced behaviour is to reduce consumption of alcohol.

In an essay entitled 'Flawed policies from flawed premises: pseudo-science about alcohol and drugs', he explained how the intellectual cornerstone justifying government policies to control the availability of alcohol was a report from a meeting of scientists held in Finland in 1975. They had been studying death from liver cirrhosis in different countries and found, unsurprisingly perhaps, that the amount people drink has a bearing on their health.

This link between liver disease and alcohol consumption morphed into a more general assertion that if you reduce the amount people drink, you will reduce all alcohol-induced harms. And yet, when Professor Heath checked with some of the experts who had gathered in Finland, he found that that is not what they had been suggesting at all. Four of the original panel subsequently published a paper asserting that there were actually very few links between the amount people drink and the incidence of social problems. In fact, they went even further, arguing that the correlations between consumption and antisocial behaviour were 'frequently negligible or negative'.

The science justifying alcohol control was as thin as the head on a pint of light ale and yet it became the foundation upon which policies at the United Nations, in the United States and Europe were based. Professor Heath wondered why it was that the 'cautious and nuanced conclusions' from the Finnish forum were converted into a 'dogmatic and slanted' guide to global policy-making. 'When the Director General of the World Health Organization (in 1978) asserted unequivocally that "any reduction in per capita consumption will be attended by a significant decrease in alcohol-related problems" too many journalists, bureaucrats, and other non-specialists unquestioningly accepted that apparently authoritative judgement,' Heath wrote.

So how should politicians respond to the apparent spread of British 'intoxication culture'? The advice to Europe's leaders from social scientists and anthropologists seems to be that the 'control' model is counter-productive and they would be much better basing policy on a 'socio-cultural' model instead. As the authors of the SIRC report put it: 'A new approach is required, based on the recognition that different European cultures have different levels and kinds of alcohol-related problems, that these problems are directly related to specific patterns of beliefs and expectations and that measures designed to preserve and promote more positive beliefs are most likely to be effective.' The experts had a clear message for Britain: what matters is not what you drink but what you think.

The British government did introduce more relaxed licensing laws and, despite all the dire warnings of social collapse, analysis later suggested drinking patterns and behaviour barely changed. People scratched their heads and wondered why. No one thought to question whether the central assumption, the driving force behind our nation's relationship with alcohol, might be built on a fundamental misunderstanding.

I imagine myself back in the King and Keys thirty years ago. It is a few minutes after opening time and Bill Deedes is presenting me with a large glass of single malt. This, I now believe, was not the act of some mischievous old hack trying to prod me down the road to ruin – quite the reverse. He knew that the way to help the young man in front of him survive Fleet Street and its dysfunctional relationship with drink was to strip alcohol of its dark magic and its dubious morality. Scotch at 11am? Chin-chin!

B IS FOR BOBBIES

With his classic custodian helmet and simple truncheon, the British bobby is seen internationally as a charming symbol of this country's nostalgia for the values and headgear of the Victorian era (see 'S is for Silly Hats'). Tourists from around the world flock to have their photograph taken beside the quaint, familiar form of a policeman on his beat. His slow even plod contrasts with the frantic dash of tooled-up cops elsewhere, a solid reliable pulse setting the tempo for our nation's soundtrack.

It is not just foreign holidaymakers who love the bobby, of course. The British beat constable is regarded as a national treasure, clothed in the uniform of reassuring tradition and echoing the principles that coincided with imperial supremacy. I have listened to countless speeches from politicians demanding 'more bobbies on the beat', a phrase which for many in Britain instantly brings to mind the face of fictional TV cop PC George Dixon, who to this day has as much impact on criminal justice policy as any flesh-and-blood Home Secretary.

Dixon of Dock Green, eponymous hero of a television series that survived two decades from the mid-1950s, is shorthand for old-fashioned common sense, decency and humanity – values associated with a more straightforward age where ordinary coppers could clip mischievous urchins around the ear and, with a salute and a wink, restore order and calm to the streets. But Dixon's continuing influence stems, not from concern about policing or crime, but something more fundamental. It is about our changed relationship with our neighbours and our neighbourhood.

The original 'peelers' or 'bobbies' marched out of the station in 1829, shortly after Sir Robert Peel had created the first police force in London. Eight constables were dispatched to independent positions within the local area and ordered to walk around a small network of streets in a regular pattern. According to the instructions written by the capital's first police commissioner, Sir Charles Rowan, the constable 'should be able to see every part of his beat at least once in ten minutes or a quarter of an hour'.

However, it quickly became clear that this system of policing was, frankly, rubbish as a crime-fighting tool. Having constables trudging up to twenty miles a night in ill-fitting boots in all weathers cost a fortune and left officers exhausted. If the perception was that it prevented vandalism, prostitution and drunkenness, the reality was that a great many PC Plods were forced to retire early with the entry 'worn out' on their pension papers. Home Office research in 1984 revealed how inefficient the foot patrol was at catching criminals: 'A patrolling police officer could expect to pass within 100 yards of a burglary taking place roughly once every eight years. Even then they may not even realise that the crime is taking place.'

Nevertheless, the bobby on the beat remained the cornerstone of British policing for well over a century because, it was believed, he discouraged potential villains and made the law-abiding feel safer. The uniformed foot patrol was a comforting presence within what was busy public space, pounding the pavement and keeping a trained eye on all that was going on.

Reading George Dixon's police notebooks from the 1950s to the 1970s, however, would have revealed evidence of a transformation. In his early years patrolling Dock Green, nine out of ten households didn't own a car. People walked. Within twenty-five years, it was the other way around. Almost everybody drove. They left their front door and were quickly cocooned in their vehicles. On their return home, the risk of having to negotiate an encounter with a neighbour was reduced to a few seconds as they locked the car and briskly headed indoors to be reunited with another piece of technology that was changing the social dynamic – television. In 1951, virtually no one had a TV on Dixon's beat. By 1971, virtually no one was without access to the telly. Where previously crowds of people would walk to the pictures or the pub in the evening, now they stayed at home to stare at a flickering screen in the comfort of their own front room. It wasn't the bobby that was changing, it was the beat.

The arrival of the motorcar and the television depopulated the pavement and changed the status of the pedestrian. Towns and cities were redesigned around the needs of the driver, those on foot often forced underground into poorly lit tunnels and intimidating underpasses. The character of urban public space changed from common resource to the habitat of the excluded and the dangerous. 'Good evenin' all' would often have echoed along subterranean walkways without response, save the uncomfortable shuffling of a tramp trying to sleep in a corner. It was the mid-1960s when police chiefs ordered that Plod, too, should get behind the wheel. The retreat of the constable into his radio-equipped rapid response patrol car further changed society's relationship with the street.

The boundary between private and public might once have been described as the threshold between 'mine' and 'ours'. What Dixon witnessed was the shared tenure of his beat being transferred to a single faceless other. Once, residents would have proudly swept the pavement beyond their front gate. Now, people sweep their front path onto the pavement for someone else to clean up. The amount of litter dropped on our roads has increased five-fold since the 1960s, a simple measure of how respect for our public spaces has been lost.

The British are said to be uncomfortable with continental piazza culture: the ritual occupation of public space by all generations. It is all right for Italian, French or Spanish families to promenade around the town square on a sunny evening, but it would never work in Dock Green. Except that when people talk about the days when they could leave their front doors open, confident that trusted neighbours would be around to keep an eye, or take their evening constitutional without fear of being mugged, they are nostalgic for the days when we also routinely occupied our public spaces.

Britain may complain that the bobby abandoned the beat, but it was the beat that abandoned the bobby. In our search for security we fled the street, and in retreating we ended up feeling less safe. We have tried to restore our confidence with barbed wire, anti-climb paint and a million security cameras but the effect has been to make us even more fearful. I remember filming on an estate in Yorkshire where the central shopping area was dominated by a breezeblock structure prickling with razor wire and CCTV cameras, the entrance reached via a security turnstile. It turned out this was the community library. The more we emphasise the boundary between public and private space, the more vulnerable we feel.

Shared urban environments are a social safety valve, a place for people of all backgrounds to mingle on equal ground. London Mayor Boris Johnson once described public space as 'the glue that holds a city together'. It is the territory where trust and confidence are forged. When people call for the return of the bobby on the beat, it is both they mean. They want the reassurance they think a greater police presence will bring, but what they really crave is their streets back.

To some extent they have been given the first: the focus on neighbourhood policing, the re-introduction of foot patrols and the creation of community support officers. But the second is not something that the police alone can do. Indeed, research suggests they may make very little difference.

In the 1970s, police chiefs in Kansas tested the widely held theory that having more officers on the streets would cut crime and make people feel safer. They split up the city patrol squads: some areas had two or three times as many uniformed cops on the streets; in others officers only went out onto the beat if they were responding to calls; the rest carried on as normal. The results came as something of a shock. There was no difference in the crime rates between the three areas and local people felt no less fearful whichever kind of patrol they had.

Kansas is not Dock Green. The American officers were in cars, not on foot. But the research was seen as evidence of the limits to what beat officers could actually achieve. They rarely catch criminals, they may not deter much crime and they don't necessarily make people feel more relaxed. Indeed, the sight of uniforms can sometimes reinforce apprehension, a reminder of the threat from criminality.

In 2000, the Joseph Rowntree Housing Trust responded to the demands of their tenants for a bobby to patrol the North Yorkshire village of New Earswick. The trustees agreed to pay North Yorkshire Police £25,000 a year for a uniformed constable, who was contracted to contribute a visible presence in the streets and provide reassurance and a sense of security to the public. The scheme achieved the opposite. Both crime and the fear of crime increased, and residents' satisfaction with the local police declined. Evaluation of the project concluded that 'seeking solutions to problems of local order through a policing and security lens alone may serve to exacerbate residents' fears'.

This paradox has inspired some profound questions as to what the police are actually for and how we might measure success. Robert Peel famously said that the test of police efficiency was the absence of crime and disorder. On that basis, and taking account of the evidence from both recorded police crime figures and the British Crime survey, they have generally been getting ever more efficient since 1995. But, of course, that's not how we measure police efficiency because, if we are honest, we don't actually believe that crime, or the absence of it, is entirely or even mainly down to the police.

Crime has fallen in pretty much every Western nation over the same period, irrespective of criminal justice or policing policies. Criminologists are still scratching their heads as to why that is but some suspect it may have something to do with the global economy or stable democracy. Perhaps it is linked to improved education systems or human rights legislation. It could be a consequence of the collapse in the price of second-hand TVs and better locks. And it may, in part at least, be down to intelligent policing – new technology and more sophisticated approaches to crime prevention and investigation.

But the idea that we can draw a line between crime levels and police efficiency is far too simplistic. When crime was rising throughout the 1960s, 70s and 80s, people didn't say it was the police's fault for not being cleverer. They blamed delinquent youth, or unemployment, or the collapse of traditional values. Equally during the last two decades, when crime has generally been falling, people haven't said it is down to brilliant detective work or the efforts of patrolling constables. In truth, they haven't even been convinced that crime is falling and still talk about social break-down being to blame for rising lawlessness.

Tony Blair's government originally tried to measure police performance against a whole panoply of targets: response times, arrests and convictions, how quickly they wrote to victims, clear-up rates, time spent on the beat rather than filling forms. Then, persuaded by the argument that actually all these targets were getting in the way, and certainly not translating into people feeling safer, they scrapped that idea and went for the one simple measure of public confidence. It was a recognition that while people may say that they want police to reduce crime, what they really want is for them to reduce fear. Bobbies on the beat were never really there to catch crooks but to be a presence: to worry potential villains and calm the law-abiding citizenry.

Shortly after taking office in 2010, the Conservative Home Secretary Theresa May announced that, in her view, the mission of the police was 'to cut crime: no more and no less'. But within three months she was saying she wanted more bobbies on the beat to tackle antisocial behaviour rather than simply criminal activity. Like almost every occupant of her post before, Mrs May appeared to be evoking the ghost of old Dixon, who knew how to deal with nuisance and mischief. 'Let's get them out from behind desks filling forms and out on the street where people want them and they want to be.'

There is a longing for a return to some mythical bygone age where cheerful constables kept neighbourhoods safe and secure. But what we really want is a return to a time when neighbourhoods kept neighbourhoods safe and secure, a time when locals would regularly stroll their own streets and offer a cheery 'Good evenin'' to all.

C IS FOR CHEESE

The ancient village of Crudgington in Shropshire has a name and a history that ring true. But don't be fooled, all is not always what it seems. The Old English and Celtic roots of the settlement's original name, Crugelton, translate as the hill-hill hamlet: it is as though the locals were determined to stress their neighbourhood's aerial aspect with a double emphasis of its hilliness. Crudgington, however, is not on a hill. The village can trace its history back to 1231; it is listed in the Domesday Book. In the search for the authentic English village, you cannot find a more reliable provenance than that. But if you sniff the air in Crudgington you might still detect the faint whiff of falsehood. This is where they dreamed up Lymeswold cheese.

In telling the story of Britain's glorious cheese industry, one encounters contradictions that still shape the national conversation: heritage versus modernity; local versus global; authenticity versus artifice. It is a journey through many ancient battlegrounds but, you may be glad to know, it has a happy ending.

Once upon a time, thousands of farmwives across Britain took paddle and churn to the fresh milk that was not consumed by the local villagers. On thousands of kitchen tables, thousands of cheeses were prepared. This was the method of preserving the protein goodness of the cowshed so the ploughman might have his lunch. But then, as the second half of the nineteeth century steamed and clanged into view, all that changed.

The arrival of the railways transformed rural life, the engine of empire dragging the local village to the global market. Crudgington was among the hundreds of places that got its own station. Instead of farmers selling fresh milk only to the community around the herd or flock, crates could be despatched far beyond, even into the hearts of rapidly expanding cities. A network of milk trains and doorstep deliverymen brought farm-fresh milk to every corner of the nation. And we lapped it up.

Farmers could scarcely cope with demand from a growing population. The need to preserve the leftovers all but disappeared. Instead, new industrial technology allowed producers to centralise cheese-making, mopping up any excess milk from across their region. To brand their product, cheeses increasingly took on the name of the area from which they hailed. But more than that, the search for consistent quality meant recipe, shape and size were controlled. From this process emerged the reputations of some of the truly great cheeses of Britain, but it also rang the death knell for small, local cheese-makers. Hundreds of varieties were lost forever; individuality did not fit with the times.

It was to get worse. Rationing in the Second World War saw the Ministry of Food stipulate that only one type could be manufactured – the National Cheese. A form of rubbery cheddar, this abomination came to define cheese in the nation's mind. To this day there are many who still think of cheese as a lump of orange sweaty fat, grated onto a slice of white.

By the 1970s, bland, processed, homogenised factory-made gunk was routinely skewered on cocktail sticks and accompanied by a chunk of tinned pineapple, a pitiful display of what amounted to British gastronomic refinement. Our plates reflected an unshakeable faith in mass production and technological advance, the qualities that had spawned an empire two centuries before.

The country was pinning its hopes on arresting economic and industrial decline through the appliance of science. Food was predicted to become space-age rocket fuel. 'Much of the food available will be based on protein substitutes,' the presenters of BBC TV's *Tomorrow's World* promised, 'delivered once a month in disposable vacuum packs.' Meanwhile on ITV, the commercial break saw robotic aliens chortling at the suggestion that people might peel a potato rather than simply add water to freeze-dried powdered mash.

Despite all this, the big cheeses in the UK's dairy industry were casting envious glances at our continental cousins with their fancy Brie and Camembert, products oozing with authenticity and sophistication. It was noted how British high-street shoppers were being sold symmetrical slices of globo-gloop in airtight plastic pouches while French fromageries offered consumers dozens of local artisanal cheeses, beautifully prepared and perfectly stored.

There was anxiety in the air. Membership of the European Economic Commuity (EEC) and the introduction of European-style decimalisation had led to disquiet over an apparent loss of British national identity. Some feared that obsession with an antiseptic future had led us to forget our rich heritage. In May 1982, at a dinner in Edinburgh for the French Prime Minister François Mitterrand, Margaret Thatcher quoted from a recently published book that had compared France and Britain and suggested it was no longer at all clear who has what, as nations copy each other so quickly. Her speech posed the question as to whether a nation's essential genius will be lost in the process of unification. Mrs Thatcher thought not. 'The nation of Racine, Voltaire, Debussy and Brie will persist,' she concluded. 'The nation of Shakespeare, Adam Smith, Elgar and Cheddar is also alive and strong.'

But within months the nation of Cheddar was attempting to copy the nation of Brie. It involved the forced marriage of cutting-edge science and traditional craft, the ceremony taking place in a shed in Shropshire. Following a two-year gestation at the cheese laboratory in Crudgington, on 27 September 1982, Lymeswold was born.

The cheese was the brainchild of Sir Stephen Roberts, an entrepreneurial farmer who ran the Milk Marketing Board. At the time, Britain's dairy industry was tormented by what it regarded as unfair distribution of European agricultural subsidies. French farmers got the curds, it was felt, while the Brits were left with the whey. Sir Stephen decided to take the French on at their own game, and lab-coated food technicians were briefed to construct a new English soft cheese, with a white mould rind but without the runny, pungent characteristics of Camembert or Brie. These properties, it was felt, would give the product the broadest appeal. From Crudgington, he hoped, a cheese would emerge to restore British pride and mount a challenge to the global dairy market.

His invention needed a name – something that would evoke the tradition and local provenance of great English cheeses. Marketing experts tested many ideas, but the one which scored best in research was Wymeswold, the name of a small Leicestershire village that had been considered as a production site at one point. Trademark considerations ruled that one out. After further discussion, the cheese was christened Lymeswold.

It was a huge success. In the House of Commons, politicians hailed it as a potential boost to Britain's balance of payments; the Agriculture Minister Peter Walker revealed that even his dog enjoyed the new cheese. Domestic demand was so great that there were soon shortages in the shops, but it was its popularity that would prove to be Lymeswold's downfall. To foodies, the cheese reeked of slick marketing, its mask of authenticity as thin as its white rind; when under-matured stocks were released to increase supply, critics were happy to encourage a reputation for poor quality. Demand quickly fell off, and ten years after its launch, Lymeswold was quietly buried. Few mourned its passing.

These were, though, desperate days for Britain's dairy farmers. The price of milk had plummeted so low it was impossible to make money from it. Resilience and imagination were all that stood between them and the collapse of their industry. What happened next is the uplifting story of how localism triumphed over centralised control; how the joyless yoke of homogenisation and industrialisation was lifted from the creativity and diversity of the British Isles. It was the moment when we realised that big wasn't always beautiful, that new wasn't always better than old, that science didn't always trump art. It was the time when we rediscovered the true meaning of authenticity.

The sharp-suited marketing men spotted it first. 'TREND: People are choosing authenticity as a backlash to aspects of modern life,' one agency's analysis reported. 'TREND: Consumers are seeking to "reconnect with the real".' The food industry could almost taste the opportunity. Farmers were advised that products should have a 'compelling brand narrative based on traditions, heritage and passion'.

Suddenly, everybody wanted authenticity liberally sprinkled on meatballs, melted on cauliflower and placed in great chunks between doorsteps of wholemeal. In the spring of 1997, amid the opulence of the luxury Lanesborough Hotel on London's Hyde Park Corner, the British Cheese Board was launched to the world. A celebrity chef was on hand to remind people of the versatility of cheese, and a survey revealed that 98 per cent of the UK population enjoyed eating the stuff. It was a self-confident affair. Supermarkets began to talk about 'provenance', with agents scouring the country for products that would allow their customers to 'reconnect with the real'. The European Union also announced a 'renaissance of Atlantic food authenticity' and bunged a bit of cash to British dairy farmers previously isolated by geography and indifference.

On the island of Anglesey, Margaret Davies was given EU help in turning milk from her 120 pedigree Friesian cows into Gorau Glas cheese. Humming with authenticity, Margaret's soft blue-veined Welsh variety was soon selling at £27 a kilo, one of the most expensive cheeses in the world. In the Somerset village of Cricket St Thomas, farmers promoted their Capricorn Goats Cheese with pictures of the individual goats. Beryl, Eva, Flo, Ethel and Dot were allegedly responsible for what was described as 'a noble and distinctive' product. This wasn't ordinary cheese, this was cheese crafted and ripened in the lush dairy pastures of a West Country valley. The man from Marks & Spencer was among the first supermarket reps to don his wellies and beat a path to the farmer's door. Britain was rejecting the global and virtual in favour of the local and real. And reality meant getting your hands dirty and your feet wet. One brand consultancy told prospective clients: 'Imperfection carries a story in a way that perfection can only dream about.'

The affluent middle classes entered the new millennium demanding real ale, slow food, organic turnips and unbranded vintage fashion. They went to Glastonbury to dance in primeval mud, stopping off at the deli on the way home for a sourdough loaf, a bag of Egremont Russets and a chunk of dairy heritage. Urban chic sported clods of rural earth as farmers' markets and organic boxes headed to town. Localism became the mantra of politicians, bankers and grocers. From off-the-peg to bespoke, Britain lost confidence in corporate giants and turned to the little guy. Searching for distinctiveness and individuality, the country eschewed the globalising instincts associated with empire, peering further back in our history for an answer to the identity crisis of the twenty-first century.

Britain went to Crudgington. Past the aluminium and concrete shed that had incubated that impostor Lymeswold, they headed for the old stone farmhouse. On the distressed oak table in the kitchen they discovered cheesecloth and press. It was here that the country found the recipe for authenticity – a handful of heritage, a pinch of creativity and a dollop of craft. So the story has a happy ending. A lost art has been rediscovered, a tradition has been revived and a smile is being put back on the face of a nation that had almost forgotten how to say 'cheese'.

D IS FOR DOGS

In the run-up to his landslide election victory in 1997, Tony Blair's pollsters warned him that his New Labour project risked being 'outflanked on patriotism'. So, on the evening of 15 April, television viewers were shown a party election broadcast entitled *British Spirit*. Its star was a dog: Fitz the bulldog.

It was an audacious piece of casting. I met Fitz briefly as he was taken for 'walkies' in front of assembled photographers and TV cameras opposite the entrance to the Houses of Parliament during that campaign. The media was fascinated by the sheer nerve of Labour's propaganda machine, brazenly commandeering the British bulldog for its own purposes.

Britain is fluent in dog. Each breed is imbued with characteristics of class and politics that are widely understood. The bulldog growls with Churchillian patriotism: pugnacious, loyal, courageous and determined. It is a dog of the traditional working-class right and, as pure-bred Fitz cocked his leg on a Westminster lamppost, we all knew Tony Blair was employing canine shorthand. The broadcast went down badly with some ethnic minorities who accused Labour of adopting a symbol of the British National Party, a tactic described in Australian political slang as 'dog-whistling' to racists. But the party's senior spin doctor Peter Mandelson knew

Fitz had done his job. 'He is a completely New Labour dog,' he told reporters.

If Tony Blair had turned up at an event with a Labradoodle at his side, it would have been translated as a worrying tendency towards Euro-federalism; a Golden retriever – a concession to Middle England; a Manchester terrier – an appeal to Labour's industrial heartlands. Practical or sentimental, urban or rural, bourgeois or proletarian, gay or straight, conservative or progressive – all of these characteristics may be revealed by the breed at the end of the lead. Research suggests dogs really do look like their owners – one study found people able successfully to match pictures of owner and pet 64 per cent of the time. But in this country, a dog is also an expression of personality and lifestyle. It is a statement of identity.

To understand how Britain has become so adept at 'reading' dogs, one must follow the scent through history. In the Middle Ages, the breeding of a dog reflected the breeding of the master. Hunting with hounds was the pursuit of the ruling elite, an exclusive pastime that required large numbers of dogs bred for specific roles. Greyhounds and mastiffs, terriers and spaniels, the forerunners of foxhounds and bloodhounds: these prized possessions were often housed in purpose-built kennels with oak beds and staff to care for their needs. A nobleman's dogs would probably be treated better than his servants. Indeed, being sent to the doghouse might have been regarded as a luxury break by some peasants.

The pure-bred animals were valuable status symbols and the nobility would go to great lengths to ensure peasant dogs didn't dip a proletarian paw into the aristocratic gene pool. Local mongrels would sometimes be fitted with wooden contraptions designed to prevent cross-breeding, a practical form of eugenics maintaining the feudal divide.

Dogs had the cachet of designer labels, advertising the superior taste and pedigree of the owner. The most exclusive and expensive animals became both ostentatious displays of wealth and intimate companions, some invited into the home as pampered pets. The reputation of Britain as a nation of dog lovers, rather than simply dog owners, can be traced to the private chambers of the Tudor court. At one time, Mary Queen of Scots had twenty-two lapdogs, each dressed in blue velvet, dotted around her rooms. An eyewitness to her beheading recorded how 'one of the executioners, pulling off her garters, espied her little dog which was crept under her cloths.' The condemned woman had smuggled her favourite pet to the scaffold in her underwear, the lonely and terrifying walk to the block, one assumes, made marginally easier by the presence of a beloved puppy in her petticoat.

For centuries, dogs emphasised the feudal fault lines within British society: on one side, a peasant's ferocious ratter; on the other, the squire's thoroughbred hunter. Man and dog both had their place in the recognised hierarchy, but just to make sure neither the lower orders nor the growing middle classes developed ideas above their station, the Game Act of 1671 made it a criminal offence to keep hunting dogs for all but those who had inherited valuable estates or were heir apparent to the nobility. The landed gentry convinced Parliament to create a distinct canine class divide which, if crossed could result in a hefty fine or imprisonment. What kind of working dog you were allowed to own was not a matter of need nor even wealth, it was a question of land ownership.

The Game Act was justified as a measure to prevent poaching, but it was really about power and class. The aristocracy wanted to stop new money upsetting the old order and, by including petty rules about dog ownership, hoped to ensure the aspirational industrialists could only aspire so far. It didn't last, of course. Money spoke. Rich cotton barons and ironmasters began buying up the estates and pumped millions into packs of foxhounds and gun dogs, determined to confer the ancient social status of hunting upon themselves. The aristocracy's vain attempt to oust the arrivistes finally ended in 1831 with the passing of the Game Reform

Act, which did away with many of the class-ridden regulations, including those relating to dog ownership.

There was some blue-blooded fury at how the new law would damage Britain's traditional class structures now that 'the black-smith, the butcher, the hog jobber, the fisherman and the cadger . . . all have certificates'. A letter in *New Sporting Magazine* that winter despaired at a law which meant 'all men shall be equally qualified to keep and use dogs'. This class battle, however, had been decided.

The wealthy middle classes had made their money in town but strove to be accepted in the countryside. They yearned to demon-strate they had mastered rural ways, that they had what it took to be fully fledged members of the landed gentry. An understanding of dogs and their breeding was a pre-requisite for such aristocratic pretensions, and so an industry developed to teach the bourgeoisie the secrets of the kennels. *The Field* magazine saw the new rich as its target market and one of its early editors, John Henry Walsh, used its pages to develop the association between well-bred people and well-bred pooches.

Writing under the pseudonym 'Stonehenge', Walsh imparted ancient wisdom, setting out the qualities of numerous dog types for the first time. He was a judge at the earliest recognised dog show, held in Newcastle in 1859, at which sixty pointers and setters were divided into categories and marked according to Walsh's descriptions of perfection. From this, Walsh was instrumental in the foundation of The Kennel Club, the organisation that sets the rules and standards for every British pedigree dog to this day. He compiled his principles of breeding, ideas that echoed the importance society placed upon parentage. 'Breeding in-and-in,' Stonehenge stated solidly, 'is not injurious to the dog, as may be proved from theory and practice; indeed it appears, on the contrary, to be very advantageous.' The idea that inbreeding could produce a flawless purity seemed eminently plausible in the evolution revo-lution that followed the publication of Charles Darwin's *On the Origin of Species*. It also played to the prejudices of a country which had long assumed that ancestry begat status, that blood dictated class.

As people moved from the countryside into rapidly expanding cities, so did dogs. The mysterious science of breeding travelled into town too, stolen rural magic to be peddled on urban streets.

Queen Victoria's private vet, Charles Rotherham, told a parliamentary committee that the canine population had soared between 1865 and 1887 as the middle classes purchased pure-bred animals as domestic companions. As one breeder put it: 'Nobody who is anybody can afford to be followed about by a mongrel dog.'

Inspired by the monarch herself, Victorian society demanded ever more exotic and spectacular pets. Doggie fads changed with the season: one year, the miniature schipperke was the must-have canine accessory because its short, black coat was less likely to leave unsightly hairs on the chaise longue. The lapdog was as much a part of a lady's paraphernalia as bonnet and parasol, a fashion statement requiring replacement with each change in vogue.

Soon hundreds of thousands of dogs had infiltrated every part of city life, from the mollycoddled 'toys' in her ladyship's boudoir to the feral packs of strays living on rats in the slums. Anxious humanitarians set up charities to deal with what was rapidly becoming an urban problem: the Royal Society for the Prevention of Cruelty to Animals (RSPCA), the Metropolitan Canine Defence and Benevolent Institute and London's Battersea Home for Lost and Starving Dogs were among the organisations founded to civilise the beastly mayhem. But they could do little about a terrifying canine threat that was oblivious to the social architecture. Rabies.

The first 'Mad Dog' panic had been in the summer of 1830, just as the aristocracy was warning of the disaster that would result from ending the restrictions on dog ownership. In fact, there had been very few confirmed cases, but each rare example unleashed snarling prejudice. The aggressive poaching and fighting dogs of the poor were fingered as those most likely to carry the disease; the inbred curs, lurchers and ratters from the squalid hovels and slums were regarded with the deepest distrust. The disease had a moral dimension – rabies was seen as deviant and dirty, rabid dogs were guilty rather than sick. During official outbreaks, beat constables were instructed to keep an eye out for suspicious-looking animals. If a dog appeared shifty, the officer had powers to impound or kill it.

The disease, however, failed to conform to this simplistic model and blame spread along with contagion and panic. The inbreeding associated with some 'luxury' dog breeds was considered to have debilitated or exhausted the pets' nervous systems, making them more susceptible. This was exacerbated, it was suggested, by the introduction of foreign bloodlines – notably French and German breeds. Another theory, popularised by animal welfare groups, was that over-feeding and pampering of pets led to a greater risk of contracting the disease – a parable on the consequences of indulgence and extravagance. The expensively assembled packs of foxhounds and gun dogs serving the rural elite were not immune from blame, much to the fury of the aristocracy new and old; rabies exposed all the snobbery, self-righteousness and bigotry associated with dog ownership in Britain.

Yet strange alliances were made across social divides as the debate coalesced into two distinct camps, described in the press as 'dog maniacs' and 'muzzle maniacs'. The former argued that the whole rabies panic was based upon an urban myth, the latter that the only sensible way to deal with the risk was to muzzle every dog in Britain for a year and eradicate the disease. Rabies had infected British society with a madness that muddled traditional class understanding.

The newspapers revelled in the gruesome suffering of its victims, publishing regular bulletins on cases confirmed and imagined. Public terror and outcry led to numerous parliamentary inquiries and initiatives, with campaign groups springing up to press their various causes. The Dog Owners Protection Association and Anti-Muzzle Association were joined by the RSPCA in claiming that the country had fallen victim to 'hydrophobia-phobia' – the irrational fear of rabies.

They had a point. Annually, registered rabies deaths rarely exceeded more than a couple of dozen. In the seventeen years following its opening, Battersea Dogs Home received 150,000 animals, of which only one was rabid. You were ten times more likely to be murdered than die from an infected dog, but public hysteria demanded a political response, and so control measures were introduced to extirpate the disease from Britain once and for all.

Muzzling and restricting the movement of suspect animals in outbreak areas led to fury, inspiring verbal dog fights between groups of owners. When Walter Long, then President of the Board of Agriculture, decided in 1897 that new widespread controls should apply to lapdogs but not to sporting dogs, he tore open barely concealed enmities. His rules set town against country, working dog owners against pet dog lovers. The rabies controls were ultimately effective in banishing the disease from the United Kingdom in 1922 but, in their wake, the once straightforward hierarchical structures of dog ownership had been left twisted and tangled. It required expert local knowledge to decipher the subtleties of station and status still inherent in the choice of beast and breed, a skill Britain quickly acquired.

There are now more than 8 million dogs in the UK, a population growing faster than the human one. Canine companions still tend to reflect personality and class identity: an English setter, for example, is likely to mean 'I am posh'; a French poodle might be saying 'I am gay'; a Staffordshire bull terrier suggests 'I am hard' (or afraid). Questions of ownership and breeding continue to tug at society's leash. The Dangerous Dogs Act, passed in 1991 in response to press and public anxiety over dog attacks, echoed the Game Act of 1671 in banning the ownership of certain breeds – legislation that had its impact almost exclusively among the urban poor. The new law did nothing to diminish the popularity of aggressive animals on the toughest estates – if anything the fashion intensified.

Nor did it deal with the greatest threat from domestic pets: according to a study of 6,000 dog owners, the most aggressive breed was the dachshund – the little 'sausage dog'. The chihuahua, Jack Russell, beagle and Border collie were all found to be more likely to sink their teeth into someone than the dreaded pit bull – suggesting to some that Parliament was once again responding to fears about the 'underclass' rather than a genuine canine threat to public safety. Although there have been tragic deaths and horrible mutilations, the average number of people killed in dog-related incidents in Britain stands at less than three a year. Around ten people a year are killed in horse-related incidents and yet few would want to ban riding or introduce strict limits on ownership.

There are clearly negative consequences of having such huge numbers of dogs inhabiting every corner of our daily lives, but Britain's passion for them shows no sign of diminishing. Quite the opposite. With more people living alone and families scattered, we look to dogs for communion in a less supportive society. A survey recently found that among singletons in Britain, 60 per cent had bought a dog or cat for companionship, with 39 per cent agreeing they had replaced a former partner with a pet. Often the trigger for inviting a dog into a family home is when the children are preparing to leave it. Dogs have become loyal surrogates in a land of restless relationships. Once we called them Spot, Rover or Fido. Today the ten most popular dog names read like the register of an upmarket nursery school: Poppy; Alfie; Molly; Charlie; Max; Bella; Ruby; Millie; Daisy; Rosie.

The life of a dog is no longer a dog's life: it reflects the behaviour and routine of its owner. As the nation's waistlines have expanded, so have our pets. The doggie-snack market is currently worth more than £215 million a year. Fat people, research shows, tend to have fat dogs: a third of British pooches are now overweight, with vets warning that if trends continue, nearly half may soon be dying early because of obesity-related illness.

Overweight dogs are also more likely to sleep in their owners' beds, a throwback to the comforter spaniels of Tudor nobility, but now regarded as a sign of dangerous anthropomorphism. We treat pets like people and deny them their animal integrity. Just as owners go on diets, so may their canine companions. There are UK slimming clubs for fat pets and weight-loss drugs specifically designed for dogs. If matters get really serious, overseas clinics encourage dog lovers to buy their porky pooch a tummy-tuck or a course of liposuction. High-street stores offer the 'trendiest' designer wear: sunglasses, jewellery and homeopathic remedies – all for dogs. Would our furry friend like some tree bark powder to aid digestion? Or skullcap and valerian tables 'for symptomatic relief of anxiety, nervousness, excitability and travel sickness'?

Increasingly, owners look for human answers to the psychological problems they perceive in their pets. Your puppy is a bit boisterous; get a diagnosis for ADHD and a vet to prescribe Ritalin. Poppy has lost some of her bounce; perhaps she needs anti-depressants, which, we are told, 'can have a positive effect on dogs when used in conjunction with behaviour therapy'.

Dogs have been granted an extraordinary place in British daily life. They reflect our history, our politics and our prejudices. For those who can interpret the meanings, the breed at the end of the lead reveals something of the lifestyle, personality and temperament of the owner. To outsiders, perhaps, it is simply a pet. But not to us. Britain is fluent in dog.

E IS FOR ERROR

It is dark and I am standing alone in the centre of London's Olympic stadium. Suddenly, 500 huge floodlights crackle into life; 80,000 pairs of eyes turn to focus on me. With a jolt of panic, I look down and realise my dreadful error. I have forgotten to put my trousers on.

Most of us have endured this kind of anxiety dream at some point. It is the subconscious just wanting to remind us that, while we all make mistakes, it is really far better to make them in the privacy of our bedroom than in the middle of a packed sports arena, where every member of the crowd has a pair of powerful binoculars trained on one's underpants.

The information age, however, means that these days such nightmares can easily become reality. Our failures, faults and foolishness may leak from the narrow confines of personal life into a public arena where, in Britain particularly, the lights are brighter and the eyes more numerous than any physical amphitheatre. We are all a misjudged mouse-click away from email embarrassment, a digital movie clip away from national humiliation, an injudicious tweet away from international ignominy. These are small (if nightmarish) risks for people whose lives are essentially private, but for anyone who flirts with fame or has a role on the public stage, error can be terminal.

Albert Einstein once said, 'The only sure way to avoid making mistakes is to have no new ideas.' There are dozens of business and lifestyle books informing readers how failure is the route to success, how progress is built upon trial and error. Military training is designed to take soldiers to breaking point, to force them to stumble. Major General Patrick Cordingley, commander of the Desert Rats during the first Gulf War, noted how senior army instructors 'were more interested in our failures than in our successes, because they felt that everyone learnt something from an error'.

To err is human; to forgive, divine, suggested Alexander Pope. But we live in a secular society where to err is to risk public damnation and forgiveness is in very short supply. The arc lights of the media shine day and night; the protective varnish of deference has been removed; mistrust and contempt abound. One misjudgement, one moment of carelessness, can quite suddenly become a calamity. The recent scandal over illegal and immoral methods employed by Fleet Street reporters prompted national soul-searching about the dark arts of British journalism. But it also posed questions about the hostility of our public sphere, a brutal environment that has disfigured our politics and our way of life. The wealthy, the famous and the powerful have become preoccupied with risk management.

Over recent years, tens of thousands of advisors, officials and consultants have been recruited to maintain the defences against public gaffe or blunder. In Westminster, spin doctors and crisis managers are now vital cogs in the political machine, charged with shaping narrative and limiting damage. The media, meanwhile, sees its role as trying to breach the barricades, to expose every flaw and transgression. It is a constant tension that soaks up the energy of government and media alike.

Both sides claim the moral high ground: the press lobby argues that exposing the frailties of the body politic is vital for a healthy democracy; Parliamentarians maintain that effective administration is impossible in the full glare of publicity. Ministers must be able to learn from their mistakes or else they will adopt a safety-first principle that militates against innovation and change, Whitehall argues. The powerful must be held to account or canker and complacency will develop, journalists respond.

So the executive has put greater store on hiding errors and spreading blame, in the 'national interest'. Meanwhile, the media applies ever greater effort to exposing and apportioning fault, in the 'public interest'.

In such an environment, the stakes can rise fast. When a mistake comes to light, it may well dominate the national conversation for days or weeks. Promising political careers can be reduced to ash in the media firestorm that follows some perceived miscalculation or folly, an inferno potentially even more intense with the growth of instant political blogging and tweeting. Attempts to protect ministers from such a fate have seen the introduction of 'special advisors', political heavies with duties to shield their employer's reputation from harm.

On the afternoon of 11 September 2001, as Westminster watched live pictures of the horrifying events unfolding in New York, one such advisor sent a now notorious email. Both towers of the World Trade Center were in flames, having been hit in terrorist attacks, and Jo Moore told the departmental press office: 'It's now a very good day to get out anything we want to bury. Councillors' expenses?' The missive, when it came to public attention, created just the furore it was intended to avoid. In the bear pit of rolling news, spin doctor Moore was torn apart, and trust in government was left sporting another black eye. But there was something inevitable about the scandal: it was the unedifying fallout from a society that pretends one can have trial without error and whose response to failure is retribution.

The fear of the voracious 24/7 news monster, gorging on poor judgement and spitting out public disgrace, extends far beyond Whitehall. Every individual, institution and enterprise with a reputation to protect is well advised to shore up its defences. Fortunes are made by those adept in risk analysis and blame avoidance. The famous beat a path to the door of consultants such as Max Clifford, whose business brochure explains how his job is 'protecting' as well as promoting clients. He boasts of his firm's 'valuable media relationships' while simultaneously accusing the press of being 'increasingly intrusive and vitriolic'. Clients trip along the narrow path between celebrity and notoriety, sometimes dancing with a foot on both sides.

PR agencies have become as much about privacy as publicity. Members of the Public Relations Consultants Association in the UK saw incomes rise from £18 million in 1983 to £401 million in 2001, a phenomenal expansion explained in part by anxiety about protecting the reputations of the rich and famous in the media age.

From its earliest days, the PR industry involved itself in reputation management. Ivy Lee, regarded as one of the founders of modern public relations, convinced the Pennsylvania Railroad to publicise rather than hide details of the 1906 Atlantic City train disaster, issuing what is said to be the first ever press release. It proved an effective way to calm the angry mob.

A century later, with company executives increasingly conscious of corporate identity and reputation, the polished skills and black arts of PR were in greater demand than ever. Manning the institutional defences, the spin doctor and publicity consultant were joined by a third key figure – the corporate lawyer. The legal representative's role was to defuse the danger from accident and error by treating them as technical matters, events to be dealt with by experts in insurance, health and safety, litigation and risk analysis.

In the first decade of this century, the corporate legal sector in Britain grew exponentially. Law Society figures suggest the number of qualified solicitors directly employed in company legal departments more than doubled. It is estimated that there are now at least two hundred city lawyers being paid more than a million pounds a year in the UK. Protecting big business from accident and error has become big business itself. A government report in

2010 described the environment in which firms attempted to respond to such risks as 'a climate of fear', where health and safety consultants, insurance companies and legal experts contrive to create a growing view that if there's a blame, there's a claim.

The author of that report, Lord Young, was later to be a victim of the changed relationship with error and misjudgement himself. What would once have been a private indiscretion, a candid remark to a friendly journalist over lunch, was splashed on the front page of a national newspaper and from there quickly accelerated into a national media storm. The Conservative peer had been secretly recorded saying that, despite the recession, most people had never had it so good. Before the sun had set, David Cameron's enterprise tsar was out on his ear.

Of course, corporate negligence and political incompetence need to be exposed. Hypocrisy and humbug are fair game. But the climate of fear for those in public life, the terror of being caught with your trousers down, has seen an increasingly defensive response to accident and error. That, in turn, has resulted in a more distrustful attitude from the general public, which encourages the press to search out stories that play to that anxiety. It can look like a market dealing in suspicion and dread.

The tactics to deal with accident and error have become more sophisticated. Take the apology: once an ignominious admission of fault, it has become a vehicle for neutralising blame and parading humility. Greg Dyke, when Director-General of the BBC, realised that a new electronic expenses system he'd introduced was an unmitigated disaster. It was time to eat humble pie. 'I sent out an email to everyone saying, I'm sorry, we got it wrong,' he later explained. 'Management generally have a terrible habit of failing to admit when they've made a mistake. We all mess up. If you admit it, everyone likes you.'

Such candour may seem refreshing when public figures are increasingly guarded about admitting their shortcomings. But contemporary apologies constructed with the help of PR advisors have their roots in the public acts of penance once demanded of way-ward public figures by the church. After his knights had murdered Thomas à Becket in Canterbury Cathedral in 1170, for example, Henry II eventually accepted the Pope's order for contrition. In a highly theatrical act of atonement, the king walked barefoot to the crime scene, thrust his head and shoulders into one of the openings of Saint Thomas's tomb, and allowed himself to be flogged by monks and prelates.

These days, political apology has become such a feature of contemporary governance that social researchers have begun cata-loguing hundreds of examples. Tony Blair features prominently in the archives of regret. In 2005, he barely opened his mouth without apologising for something or other. In that one year he said sorry to the Guildford Four and the Maguire Seven, Irish men and women wrongfully convicted of IRA pub bombings years earlier; he for-mally apologised to British survivors of Hurricane Katrina for a disorganised response from the Foreign Office; he made a public apology to Walter Wolfgang, a Labour activist expelled from his party conference for heckling; he apologised in advance to the people of Auchterarder in Perthshire for the disruption and incon-venience of hosting the G8 summit there. On other occasions, Tony Blair said sorry for the Irish potato famine and the slave trade.

He was a political leader who recognised there was capital in contrition. But would he, could he say sorry for the one decision of his political career for which many of his own supporters demanded an apology – the invasion of Iraq? As Mr Blair prepared to address party delegates in Brighton in 2004, his spin doctors briefed the press that his speech would include a statement of regret. When it came to it, however, it was far from the admission of guilt that his critics wanted. 'The evidence about Saddam having actual biological and chemical weapons, as opposed to the capabil-ity to develop them, has turned out to be wrong,' he said. 'I can apologise for the information that turned out to be wrong, but I can't, sincerely at least, apologise for removing Saddam.'

The writer and commentator Allan Massie thought the media had been hoodwinked and the public short-changed. 'When we demand apologies from a politician, we are not looking for an act of healing as a prelude to reconciliation, though we may persuade ourselves that this is what we are doing,' he wrote. 'Instead we are hoping to see him abase himself. There is in reality for the politician only one satisfactory form of apology, and it is resignation.'

Apologies may imply swallowed pride, painful humiliation and negative consequences. But in the media age they have become a first line of defence in reducing the damage from some highly public error.

Analysis suggests there are three keys to their successful use: a statement of regret; an admission of responsibility; an offer to remedy the situation. When President Bill Clinton went on US television to apologise for lying about his affair with Monica Lewinsky, he offered a model of how to do it.

'I misled people, including even my wife. I deeply regret that.' *Tick.*

'I must take complete responsibility for all my actions, both public and private. And that is why I am speaking to you tonight.' *Tick.*

'I must put it right, and I am prepared to do whatever it takes to do so.' *Tick and a gold star.*

Such is the power of the apology that the British justice system is increasingly incorporating it in its response to crime. Restorative justice is popular with legislators because it is cheap and appears effective: studies suggest it can cut reoffending by a quarter and reduce stress in those affected. Most victims of youth crime now accept the chance to meet the perpetrator face-to-face for a structured meeting that usually follows the classic apology script: an admission of guilt; a statement of regret; a discussion of how to repair the harm caused and prevent it from happening again.

It is, of course, entirely sensible for institutions to try to learn from error. The phrases 'something must be done' and 'it must never happen again' routinely echo around when fault or failure are exposed. But the environment of rolling news, what my BBC colleague Nik Gowing described as 'the tyranny of real time and the tyranny of the timeline', requires an immediate and vigorous response to mistakes.

Within hours of some revelation one can guarantee there will be calls for urgent structural and systemic reform. Woe betide anyone who suggests a sense of perspective or a time for reflection are needed: such calls are likely to be condemned as complacency or callousness. Indeed, in the febrile atmosphere that accompanies public outrage, the voice of calm can also end up being drowned in the duck pond by the angry mob.

Policy shaped by panic almost always turns out to be a bad idea. Systems hurriedly assembled as a response to headlines can prove to be blunt and inefficient tools, unnecessary or counter-productive. Many institutions are hampered by the bureaucratic legacy of some long-forgotten scandal that demanded something be done. Britain's Vetting and Barring Scheme is a child of just such a moral panic: a textbook case of how media storm and political expediency combine to demand reform that later appears disproportionate or simply daft.

The saga began in the summer of 2002. That August, like every August, news desks were searching around for stories to fill their papers and bulletins. With Parliament on holiday and little else happening, an appalling child abduction story from Cambridgeshire dominated the front pages. The Soham murders became a national talking point and when it emerged that the killer, school caretaker Ian Huntley, had previously been investigated for sexual offences, the question of responsibility extended from the criminal to the political sphere. Would any blame for the deaths of Holly Wells and Jessica Chapman be pinned on the government? Political opponents were circling. Ministers had to respond, and respond quickly.

The Home Secretary David Blunkett bought time in the

traditional manner: he announced an inquiry. The man he chose to lead it was Sir Michael Bichard, a Whitehall mandarin whose crisis management skills had impressed Mr Blunkett as Education Secretary five years earlier. At that time, according to press reports, details of Mr Blunkett's complicated love life were threatening to spill out into the public arena and Sir Michael had been instrumental in ensuring tempers were calmed and details hushed.

Mr Blunkett hoped that the Bichard inquiry into Soham would both satisfy the demand that lessons must be learned and help shift any blame away from the department. Sir Michael delivered. He severely criticised the chief constable of Humberside, David Westwood, for not keeping records of child abuse allegations concerning Ian Huntley, and demanded the officer take personal responsibility for 'very serious failings'. The scandal had its fall guy and, despite support from his local police authority, David Blunkett used new executive powers to order Mr Westwood's suspension. The chief constable subsequently took early retirement.

Sir Michael's report, though, went much further, recommending the creation of a huge vetting system requiring those who wish to work with children or vulnerable adults to be registered. The government had little option but to accept the idea – rejecting it would have left ministers potentially open to blame for every case of child abuse thereafter. Lawyers and legislators spent years working out how this new register might work, eventually announcing a system that was likely to see one in four of all adults being vetted by the state. An attempt to ensure an error could never happen again had resulted in the development of a giant, expensive and intrusive bureaucracy that many argued would actually damage the relationship between adults and young people.

Within weeks of taking office in 2010, the new Conservative Home Secretary Theresa May announced that the registration scheme would be scrapped, the vetting process scaled back and 'common sense' would be used to protect children and vulnerable adults. There was barely a murmur of opposition.

Public life is, of course, riddled with misjudgement and failure. It is quite right that mistakes are identified and, where necessary, acted upon to reduce future harm. Health and safety systems backed by inspection regimes have undoubtedly made our world less hazardous. But the harsh climate of Britain's public domain has changed our relationship with error. The consequences can be buck-passing, spin, insincerity, waste and cynicism. Our aversion to risk poses risks of its own.

F IS FOR FAMILY

There's an old saying that one should never discuss politics or religion in polite company. These are subjects regarded as simply too dangerous to bring up over dinner; passions are almost bound to be unleashed, with the distinct possibility of raised voices, broken crockery and severed friendships. I would, perhaps, add a third category, a subject that mixes the first two in a most combustible fashion: family.

Discussions about family quickly get personal because, well, it is personal. For better or worse, we all have a family and tend to regard ourselves as something of an expert on the topic. From often painful experience, we are convinced we know what works and what does not: we remember bitter Uncle Frank who ended up living alone; mad cousin Dorothy who was pushed into a most unsuitable marriage; and then there was sad Vera who, frankly, tarnished the family name in a manner best forgotten.

Every family has its cautionary tales, parables that reinforce our moral values and shape our political views. The family is seen as the building block of society, its composition and structure essential factors in preventing the collapse of our very way of life. It is a subject so contentious that, for a moment, I find myself questioning the wisdom of even continuing with this chapter. But

I don't have enough to say about flamingos or fezzes so ... here goes with 'F is for Family'.

There is a paradox about our attitudes to family life in Britain. According to a report by the Conservative Party's policy advisors in 2007, 'peculiarly high levels of family breakdown found in Britain are at the heart of the social breakdown which is devastating our most deprived communities and fracturing British society in general.' It is a view that enjoys widespread public agreement. Yet, when one asks people about their own families, a rather different picture emerges.

A few years ago I helped commission a survey for the BBC on people's experience of British family life, choosing questions that had been posed previously to see how attitudes had changed. In 1964, pollsters had asked whether people were optimistic about the future facing their family. It was the swinging sixties, we'd apparently never had it so good, and Britain was a nation excited about the promise held by the white heat of technology. Just over half of respondents (52 per cent) were positive about their family's prospects. After four decades of what traditionalists describe as 'continuous decline' in family stability, how confident would Britain appear when we asked the same question again? The answer was unexpected: the proportion of people who were upbeat about their family had risen markedly – from half to three quarters (76 per cent) of respondents.

There were to be more surprises in our survey. In 1951, social scientists asked people whether their parents had done the best for them when growing up: nine out of ten (90 per cent) agreed their mother had; eight out of ten (80 per cent) said their father had done his bit. More than half a century of concerns over parenting later and the figures in our BBC poll showed that appreciation levels had gone up: mums scored 94 per cent and dads 86 per cent.

Are twenty-first-century men behaving badly – spending too much time down the pub with the lads? Back in 1957 one in five married women reported that their husband didn't spend enough of his spare time with the family. Fifty years of family disintegration afterwards and the figure had fallen to one in twelve.

At first sight, this doesn't make sense. Marriage levels in Britain are at an all time low and commitment seems to have become a dirty word. For every two weddings there is one divorce and cohabiting couples are even less likely to stay the course than those who have tied the knot. We have the highest proportion of lone parents in Europe – almost a quarter of UK children live with just Mum or Dad. It is a catalogue of marriage break-up and relationship breakdown that we know is associated with depression, delinquency, unemployment and poverty. Yet when asked in 2010 whether they were happy with their family life, a remarkable 97 per cent replied 'yes' – a more positive view than in any similar survey I have seen.

Much of the general anxiety about the British family relates to its changing structure, particularly a concern that we are moving away from the model family, whose uncomplicated life shaped the attitudes of the baby-boomer generation.

'This is Janet. This is John.' The *Janet and John* books were first published in Britain in 1949 and, by the 1960s, 80 per cent of schoolchildren were following their lives as they learned to read. There was Mother in the kitchen, Father in the garden playing with Darky the dog, and the two children, scrubbed and ready for another trip to the shops. In their most formative years, millions of young Britons were encouraged to believe that Janet and John's 'nuclear' family was what normal life looked like. It was a reassuringly straightforward and stable world, in contrast to the social turmoil of post-war Britain.

Hitler's bombs had not just smashed the country's buildings and bridges; war had torn families apart and left countless marriages wounded or doomed. There was genuine concern that the fabric of British life might have been damaged beyond repair. Into this anxiety walked John Bowlby, a psychologist whose own experiences of family life had inspired a fascination in child development.

Son of the king's surgeon, John's childhood was typical of an upper middle-class British boy at the opening of the twentieth century. In his earliest years, he saw his mother for only one hour a day, after teatime, and was looked after almost exclusively by a nanny. His parents shared a common belief that parental attention and affection would spoil a child. At the age of seven, John was dispatched to boarding school, later reflecting, 'I wouldn't send a dog away to boarding school at age seven.'

Driven by his personal traumas, Bowlby developed his 'attachment theory', the idea that an infant needs a close relationship with at least one parent or carer in order for social and emotional development to occur normally. It was a hypothesis that gained ground during the Second World War, as welfare officials tried to look after thousands of small children separated from their parents or orphaned.

When peace had been restored, Bowlby published a book that took the theory further and became influential in the development of family policy. Entitled *Forty-four Juvenile Thieves*, it focused on children with emotional problems. Half the study group of eighty-eight youngsters had been reported for thieving while the remainder had not committed any crime. Having compared the backgrounds of children in the two groups, he concluded that 'broken homes' *caused* delinquency.

Bowlby later clarified his thinking, explaining that he had meant the cause was 'broken mother–child relationships', not necessarily broken marriages. Nevertheless, the report was seized upon by those who argued that marriage itself protected against criminality, that the nuclear family structure directly improved social outcomes, and that D.I.V.O.R.C.E spelled disaster.

They are theories that still dominate political debate about the family today. In the Conservative Party's 2009 policy paper 'Breakthrough Britain', former Tory leader Iain Duncan Smith claimed to have evidence justifying government encouragement of marriage in the national interest. 'You cannot mend Britain's broken society unless you support and value the institution that is at the heart of a stable society.'

In the post-war years, the British government had also been persuaded that the social dangers associated with marriage breakdown required state intervention. The Archbishop of Canterbury Geoffrey Fisher rose in the House of Lords in March 1947 to say that each single divorce created 'an area of poison and a centre of infection in the national life'. Government, he argued, should convince the ordinary level-headed citizen that marriage was an obligation and that adultery and fornication were deadly sins. 'Divorce,' he said, 'is always the final record of a human disaster.'

With divorce rates having increased forty-fold in forty years, ministers agreed to set up state-funded Marriage Guidance Centres to try to stop the rot. A founder of the counselling movement, the Reverend David Mace, was invited to deliver a series of lectures on marital life and strife on the BBC's Home Service. 'Don't let things drift on from bad to worse, and then come for help about your marriage after it has crashed in ruins at your feet,' he told his audience. 'There isn't a minute to waste.'

As Britain rebuilt its infrastructure, the model of the ideal nuclear family was also being renovated to take account of the social legacy of war – particularly the changing ambitions of women. The traditional pre-war marriage assumed the man ruled the roost: wives undertook parenting and domestic duties while their husbands were the breadwinners and paternal protectors. But when men went off to fight, women were invited to enter the labour force and proved reluctant to resume their place in the kitchen after the troops returned home.

Prominent social commentators argued it was mothers neglecting their household responsibilities who were to blame for the wave of divorce and delinquency: latch-key children up to mischief while their parents were both at work; the birth-rate tumbling as marriages failed. The question became how to woo women back to the hearth. The answer was to redraft the contract. Men and women should resume their traditional roles, it was decided, but with husband and wife enjoying equal status. Education programmes trained girls for domesticity and motherhood, while promising personal fulfilment in a 'relationship' rather than an 'institution'. This romantic ideal proved popular with women, even if the reality was often very different. Many men struggled to adapt.

The hope had been that the 'companionate family' model would sustain the institution of marriage through a tricky patch. The reality was that it often raised unattainable expectations and was later accused of being a major contributor to marital disillusionment and the rise in the divorce rate. By the end of the 1960s it was clear that government would have to think again if the traditional family was to survive the fallout from revolutionary sexual politics.

It was no longer possible to try and shame married couples into staying together. Plan B was to encourage those who did divorce to re-marry. It was an admission that not every couple could or should stay together 'til death us do part. Instead, the idea was that even when individual marriages failed, the institution would survive.

The Divorce Reform Act of 1969 made it much quicker and easier for couples to split and re-tie the knot, and initially it seemed the tactic might work. In 1972, the year after the law came into force, more veils were lifted, brides kissed and confetti scattered than at any time since the frantic days of 1940 when the troops were leaving. The number of marriages dissolved had jumped 60 per cent to 119,000 but, crucially, the number of divorcees who remarried was 121,000.

Optimism was short-lived, however: 1972 marked a highpoint for marriage in the UK. It has been in continuous decline ever since, a steep downward curve that provided traditionalists with a graphic depiction of how British society slid into a moral cesspit of deviance, selfishness and sin.

What had really changed, though, was Britain's understanding of what constituted 'normal' family life. An unmarried couple sharing a bed had moved from scandal to convention within thirty years. By 2010, almost half of children in the UK were born outside wedlock. Indeed, the majority of babies in Wales and the north of England were delivered to parents who were not married, rising to 75 per cent in some towns.

For Britain's ethnic minorities the definition of a normal family varied substantially, dependent on cultural heritage. Within the British-born Caribbean community, the key features had become very low rates of marriage, high rates of single parenthood and high rates of mixed marriage: 63 per cent of men with a partner lived with a white woman; 45 per cent of women with a partner lived with a white man; only around a quarter of Caribbean children lived with two black parents.

In contrast, the key features of family life in South Asian communities were very high rates of marriage, low rates of single-parenthood and low rates of mixed marriage. Around three quarters of Pakistani and Bangladeshi women were married by the age of twenty-five, and a clear majority saw their role as looking after the home and family.

Interpreting the data, academics at the Institute for Social & Economic Research concluded that there had been a general shift from what they called 'old-fashioned values' towards 'modern individualism' among all ethnic groups in Britain, but changing at different paces. 'Pakistanis and Bangladeshis are behind that trend. Caribbeans are in front. In fact, all the groups studied are moving in the same direction.'

Britain's white population was somewhere in between, with a range of acceptable family options now available. Gay or straight, married or cohabiting, open or monogamous, when it came to family structure in the twenty-first century, researchers concluded there was no longer a recognised thing to do.

Reaction to the 'anything goes' attitude to family life could be divided into two camps. For some it was evidence of the corrosion of society and character by an increase in selfish individualism. For others it was the victory of personal liberation and freedom over outdated moralist values and structures.

During the New Labour era, government thinking on family life was heavily influenced by the ideas of Anthony Giddens, the architect of Tony Blair's 'third way' political philosophy. He argued that marriage and the nuclear family had become shell institutions, urging ministers to base their social policy, not on shoring up traditional structures, but on encouraging what he called 'pure relationships'. He imagined these being based on 'the acceptance on the part of each partner, until further notice, that each gains sufficient benefit from the relationship to make its continuance worthwhile'.

Giddens called it a democracy of the emotions, but to more conservative commentators, it was the road to hell, a philosophy for a society set to self-destruct on selfishness and sin. The ideological battle lines were clearly drawn, with Giddens describing the potential showdown as fundamentalism against cosmopolitan tolerance. It was clear where the loyalties of Tony Blair's guru lay. 'Cosmopolitans welcome and embrace this cultural complexity. Fundamentalists find it disturbing and dangerous. We can legitimately hope that a cosmopolitan outlook will win out.'

The politics of the family were heating up to the point where, in 2009, the British Academy (a learned body which acts as a mother-ship for social scientists) decided that analysing family patterns should be a top priority. A report the following year noted how many political claims on the topic were based 'solely on value systems' and 'vary hugely in their source and solidity'. In short, the boffins were saying that politicians often talked a lot of tosh when it came to families, confusing personal views with objective evidence.

The academy set out to separate the science from the politics, a delicate operation at the best of times, but particularly fraught in the area of family policy. First, they examined the assertion that divorce *caused* delinquency. When they looked at the data, they found the link to antisocial behaviour in children 'applied to unhappy separations but not to happy ones'. A second experiment supported the finding, comparing the absence of a parent as a result of a divorce with loss through a death. 'The association with anti-social behaviour applied to divorce, but only very weakly to bereavement,' they found. The conclusion was that it is not the broken home that makes the difference, but whether conflict and discord accompanied the break-up.

Family break-up had also been linked to children doing badly at school and suffering depression, but was it *causing* the difficulties? Again, the evidence suggested it was parenting that was the real problem. 'Poor parenting constituted a risk even in the absence of family break-up, whereas family break-up carried little risk if it was not also followed by poor parenting.'

What about the claim that traditional marriage is better for children than cohabitation? The report found 'abundant evidence to conclude that committed loving relationships between parents benefit children' and 'married people are more likely to be strongly committed to living together than was the case with the unmarried but cohabiting.' But this didn't mean that marriage itself was better for children. It might well be that the kind of people who get married are better at bringing up kids.

When the researchers looked at the profile of parents who have children outside marriage they found they were likely to have less money and lower educational attainments than couples who were married. They were also more likely to have had underage sex and to have been a teenage parent – factors statistically linked to poorer parenting.

The scientists wondered what would happen to marriage stability if more people in the high-risk group tied the knot. 'The evidence suggests that probably it would lessen and that the differences between the married and cohabiting would diminish.' In other words, it wasn't marriage that improved children's chances, but the kind of people who chose to marry.

At the same time as the British Academy was questioning the magic of marriage, the OECD (the Organisation for Economic Co-operation and Development, the think tank for rich countries) was questioning the received wisdom that children raised by single mums do less well than those brought up by two parents. Having examined the evidence from twenty-five countries, they suggested the causal effects of being raised in a single-parent family were smaller than hitherto believed, or even zero. The OECD was honest about the limitations of its analysis but it summarised the research findings like this: 'Overall, if there are indeed negative effects of being raised in a single-parent family, the effect is small.'

Once again, the point was that the important driver in successful families was less its form than its function. The focus, it was argued, should not be on trying to revive or sustain traditional structures, but in teaching and supporting good parenting and relationships. Here, potentially, was the answer to the riddle of why people's experience of family life in Britain appeared to be improving despite the collapse in marriage and widespread relationship breakdown. As one academic put it: 'Families are doing the same business in different conditions.'

It might just be that our society's interest in good parenting and children's rights, the emancipation of women and the changing role of men, the greater acceptance of gay and lesbian relationships and the challenge all these changes throw down to traditional cultural orthodoxies has, actually, produced happier families. Maybe, but I wouldn't, necessarily, mention that in polite company.

G IS FOR GRASS

As a reporter, my natural habitat tends to be on untended grass, among the litter and dog mess of a British sink estate. In my BBC suit, tie and shiny shoes, I have stood in countless neglected urban parks, like an erratic boulder abandoned by a glacier. The local park is a good place to judge a neighbourhood. Look around. Is the description that leaps to mind 'refuge'? Or 'no-go area'?

Just as the condition of the village green might once have reflected the social health of an ancient British settlement, so the patches of public open space in contemporary communities are an indicator of the resilience of local people. And the biggest clue of all is the state of the grass. If a community is functioning well, the grass will tell you. The football pitch, cricket square, bowling green or public lawns: if they are cared for, the people almost certainly care for each other.

Trendy gardeners may dismiss the lawn as a monocultural abomination, but the British relationship with closely cropped turf runs too deep to be troubled by mere horticultural fashion. Our passionate affair with grass is founded upon a fierce and bloody civil war that stretches back to Tudor times and beyond: each blade is a sharp reminder of a power struggle that lasted for centuries. The battles that shaped Britain's social structure were fought on fields of grass.

Some sociologists suggest that our love for verdant shaded lawns is based upon a primeval urge described as Savannah Syndrome, a throwback to the tree-dotted grasslands of Africa on which humanity evolved. As the philosopher John Stuart Mill wrote: 'The foot is freer and the spirits more buoyant when treading the turf than the harsh gravel.' However, walking on the grass in Britain came to be regarded as a privilege rather than a right, prompting inevitable unhappiness and upheaval.

When Henry VIII dissolved the monasteries, land previously controlled by the church was purloined by the increasingly powerful gentry. Walls were built and fences erected around commons and greens, once public spaces now enclosed for sheep rather than people. Land became a privately owned commodity. The king himself acquired vast tracts in the 1530s, including numerous acres farmed by the monks of Westminster, which he intended to turn into hunting grounds; the London parks we now know as St James's, Regent's Park and Hyde Park became the exclusive domain of His Royal Majesty 'for his own disport and pastime'.

A proclamation of 1536 spelled out the pain and punishment that would befall any commoner who presumed to hunt or hawk anywhere from the palace of Westminster to Hampstead Heath. Henry had tied land ownership to social status and entrenched in British culture for centuries to come the demand for public access to green spaces. The English Civil War was essentially a power struggle between the new land-owning gentry and the older feudal landlords, a re-ordering of rights that swung to and fro with each passing decade.

Admission to the royal parks in the capital reflects the complexities of the tussle. Charles I allowed some general public access but, after the king's execution, Oliver Cromwell closed Hyde Park and demanded an entry payment of one shilling for a coach and 6d for each horse. The Puritans had little interest in playgrounds. With the restoration of the monarchy in 1660, the park gates opened wide once more, although free entrance would always be dependent on the grace and favour of the Crown. I am reminded of the limitations of the royal welcome to many of London's glorious parks whenever I wish to place a BBC camera tripod upon their lawns. It is not public space and, unless we have obtained a permit from the sovereign, the Palace's park keepers will, politely but firmly, escort us to the exit.

In the 1730s, Queen Caroline, the cultured German wife of George II, developed grand plans to enclose St James's Park and the whole of Hyde Park into private royal gardens. When she enquired of the Prime Minister Sir Robert Walpole what it would cost, he replied simply 'three crowns'. The Hanoverian dynasty, which had recently succeeded to the crowns of England, Scotland and Ireland, did not dare alienate its subjects and the plan was shelved.

European observers thought there was something peculiarly British about this idea of general access to green spaces. The French novelist Abbé Prévost was amazed to witness in St James's Park 'the flower of the nobility and the first ladies of the court mingled in confusion with the lowest of the populace'. However, Prévost also noted the tensions within the relationship. 'Who could imagine, for example, that the most wretched porter will contest the right of way with a lord, of whose quality he is aware, and that if one or the other stubbornly refuses to yield, they publicly engage in fisticuffs until the stronger one remains master of the pavement? This is what sometimes happens in London.'

The city park was to become the battleground for class struggle, increasingly so as hundreds of Parliamentary Enclosure Acts stripped agricultural workers of their access to pasture and meadow, forcing a landless population from the fields to the factories. As the commoners lost their commons, so the mighty landowners competed to show off their vast sweeping lawns. Hugely labour intensive, only the wealthiest could afford to maintain the acres of immaculate turf, hand-produced with scythes and shears. This was grass as a statement of authority, a display of power as emphatic as a parade of North Korean tanks in Pyongyang.

These days, landscape gardeners advertise in the local services directory between kissograms and launderettes, but in the nineteenth century, they were both culturally and politically influential figures, shaping not just the great estates but wider society.

John Loudon was among the most celebrated landscape planners of the age, engaged by the wealthy Stratton family in 1808 to redesign Tew Great Park in Oxfordshire. His landscaping was held up as a model of elegance and refinement, but as he marked out lawns and drives he was thinking about soot and smoke. Sniffing the changing wind, Loudon determined to establish himself as one of the first urban planners.

In 1829, more than a century before the creation of London's much beloved Green Belt, Loudon proposed just such an idea in his work *Hints on Breathing Places for the Metropolis*. He knew what enclosure had done to rural communities such as Cambuslang in Lanarkshire, where he grew up, and feared a worse fate was about to befall the rapidly expanding industrial towns and cities.

Loudon came up with the idea of concentric rings of turf and gravel, which would ensure that 'there could never be an inhabitant who would be farther than half a mile from an open airy situation, in which he was free to walk or ride, and in which he could find every mode of amusement, recreation, entertainment, and instruction'.

He instinctively believed that civic health was closely linked with access to grass, a view shared by some Parliamentarians who feared rapid industrialisation was throwing up towns and city districts unable to cope with the influx of hundreds of thousands of workers and their families. Forced to live in cramped and squalid conditions, cholera, diphtheria and small pox quickly spread among the urban poor. It was the perfect breeding ground for disease and social unrest.

In 1833 the Select Committee on Public Walks concluded that it was advantageous to all classes that there be grassy places to which wives and children (decently dressed) could escape on a

Sunday evening. It seems an innocuous enough idea today, but the committee had used the phrase 'all classes' and, in so doing, inspired the reformers Jeremy Bentham and John Stuart Mill to pen a furious demand for universal access to green spaces like Regent's Park. 'To call such a spot a public park is an impudent mockery,' they wrote. 'It is not a public park, but a place set apart for the use of the wealthy only, and the people are permitted to grind out their shoes upon the gravel, merely because they cannot be prevented.'

Although the Crown claimed that there was open access, the keys to Regent's Park were only available to those who paid two guineas a year, a restriction justified on the basis that young trees would be injured by the mischievous and the park would become a place of assignation for young lovers. 'Heaven preserve us!' Bentham and Mill's fury at the injustice explodes in mockery from the pages of their letter to the Public Walks Committee. 'Righteous souls, who deprive thousands of your fellow-beings of the means of taking the most innocent and healthful enjoyment, lest the chaste park should be polluted by the whisper of ungodly passion.' As for the risk of vandalism, Bentham and Mill accepted that the English were more destructive than other nationalities, but said that this was because 'the people of the Continent have long been trusted in all public places... while the people of this country have been trusted scarcely anywhere, except where money has procured admission.'

It was rousing rhetoric, a poetic rallying cry: the 'toiling and smoke-dried citizens' of the 'great Babylon' denied even the opportunity to walk upon the 'innocent lawns' or 'gather a cowslip from the grass'. The demand for access to green spaces was growing louder.

Public parks were imbued with powerful symbolism as the massive social upheaval of industrialisation swept across Britain. Victorian romantics saw them as much more than a vital public health measure in overcrowded cities. They represented a heavenly idyll contrasting with the satanic mills of untrammelled capitalism. Denied access to God's natural landscape, the poor would succumb to earthly temptation.

It was at this point that what we now think of as the great British public park was conceived, complete with bandstand and duck pond, peacocks and perambulators. Among its chief architects was John Loudon, who had big ideas for the nation's pleasure grounds. As well as the requisite turf, he envisaged 'water, under certain circumstances (especially if there were no danger of it producing malaria), rocks, quarries, stones, wild places in imitation of heaths and caverns, grottoes, dells, dingles, ravines, hills, valleys, and other natural-looking scenes, with walks and roads, straight and winding, shady and open'.

Loudon set the benchmark on 16 September 1840 with the spectacular opening of Derby Arboretum, the first public park in England, possibly the world. It is hard to imagine from the contemporary viewpoint of a neglected patch of green in some struggling post-industrial town just what excitement a new park could engender. For hundreds of years, ordinary workers had seen their limited access to grass gradually stolen from them; commons enclosed, fences erected, the threat of prosecution or summary justice should they dare to trespass on private lawns. Now, unexpectedly, the pendulum seemed to be swinging back the other way.

Wealthy Derby mill owner Joseph Strutt had concluded that in order to gain the respect of the working classes and reform them from 'their brutish behaviour and debasing pleasures', they must be allowed to walk upon the lawn. He handed the deeds of his arboretum to the town council and inspired the biggest party in Derby's history. 'The balls and bands, the feasts and the fireworks, the dejeuners and dances, continued from Wednesday to Saturday,' the local paper reported. Tradesmen closed their shops and Derby's mental condition was described as 'an effervescence of delirious delight, of rollicking rapture'.

Suddenly, every self-respecting industrial town wanted one of these new civic parks and influential figures were recruited to the cause. The Duke of Devonshire, one of the richest and most powerful landowners in the country, agreed that his head gardener at Chatsworth, Joseph Paxton, could work on public parks for polluted mill towns and industrial centres in northern England and Scotland.

The Prime Minister Sir Robert Peel, son of a wealthy Lancastrian mill owner, donated some of his personal fortune to Manchester's Committee for Public Walks, Gardens & Playgrounds, which spent seven years co-ordinating three new parks, each to open on the same day. To the sound of cannon fire and trumpets, 22 August 1846 saw tens of thousands of people stream into Peel Park, Queen's Park and Philips Park, green spaces hailed as the clean lungs of the working city of Manchester.

On Easter Monday the following year, the Paxton-designed Birkenhead Park on the Wirrall opened its gates. Again, tens of thousands came to mark the occasion and there were 'rural sports' freely and joyfully played on the open grass: a sack race, chase the pig with the soapy tail, a blindfold wheelbarrow race and, apparently, a grinning match through six horse collars – the ugliest to receive five shillings. In that moment, it appeared, the village green had been reclaimed.

Among the crowds who thronged to Birkenhead over the next few years was the celebrated US landscape architect Frederick Olmstead. Impressed by what he saw, he took both the landscape features and the egalitarian principles of Birkenhead Park back across the Atlantic and incorporated them into US culture. His design for New York's Central Park borrowed heavily from Paxton's parks in northern England, but the journey to the Wirrall was to have an even more profound impact on American suburbia.

The Riverside district of Chicago, laid out by Olmstead after his visit, was to become the model for suburban communities across the States. He set each house thirty feet from the road, with no dividing wall in between. Instead, the front lawns converged into a seamless river of green without obstruction or boundary. This was Olmstead's and America's homage to Britain's anti-enclosure movement and to our community parks.

Back in the UK, however, for all the rollicking rapture, there was also dark muttering – warnings that the brutish working classes could not be trusted to respect the lawns and gardens, and no good would come of such generosity. A letter in *The Times* revealed how, just as the working classes in the north of England were enjoying new access to green spaces, the Royal Parks in London were trying to evict the vulgar plebs. 'Last Wednesday every decently dressed mechanic was turned out of Hyde Park,' the epistle began, hinting at bubbling disquiet. 'The warden in green said this was in accordance with new orders received from the ranger. It strikes me that these very green underlings are acting in a way, whether with or without authority, most conducive to encourage revolutionary principles, and I expect some day to hear of their getting a good ducking in the Serpentine. What is the use of this excessive exclusiveness with regard to parks which used to be considered public? It is enough to make any person's blood boil.'

With London still expanding rapidly, landowners around the capital continued the policy of enclosure, fencing and carving up traditional common land for housing. The developing commuter belt became a battleground over access to grass. In the spring of 1870, rioting erupted south of the Thames.

In Wandsworth, hundreds of people armed with hatchets and pickaxes re-established a footpath enclosed by a Mr Costeker at Plough Green. 'At each crashing of the fence there was a great hooting and hurrahing.' At Plumstead Common 'a party of women, armed with saws and hatchets, first commenced operations by sawing down a fence enclosing a meadow.' Reports at the time spoke of 'the lower class . . . resolved to test their rights'.

When a golf club in Camberwell enclosed a popular beauty

spot, One Tree Hill, in 1896 it provoked a wave of anger. The erection of a six-foot fence around immaculately trimmed greens for the exclusive benefit of the well-to-do members of a private club unleashed the pent-up fury of hundreds of years of class struggle to walk upon the grass.

On a Sunday in October, a crowd of 15,000 people assembled close to the hill and began attacking the fence. Police reinforcements were summoned and calm was, eventually, restored. But a week later the protestors returned in far greater numbers. Some reports said that 100,000 people crowded around the golf club that day with 500 foot and mounted police lined up to protect the fence. 'Stone throwing was freely indulged in, and the police were more than once hit.' One officer was badly wounded as the battle intensified. 'Rushes on the part of the roughs were quickly responded to by charges of the police, when mounted police and fleeing public were mingled in what, at times, appeared to be inextricable confusion.'

However, as the Victorian era drew to a close, from the inextricable confusion of urban development and industrialisation emerged a country fanatical about grass: tennis courts, croquet lawns, bowling greens, golf courses, football pitches, cricket squares. The invention of the mower had seen the lawn escape over the high hedges of England's great estates and into the gardens of a million humble suburban homes. Urban planners had become convinced of the need for green spaces and municipal authorities vied to recruit the finest lawn-makers for their locality.

The last decade of the nineteenth century saw a thousand acres of town gardens and ornamental grounds open in London alone. The Garden City movement of Ebenezer Howard revisited some of Loudon's ideas, creating new towns built around concentric circles of green. The National Trust was born, with a mission to protect 'the public interest in open spaces'. The trust would go on to care for more than 600,000 acres of land 'for the benefit of the nation'.

It appeared the long and bloody fight for the right of all to walk upon the green grass had been won. But then it all started to go backwards again. It was as though we gradually but inexorably lost our memory of the struggle we had been through, a communal dementia in which hundreds of years of campaigning and fighting was forgotten.

Perhaps Britain had new battles to win; the Second World War saw parks, commons and greens ploughed up for food production. In the 1950s, cash-strapped local authorities attempted to restore municipal gardens, but they couldn't finish the job. The 1960s was a decade with eyes on a concrete future rather than nostalgia for some organic past. (It was also a time when a passion for grass meant something entirely different.) The 1970s and 80s were an economic roller-coaster ride in which any remaining park keepers found themselves and their peaked caps flung out at the first hint of danger.

Which led us to the 1990s, when my professional wandering led me to countless residential parks to take the civic temperature. What struck me was just how deserted these places felt. Where was everybody? The answer was indoors.

If 'toiling and smoke-dried citizens' wished to take a little exercise, they drove to the breezeblock leisure centre, a development constructed and maintained with the money that used to be spent on the local park. If they wanted to find some 'amusement, recreation, entertainment, and instruction', they headed for the shopping mall, with its artificial trees and canned muzac. The commercial had replaced the civic. Public space had been abandoned in favour of the private sphere.

When plans were revealed to build on the last remaining patch of public grass in central Washington in north-east England, a few local residents launched a campaign to try to save it. They had watched how developers had transformed their town, effectively enclosing previously public areas within The Galleries shopping centre. In April 1998, a small group began setting up their stall in the mall hoping to collect signatures for a petition but, in a powerful reflection of what had already been lost, they were refused permission by the shopping centre owners. Mary Appleby, Pamela Beresford and Robert Duggan went to the European Court of Human Rights to argue that they were being denied their freedom of expression, but the judges disagreed. Washington's proud civic centre was now private retail space. Once more, rich traders would decree who could walk on the grass.

An emergent environmentalist movement saw the neglect of green spaces and the privatisation of town centres as a new policy of enclosure that needed to be challenged. The political activist George Monbiot, writing in the *Guardian*, demanded citizens 'reassert our rights to common spaces' and 'where necessary wrest them back from the hands of the developers'. The call to arms attracted a broad range of recruits: hippies and anarchists; eco-warriors and anti-capitalists. They were a noisy, diverse and angry crowd with often contradictory and pretty unrealistic global ambitions. The *Daily Mail* described the coalition of activists as 'a grouping of organisations from Lesbian Avengers to cloaked members of the Druid Clan of Dana'.

Up in the trees of a public park in Derby in 1998, close to the scenes of rollicking rapture a century-and-half before, activists built tree houses in an attempt to thwart developers who wanted to build a road and a roundabout. But such protests were fringe affairs lacking broad popular support. Far from wanting to see the end of capitalism, most people preferred the air-conditioned comfort of the private shopping mall to the intimidating atmosphere of the public park.

It fell to a committee of MPs in 1999 to take stock. 'We are shocked at the weight of evidence, far beyond our expectations, about the extent of the problems parks have faced in the last thirty years,' their report concluded. 'It is clear that if nothing is done many of them will become albatrosses around the necks of local authorities. Un-used, derelict havens for crime and vandalism, it would be better to close them and re-use the land than to leave them to decay further.'

Created as a refuge, the public park had become a no-go area. One witness told the MPs that the parks could not be made safe by 'two men in a rundown vehicle and an Alsatian dog driving through every day at four o'clock. The kids went at five to four and came back at five past four and carried on burning.' The traditional park keeper, if one existed, was an object of ridicule. Local youths began to see the (often elderly) 'Parky' as impotent and laughable.

It is a rule of contemporary British politics that when ministers discover they have neglected some vital aspect of government they announce the creation of a 'taskforce'. The word has a sense of urgency and military efficiency. So it was that in January 2001 the Urban Green Spaces Taskforce was established. There was much political discussion about urban renaissance amid growing anxiety about antisocial behaviour. Focus groups kept coming up with the same three words to describe what the public wanted: cleaner, greener and safer communities. In short, they needed their park back. They wanted to walk on the grass again. 'Cleaner, Greener, Safer' became the mantra of Deputy Prime Minister John Prescott, who told Parliament that 'litter, graffiti, fly-tipping, abandoned cars, dog fouling, the loss of play areas or footpaths, for many people is the top public service priority.' He said that public spaces were a barometer of a community, and successful neighbourhoods were characterised by parks and open spaces that local people were proud of and where they wanted to spend their time.

The government knew, however, that bunging a bit of cash at the problem might make sense in a time of relative plenty, but a good lawn needs to be cared for during hard frosts and baking sun. 'Central government expects local green space managers to make the case for green space expenditure against other pressing priorities,' Mr Prescott helpfully announced. 'Otherwise there is the danger that when budgets are tight, the case for green space will not be made effectively, will slip down the local priority list and decline will set in again.'

Standing on untended grass, among the litter and dog mess of a British sink estate, I survey the scene. Budgets are tight and some regard spending on parks, pitches and playgrounds as an indulgence in austere times. But hundreds of years of struggle should not be dismissed lightly. If a society is functioning well, the grass will tell you.

H IS FOR HAPPINESS

If you had walked into my family's sitting room in 1969, you would have seen a piece of furniture designed to look like a small mahogany drinks cabinet. In fact, when you folded back the little doors, it revealed itself as a television set. The object encapsulated my parents' wary relationship with modernity. They would rather pretend to their friends they had bottles of alcohol stashed in the house than a TV.

For me, though, the wooden doors opened onto a glorious future – my destiny. On the black and white screen inside the box I watched a man step foot onto the moon and, with that one small step, confidently assumed humankind was striding along a conveyor belt to a better and better world. Adventure and discovery would bring flying cars, everlasting gobstoppers and answers to every question – the definition of 'progress' to an optimistic 10-year-old boy.

More than four decades on and I am still waiting. Not for flying cars and everlasting gobstoppers, I gave up on them years ago. But for an answer to one question: how should we define progress? It is a puzzle that haunts our contemporary politics: the Prime Minister has ordered official statisticians to come up with a way to measure levels of well-being in Britain, initiating a debate as to what exactly social progress looks like.

But David Cameron is following a well-worn path. It is a mystery that has been bugging people for at least two-and-a-half thousand years, ever since Confucius in ancient China, Plato in ancient Greece and the Gautama Buddha in ancient India each tried to define it. For all of them, 'progress' had an ethical or spiritual dimension. It was a process of development leading to greater contentment, fulfilment and happiness in society – the good life, the ideal state, nirvana.

The first European voices to challenge the notion that human advancement was a religious or spiritual journey were probably heard in the fourteenth century. Renaissance thinkers began to ask whether progress might also be linked to a better understanding of science and appreciation of culture, that there was a human as well as a divine element to it.

This thought was taken up by the philosopher Sir Francis Bacon in his novel of 1624, *New Atlantis*, in which he introduced readers to the perfect society of Bensalem, a utopia achieved entirely through learning, experiment and discovery. It might not sound like much of a blockbuster plot, but in the seventeenth century this was heady stuff. The book inspired the foundation of the Invisible College, a group of a dozen eminent scientists which later became the Royal Society, one of the world's most respected scientific institutions to this day.

There was a conflict between a church that saw progress in terms of a journey towards individual Christian salvation and scientists who argued that humanity's destiny lay in its own hands by the acquisition of knowledge and application of rational thought. In the spring of 1776, the English philosopher Jeremy Bentham published an anonymous pamphlet entitled 'A Fragment on Government', in which he argued, 'It is the greatest happiness of the greatest number that is the measure of right and wrong.' He maintained that the purpose or 'utility' of every government action should be 'to add to the happiness of the community'. It was a vision that borrowed heavily on the ideas of ancient Greece, but the problem remained as it had for thousands of years: how to measure such progress?

Bentham defined happiness as the excess of pleasure over pain or the difference between well-being and ill-being. 'Taking the whole of mankind together,' he mused, 'on which side of the account does the balance lie, on the well-being or ill-being side?' Despite extensive lists of pleasures and pains, Bentham never found a convincing way to measure social well-being. Nor did other utilitarian thinkers. Happiness appeared to be a candyfloss concept, attractive but ultimately fluffy and insubstantial – hardly the handy ready reckoner that government needed to decide its priorities.

So it was that another yardstick for progress came to be accepted: money. Economists, not social scientists, were invited to sit closest to the seat of power. Tangible wealth, rather than ethereal well-being, became the fundamental political goal.

Even finding a single accepted measure of affluence proved tricky, and it wasn't until the 1930s that Russian-born economist Simon Kuznets came up with the concept of Gross Domestic Product (GDP). For industrialised countries such as Britain, trying to recover from the deprivations of the Second World War in the 1940s and 50s, GDP was embraced as the best way to monitor material and social development. Despite Kuznets' own warning that his measure should not be used as a surrogate for well-being, those three letters became the focus of UK government activity, recited mantra-like as an incantation for a better life. National advancement and greater GDP became almost indistinguishable.

However, not everyone was content with this state of affairs. In 1960, a paper published by the United Nations warned that 'one of the greatest dangers in development policy lies in the tendency to give to the more material aspects of growth an overriding and disproportionate emphasis.' Poorer nations, particularly those looking to break free of a colonial yoke, argued there was more to progress than money. 'The end may be forgotten in preoccupation of the means,' the UN report added.

Eight years later, Robert F. Kennedy, campaigning for the US Presidency in Kansas, gave an impassioned speech arguing the same point:

> Our Gross National Product ... counts air pollution and cigarette advertising, and ambulances to clear our highways of carnage. It counts special locks for our doors and the jails for the people who break them. It counts the destruction of the redwood and the loss of our natural wonder in chaotic sprawl. It counts napalm and counts nuclear warheads and armoured cars for the police to fight the riots in our cities ... and the television programmes which glorify violence in order to sell toys to our children. Yet the Gross National Product does not allow for the health of our children, the quality of their education or the joy of their play. It does not include the beauty of our poetry or the strength of our marriages, the intelligence of our public debate or the integrity of our public officials. It measures neither our wit nor our courage, neither our wisdom nor our learning, neither our compassion nor our devotion to our country. It measures everything, in short, except that which makes life worthwhile.

The following year the UN General Assembly issued a declaration stating 'each government has the primary role and ultimate responsibility of ensuring the social progress and well-being of its people.' It might almost have said 'happiness'. The Assembly stressed it should be the objective of every state to raise not just material, but spiritual standards of living. The list of goals included the elimination of hunger and poverty, the eradication of illiteracy, adequate housing, and the highest standards of health. But the UN went much further, demanding nations strive for 'a just and equitable distribution of income', 'the encouragement of creative initiative under conditions of enlightened public opinion' and an 'integrated society'. Getting rich was not enough – progress was about human rights and social justice.

This was 1969, and I was watching Neil Armstrong and thinking of everlasting gobstoppers, the UN was watching anti-Vietnam protests and thinking of world peace, and thousands of hippies were heading for Woodstock and thinking of free love. But none of these visions of progress was embraced by political leaders around the world who, for decades to come, would still stick doggedly to the idea that increasing GDP should be the basis for deciding policy.

Then something changed. Perhaps it was the impending millennium that prompted a reflective mood. Or maybe it was environmental concerns about the state of the planet. It might simply have been that, in the developed world at least, enormous new wealth was not really making people any happier. With the imminent arrival of the twenty-first century, old questions began to be asked once again.

In 1998, for instance, an article appeared in the magazine *Forbes ASAP*, by Peggy Noonan, a former speechwriter for US Presidents Reagan and Bush Sr. 'History has handed us one of the easiest rides in all the story of man,' she wrote. 'It is all so fantastically fine.' Then she added: 'Lately this leaves me uneasy. Does it you?' Here was someone who had spent her life arguing the case for capitalism, writing in a journal for the super-rich and questioning the comforts of wealth. 'The more you have, the more you need, the more you work and plan,' Noonan observed, complaining that affluence 'carries within it an unspoken command: More!'

The article was to gain prominence because, three years before 9/11, it contained within it a prediction of a terrorist attack on New York, 'the psychological centre of our modernity, our hedonism, our creativity, our hard-shouldered hipness, our unthinking arrogance'. But, for me, the anxiety that drove the essay was an almost visceral fear that the richest nations on the planet might have missed the point, that the West had got its priorities wrong, was so busy making money it had lost the plot. 'Does family life spill over into work life? No. Work life spills over into family life,' Noonan argued. 'This is not progress.'

At almost the same moment, three eminent American professors completed a book that would, ultimately, transform British politics. Entitled *Well-being: The Foundations of Hedonic Psychology*, Daniel Kahneman, Ed Deiner and Norbert Schwartz announced the existence of a new field of psychology striving to achieve what Jeremy Bentham and the utilitarian movement failed to do – to measure happiness. 'Our hope is that hedonic psychology will be relevant to policy,' the authors wrote. 'We recognise, with a large degree of humility, that scientific understanding in this field is currently woefully inadequate to provide a strong underpinning for national policies. We believe, however, that in the decades to come there will be much greater success in understanding hedonics, and that principles will emerge that can be used by policy makers.' The book was hailed as 'the handbook, guidebook, compass and bible' for what might be called the new utilitarians – a global group of academics and intellectuals pledged to transforming economics and politics around well-being rather than wealth.

It was a damp November afternoon in 2002 when, over tea and biscuits at Her Majesty's Treasury in Whitehall, a cell of British new utilitarians plotted their opening gambit. A pamphlet entitled *Life Satisfaction: The State of Knowledge and Implications for Government* was circulated the following month and clearly stamped: 'This is not a statement of government policy.' Its motive was far more radical.

The apparently innocuous conclusion of the 2002 tract was that 'there is a case for state intervention to boost life satisfaction.' Who could argue with that? But it implied a redefinition of political purpose. 'This is a revolution in how we think about everything,' argued the economist Professor Richard Layard, one of those gathered in Room 2/18 that day. 'Government has got to rethink its priorities,' he insisted. 'I am hoping that each department will review its objectives and see how closely they are in line with the idea of promoting the happiness of the people.'

What lay behind the challenge was the claim that it was now possible to measure well-being at least as well as economists measure wealth. The hedonic psychologists had produced good evidence that happiness was an objective phenomenon and that there were ways of counting it.

At around this time, I paid a visit to Daniel Kahneman – author of one of the gospels in the happiness bible. 'It turns out,' he told me, 'something like fifteen per cent of the overall time that people spend is bad time, unpleasant time. Now that gives you something to get your teeth into. If you manage to reduce that number from fifteen per cent to fourteen per cent, you would be doing a great service to humankind!' Kahneman was aware that the pursuit of happiness, although enshrined in America's constitution, was too easily dismissed as a nebulous and naïve ambition by hard-nosed policy advisors in Washington. Reducing unhappiness, however, was accepted as a legitimate and noble aim.

In Britain, the new utilitarians were beginning to grow in confidence: the government was pledged to evidence-based policy and they hoped the science of happiness could become a driving force in determining the political direction of travel. Within Number Ten itself, Tony Blair's strategy team included enthusiastic advocates of the new utilitarian cause. Geoff Mulgan and David Halpern were quietly encouraging the Prime Minister towards the politics of well-being, but the Labour leader was never totally convinced.

The problem was not just that the science was new, but that its findings cut across political ideologies. In fact, it appeared to turn conventional arguments on their head. The accepted wisdom in Britain was that the twentieth century had seen 'the right' win the economic case and 'the left' win the social case. Happiness science suggested, up to a point at least, that well-being was improved by conservative social policies and socialist economic policies. The left embraced findings that suggested redistributing wealth is good for our well-being; that state intervention in public services raises joy in the national heart; that policies encouraging a work–life balance are good for the general well-being. The right preferred the scientific papers suggesting that marriage (rather than cohabitation) has a hugely positive effect on happiness; and that God and the Boy Scouts add to the sum of human contentment, while entertainment TV and multiculturalism tend to reduce it.

As the Westminster party apparatchiks struggled to fit the new philosophy into old ideology, it became clear that the message of the new utilitarians was striking a chord with the public. After decades of economic growth, Britain was richer than at any point in its history. Yet, as Geoff Mulgan put it, 'society's ability to meet people's psychological and psycho-social needs appears to have declined.' Delivering almost inexorable economic growth was stubbornly refusing to create the feel-good factor politicians yearned for, and so it was that the happy evangelists were quietly able to gain access to the corridors of power.

They still tended to operate in the shadows, working in little happy cells secreted within the state machine. One group had successfully infiltrated local government some years earlier, achieving legislation stating that the 'promotion of well-being' was a responsibility of all councils in England. At national level, the Whitehall Well-being Working Group kept a low profile (W3G to those in the know) and few took much notice of the report published by the Department of Environment advocating that well-being be used to inform future policy development and spending decisions. Nevertheless, the new utilitarian message was feeding into the system.

Richard Layard became the public standard bearer for the happiness movement in the UK, an eminent economics professor with excellent political contacts. His power base was the Centre for Economic Performance at the London School of Economics, a body that included on its board Gus O'Donnell, the man Whitehall called GOD.

Then the top official at the Treasury, O'Donnell would go on to head the civil service, a bureaucrat whose professional life was devoted to measuring progress in government. Fascinated by Layard's claims that wealth was failing to translate into well-being, he became convinced that the arguments of the new utilitarians went to the very heart of what government is actually for, and how we can measure its success. The civil service and, critically, the Treasury were engaged in the debate. Senior officials had been persuaded that it was no longer a question of whether one could measure well-being, but how its measurement might change the business of government and the definition of social progress.

'It's time we admitted that there's more to life than money,' a fresh-faced politician announced in 2006. 'It's time we focused, not on GDP, but on GWB – General Well-being.' David Cameron had recently been elected leader of the Conservative Party when he gave a speech that echoed the words (if not the poetry) of Robert F. Kennedy from almost four decades before. 'Well-being can't be measured by money or traded in markets. It can't be required by law or delivered by government. It's about the beauty of our surroundings, the quality of our culture, and above all the strength of our relationships. Improving our society's sense of well-being is, I believe, the central political challenge of our times.'

The idea was mocked in the popular press, but some commentators believed the Conservative leader was on to something. I went to interview him, to see if he was serious about putting well-being at the heart of his politics. 'We should be thinking not just what is good for putting money in people's pockets but what is good for putting joy in people's hearts,' David Cameron told me.

Richard Layard's book *Happiness: Lessons from a New Science*, published a year before, had become a surprise bestseller and a must-read for both political and social scientists. He demonstrated how, beyond a certain point, additional wealth does not translate into extra well-being, the so-called Easterlin paradox. Most Western countries, he argued, had passed that threshold and the pursuit of economic growth was actually becoming counter-productive.

Suddenly, it was fashionable to question the hegemony of GDP. In the summer of 2007, representatives from many of the rich nations' clubs gathered in Istanbul to do just that. The OECD, the United Nations, the European Commission and the World Bank signed a declaration committing them to 'measuring and fostering the progress of societies in all dimensions, with the ultimate goal of improving policy making, democracy and citizens' well-being'.

The Secretary General of the OECD stood to address the 1,200 delegates in the cavernous conference hall. 'It is time to call for a global effort to find better measurements of progress,' Angel Gurría told the conference. 'In the end, what we are trying to do is not just to measure progress and well-being but to achieve it.' There was, perhaps, a hint of urgency in his remarks: a sense that the economic architecture that supported Western society had developed dangerous cracks, but no stable alternative had yet been erected.

Governments around the world recruited the greatest minds to address the problem. In France, President Nicolas Sarkozy invited no fewer than five Nobel prize-winning economists to join a panel of experts pledged to finding more relevant indicators of social progress. The Commission on the Measurement of Economic Performance and Social Progress first assembled in February 2008, headed by the former chief economist at the World Bank, American professor Joseph Stiglitz. They were not to know on that damp winter's day in Paris that severe economic storms were gathering just over the skyline. Within months, the world's banking system would teeter on the brink of collapse and, with the resulting recession, political focus would shift from the philosophy of social progress to concerns over how to restore economic growth.

The global financial crisis was a reality check to the new utilitarian movement, and the question was whether its ideas would survive in a climate of (relative) austerity. Stiglitz and his team of economic all-stars finally agreed a 300-page report in September 2009, their conclusions to be launched in the Grand Amphitheatre of the Sorbonne as outside, on the streets of Paris, more than a million protestors demonstrated at government plans for economic belt-tightening. The French President stood to speak, the marble faces of Descartes, Pascal and Lavoisier watching him from their pillared alcoves. Would he, in the face of mass public protest at spending cuts, support his experts' conclusion that the measurement of progress should focus less on wealth and more on well-being? Would he agree to be a leader in a global debate as to whether we are really striving for what is important?

Yes, he would. 'France will open the debate on this report's conclusions everywhere,' he announced. 'France will fight for every international organisation to modify their statistical systems by following the commission's recommendations.'

In Britain, those recruited to the new utilitarian cause were more circumspect but no less determined. Three months after Sarkozy's rallying call, buried in a report on mental health strategy, the UK's Labour government committed itself to putting well-being in all policy. The Health Secretary Andy Burnham explained how his officials would liaise with other departments to ensure that policies considered the impact on well-being, as well as using it to inform future policy and research.

Behind the scenes, a team of British statisticians had been quietly working on a measure of societal well-being for years, but it was not until David Cameron moved into Downing Street that the project won official approval. I was among sixty journalists, academics and civil servants invited to the Treasury in late November 2010. The PM breezed onto a purpose-built podium to address his audience. 'From April next year, we'll start measuring our progress as a country, not just by how our economy is growing, but by how our lives are improving; not just by our standard of living, but by our quality of life,' he announced.

Was he serious? 'People often regard the "happiness agenda" as being a bit like candyfloss; it is sweet but insubstantial,' I suggested to Mr Cameron. 'Will this change people's lives, do you think?'

'If I thought this was woolly and insubstantial and candyfloss-like, I would not be bothering to talk to you about it on a Thursday morning when I have got lots of other things to do,' he replied.

But would he, for instance, change his politics if the well-being measure suggested he should? 'What I believe this will do is help to provide evidence to create a debate that may encourage us to change our minds about some things we have been rather stubborn about,' the Prime Minister said. 'It could throw up things that might challenge politicians' views about equality or taxation, but that is all for the good. We should never be frightened of having a debate.'

Perhaps not. But if we are really going to see an accepted measure of well-being being used to shape our policy and politics, that prospect will prove frightening for many. Old orthodoxies and ideologies will come up against uncomfortable challenges. Having emerged from Whitehall's shadows, Britain's new utilitarians are likely to face ridicule and attack. There will be some unhappy times ahead in the pursuit of happiness. I fear, too, that my hopes of everlasting gobstoppers and flying cars are as far away as ever.

I IS FOR IMMIGRATION

Conjurors call it 'misdirection', encouraging an audience to look over there when the sleight of hand is taking place over here. Soldiers use feints or diversionary tactics to fool the enemy into believing the action is in one place when it is really in another. Governments have similar tricks, exploiting external threats to distract attention from their own domestic faults and failures.

Natural xenophobia, our primal fear of the foreign or unfamiliar, is an easy trait to manipulate. History is filled with examples of leaders feeding common prejudices to court popularity in tough times, blaming and then punishing the outsider for every social ill. Even today, Britain's tabloid press is ready to accuse 'foreigners' of being responsible for crime waves, unemployment, housing shortages, stretched public services and welfare scrounging.

Politicians argue that they are responding to some tangible social crisis when they talk up their latest immigration plan. There are complex and genuine social, financial and political concerns that flow from the movement of large numbers of people in an age of globalisation, but sometimes it is hard to see how the rules and restrictions proposed are anything more than a distraction from more stubborn problems afflicting twenty-first-century Britain.

It was forever thus. When Edward I sailed back to England

from his duchy in Gascony in 1289, he found that a succession of wars, rebellions and foreign escapades had left him deeply in debt. The taxes required to fund his battles were, of course, highly unpopular but the king urgently required more cash. So he exploited a three-letter word that had become almost as despised as 'tax': Jew.

England's Jewish population was an easy target: the foreign moneylenders, financiers and bankers were blamed by commoners and clergy alike for extortionate interest rates and anything else that came to mind. Wild accusations of ritual murder and torture were commonplace: myths about Jews hunting for children as sacrifices before Passover spread easily and widely in medieval England.

In the summer of 1290, Edward called his knights together. He needed their help to replenish the royal coffers and offered a deal. The king announced that every Jew in England would be thrown out of the country if his knights agreed to collect the new tax. The Edict of Expulsion was hugely popular and successfully distracted attention away from the extra taxation. It wasn't the first and it wouldn't be the last time that 'immigration control' was used to buy political advantage.

Wind the clock forward almost exactly six hundred years to the nineteenth century, and the story was repeated. Britain was facing a financial crisis, as the boom years of imperial expansion could no longer be sustained. Rising unemployment had forced hundreds of thousands of labourers and their families into abject poverty and conditions for those lucky enough to find work were not much better: long hours, dangerous conditions, little security and low pay.

In London's East End and around the docks, there was rising desperation and simmering anger. No family was protected from the workhouse or starvation. In early August 1889, news broke that the cargo ship *Lady Armstrong* was tying up at West India Dock and 2,000 frantic men literally fought each other to be among the first ranks of labourers when contractors selected the men for work. The elation of those picked out turned to rage, though, when it emerged that the dock's manager had cut their so-called 'plus' money, the few extra pennies' bonus they were due when a large vessel was unloaded.

The London Dock Strike followed, quickly spreading across wharf and quay. A month later and the employers gave in: a famous victory for trade union solidarity, a milestone in the development of the British labour movement, but a clanging warning bell to the Establishment. It was time to play the race card.

The leader of the Dockers union, Ben Tillett, had revealed something of the common street prejudice of the time when he told migrant workers who had backed the strike: 'Yes, you are our brothers, and we will do our duty by you. But we wish you had not come.' A Glasgow steel worker, addressing the 1892 TUC congress, said: 'The door must be shut against the enormous immigration of destitute aliens into this country.' The 'aliens' were largely Jews fleeing persecution in Eastern Europe, many of them heading through the UK on their way to the United States. The TUC duly voted for a motion demanding a complete halt to immigration.

For some ambitious politicians, the Jewish refugees represented the ideal scapegoat for many of the social ills afflicting the working classes. In 1900, Major Sir William Evans-Gordon won the East End constituency of Stepney for the Conservatives on an anti-immigrant platform. He reflected many of his voters' anxieties when he proclaimed that 'not a day passes but English families are ruthlessly turned out to make room for foreign invaders. The rates are burdened with the education of thousands of foreign children.'

Then, as now, the arguments were that housing and public services were being put under strain, not because of lack of government investment or planning, but by the arrival of foreigners. Rich newspaper owners were more than happy for their publications to stoke up anti-Semitism: the *Daily Record* and *Mail* in

Glasgow ran the headline 'Alien Danger: Immigrants Infected with Loathsome Disease'. In the House of Commons, one Tory MP likened Jewish immigration to the entry of infected cattle.

Emboldened by such public displays of intolerance, in January 1902 at the People's Palace in London's Mile End, Major Evans-Gordon chaired a 'Great Public Demonstration', 'Under the Auspices of The British Brothers League'. The league, campaigning for restricted immigration under the slogan 'England for the English', was attempting to organise along paramilitary lines.

Far from challenging popular prejudice, denouncing racist rhetoric and accepting responsibility for the plight of London's poorest neighbourhoods, the government set up a Royal Commission on Aliens to investigate the effect of immigrants upon housing, unemployment, public health and morals. One of the six members appointed to the commission was Major Evans-Gordon.

The committee's report, however, failed to provide the newspapers with the headlines they might have expected. It concluded that the aliens were not responsible for disease or a surge in crime, were not a burden upon the welfare system and there was no evidence that they posed any threat to jobs or the working conditions of the British labourer. The only 'charge' upheld was that they were partly responsible for overcrowded housing conditions in a few parts of London.

It must have been deeply irritating for the beleaguered Conservative Prime Minister Arthur Balfour. His administration was on the verge of being crushed in a Liberal landslide and had been relying on the handpicked commission to justify a populist attack upon immigrants. The evidence didn't stack up, but Balfour went ahead anyway. Parliament was persuaded to introduce the Aliens Act 1905, legislation that gave institutional legitimacy to the idea that foreigners were to blame for the problems of the white working classes.

Roll the clock forward forty years and another ship from the West Indies was tying up on the Thames. The cargo of the SS *Empire*

Windrush was not sugar but workers, however – around 500 black passengers, mostly from Jamaica, encouraged to take the month-long voyage from Kingston by the prospect of employment. Barely had the passengers stepped off the boat when eleven Labour MPs penned a furious letter to Prime Minister Clement Attlee. The missive explained they were concerned for the racial character of the English people and warned that 'an influx of coloured people domiciled here is likely to impair the harmony, strength and cohesion of our public and social life and to cause discord and unhappiness among all concerned.'

'I note what you say,' Attlee replied, 'but I think it would be a great mistake to take the emigration of this Jamaican party to the United Kingdom too seriously.' For the Prime Minister, the arrival of a few hundred Commonwealth citizens at Tilbury docks was a small part of a greater effort to encourage tens of thousands of immigrants into Britain to help rebuild the country's shattered infrastructure. 'It is traditional that British subjects, whether of Dominion or Colonial origin (and of whatever race or colour), should be freely admissible to the United Kingdom,' Attlee continued. 'That tradition is not, in my view, to be lightly discarded, particularly at a time when we are importing foreign labour in large numbers.'

The arrival of the *Empire Windrush* became the symbolic starting point for mass migration of Commonwealth citizens to the United Kingdom, but it also fundamentally changed the politics of immigration. From the moment those nervous but eager Jamaicans stepped ashore, the alien threat – privately at least – became less about economics and more about the colour of people's skin.

Front of house, post-war Britain was anxious to appear honourable, generous and loyal. The uplifting narrative was of a nation that had defeated the vile racism of Nazi Germany by occupying the moral high ground. Even as it licked its wounds, Britain promised to stand foursquare with those to whom it owed a debt of gratitude, the people of the wider Commonwealth whose citizens had joined in the fight against fascism. The newspapers were happy to endorse the idea of a multinational group hug and there was little open opposition to the 1948 Nationality Act reaffirming the right of free access to the United Kingdom for all 800 million subjects of the King around the world.

Behind the scenes, however, secret Cabinet documents reveal a tale of racism and duplicity. The government was doing everything it could to ensure only the right sort of immigrants came to help rebuild Britain's battered economy. The Colonial Office admitted to using 'devious little devices' to discourage and restrict black and Asian migration to Britain – covert administrative measures of questionable legality.

Just two years after asserting the rights of British subjects of whatever race or colour, Clement Attlee told his Cabinet he wanted more ideas for how 'to check the immigration into this country of coloured people'. The Home Secretary James Chuter-Ede pointed out to him that politically 'it would be difficult to justify . . . if no comparable restrictions were imposed on persons who are citizens of other Commonwealth countries.' The government didn't want to discourage workers from the white Commonwealth or the Irish Republic, and the Home Secretary explained that 'an apparent or concealed colour test would be so invidious as to make it impossible of adoption.' Chuter-Ede suggested, however, that such a step was also unnecessary because 'the use of any powers taken to restrict the free entry of British subjects to this country would, as a general rule, be more or less confined to coloured persons.'

When the Tories came to power in 1951, the major policy challenge was dealing with continuing labour shortages, but like Labour before it, the Conservative government was keen to find crafty ways of stopping black and Asian citizens from filling the jobs. Confidential Cabinet papers reveal how ministers told officials to discourage the immigration of 'coloured people'. They made it more difficult for black and Asian migrants to obtain travel documents, and advertisements were placed in colonial newspapers warning that jobs and accommodation were hard to find in the UK.

The public position was still that Britain welcomed all Commonwealth citizens, but privately the government was discussing even more drastic measures to keep out 'coloured' immigrants. Shorthand notes of conversations between Prime Minister Winston Churchill and Home Secretary David Maxwell Fyfe reveal the latter saying there was 'a case on merits for excludg. riff-raff' but 'Wd. have to admit in Parlt. tht. purpose of legn. was to control [admission] of coloured.'

Churchill decided that, before taking such a political risk, the government needed an economic or social justification for discriminating on the basis of skin colour. A working party was charged with assembling evidence from police reports and departmental surveys. Questionnaires were circulated in labour exchanges, asking: 'Is it true that coloured people, or certain classes of coloured people, are work shy?' and 'Is it true that they are unsuited by temperament to the kind of work available?' When the results came back, the Home Secretary was obliged to concede that the working party had found 'no such evil consequences of this immigration' to justify a policy of racial discrimination.

The search for excuses to keep out black and Asian immigrants continued, but again and again the enquiries came up with the wrong answers. A report presented to the Cabinet in 1957 found most black and Asian immigrants to be law-abiding and a useful addition to the country's labour force. If there was a problem, ministers were advised, it came from a white population becoming increasingly hostile and resentful. The Cabinet was told about clashes with Teddy Boys and warned that 'the tolerant attitude of the white people will last only so long as the coloured people do not encroach on the interests of the rest of the community.'

A year later, with a dreary predictability, racial violence spilled onto the streets of Notting Hill in London. A lynch mob of 300–400 white youths, many of them Teddy Boys, attacked the houses of West Indian residents with petrol bombs and missiles, in rioting that lasted five nights over the August bank holiday. Police reported how, at one point, crowds several thousand strong roamed the district, breaking into homes and attacking any West Indian they could find. There was open defiance to the police; one officer was told: 'Mind your own business, coppers. Keep out of it. We will settle these n*****s our way. We'll murder the bastards.'

Some black youths attempted to fight back: one large group of West Indian men was seen shouting threats and abuse, and openly displaying various offensive weapons. But the true story of what became known as the Notting Hill riots was very different from the official police report, which dismissed it as simply 'ruffians, both coloured and white, who seized on this opportunity to indulge in hooliganism'.

Six months later, and with public hostility against the arrival of immigrants enflamed by disturbances in a number of British cities, David Maxwell Fyfe – now Lord Chancellor – addressed the Cabinet in Downing Street. 'Although the real problem is in the numbers of colonial immigrants who arrive in this country,' he advised, 'public opinion tends to focus attention on the criminal activities of a small minority.' The Lord Chancellor admitted that this issue was 'undoubtedly inflated out of all proportion' but his advice to Cabinet was to respond to misguided prejudice. 'It would be better for the government to take the initiative and introduce legislation,' he said. 'Failure to take action might react unfavourably on the government's popularity.'

The link between discriminatory immigration control and party political expediency could hardly have been expressed more clearly. The Lord Chancellor proposed tough new laws for deporting 'undesirable immigrants'. The problem, as always, was that the legislation could not openly discriminate between white and 'coloured' migrants. 'For presentational reasons,' he told ministerial colleagues, 'we recommend that citizens of the Irish Republic should be liable under the Bill ... but we recognise in practice, although they could be deported without difficulty, it would be impossible to prevent their re-entry.' It wasn't the white Irish immigrants the proposals were targeting.

The secret Cabinet discussions eventually led to the Commonwealth Immigrants Act of 1962, one of the most counterproductive pieces of legislation ever passed. Until that point, Caribbean and Asian immigrants had tended to be single people, often skilled workers who planned to take advantage of labour shortages in Britain before returning home. When proposals for the new law were announced, immigration of 'coloured Colonials' shot up six-fold.

It had been widely but mistakenly rumoured that the legislation would see the UK permanently close its doors to non-white migrants, including the families of those already living here. To beat the ban, a record 125,000 people from black and Asian Commonwealth countries arrived in Britain in 1961, an influx for which the government was totally unprepared. The Act itself was intended to stem the flow by requiring new immigrants to have a work voucher but, by also enshrining the right of migrant workers to be joined by their dependents, it positively encouraged the permanent settlement of families. Those migrants who might have planned to return to their homeland now didn't dare leave.

Muddled and unprincipled politics had contrived to achieve the one thing they were designed to avoid; the ethnic character of many British cities was altered forever. For the white working classes, the cultural transformation seemed alarming and as unemployment rose during the mid-1960s, so did racial tension. Fewer Commonwealth migrants were granted permission to enter the UK – in fact, many more people were leaving the country than arriving during this period – but in the poor neighbourhoods where black and Asian families had set up home, they became scapegoats for all the stresses associated with rapid social change.

At 2.30 on the afternoon of Saturday, 20 April 1968, Enoch Powell rose to speak in a meeting room on the first floor of the Midland Hotel in Birmingham. He talked of the deep unease of his white constituents in nearby Wolverhampton, their anxiety at the rapid shift in the ethnic make-up of their neighbourhood. 'For reasons which they could not comprehend, and in pursuance of a decision by default, on which they were never consulted, they found themselves made strangers in their own country,' Powell said.

The Conservative MP did not believe the answer to racial discord was anti-discrimination laws, as the Labour government was proposing. Instead, Powell argued, the immigrants should be encouraged to pack up and leave, because it was their very presence that threatened the stability of the nation. 'As I look ahead, I am filled with foreboding. Like the Roman, I seem to see "the River Tiber foaming with much blood"', he said.

There was a candour in what Powell was saying, however sickening to contemporary ears, in marked contrast to the secret racism that lay behind two decades of immigration policy. Mainstream politicians moved to occupy the moral high ground in the furore that followed the 'Rivers of Blood' speech, but principles were in short supply.

Only weeks earlier the Labour government had rushed through emergency immigration laws that the Commonwealth Secretary George Thomson had argued in Cabinet were 'wrong in principle, clearly discriminatory on grounds of colour, and contrary to everything that we stand for'. That legislation, the Commonwealth Immigration Act, was a response to concerns that tens of thousands of Kenyan Asians with British passports might flee persecution in East Africa and come to the UK. Prime Minister Harold Wilson was told by his Home Secretary, James Callaghan, that on the one hand Britain had moral and legal obligations to the refugees, but on the other hand the Trade Union movement was already kicking up over plans to outlaw racial discrimination, and 'this would become more serious if the numbers of coloured immigrants entering the country were allowed to rise.'

By inserting a clause exempting those whose grandparents were born in Britain, the law was designed to affect Asians from East Africa, not white settlers. The Attorney General Sir Elwyn Jones admitted that the proposals almost certainly breached the European Convention on Human Rights. Fortunately, he was able to tell the Cabinet, 'although we have signed this Protocol we have not yet ratified it.'

The Times called it 'probably the most shameful measure that Labour members have ever been asked by their whips to support'. James Callaghan told Parliament: 'I repudiate emphatically the suggestion that it is racialist in origin or in conception or in the manner in which it is being carried out.' However, six weeks later, a hint to Callaghan's true motives was revealed in an internal document. 'When we decided to legislate to slow down Asian immigration from East Africa we took our stand partly on the ground that a sudden influx of this kind ... imposed an intolerable strain on the social services,' he wrote. But the memo confessed that there was little or no evidence of immigrants burdening schools, health services, housing or the welfare system.

Callaghan later admitted privately that the problem was not the impact of new arrivals upon public services but the impact of brown skin on the public. Despite assurances to Parliament and Labour's public commitment to eradicate racial discrimination, the government had forced through legislation specifically designed to deprive citizens of their rights on the basis of skin colour.

Wind the clock forwards once more to a Saturday afternoon in 2004. It was May Day and a bus bearing foreign plates had just pulled into Victoria coach station after a twelve-hour journey. Disembarking was the bleary-eyed vanguard of an unexpected and unprecedented invasion of Britain. These were the pioneers of an extraordinary exodus that would be felt in every corner of the country, transforming the politics of immigration once again.

Eight new nations in Central and Eastern Europe had just been granted membership of the European Union. At the stroke of midnight, 75 million citizens from the Czech Republic, Estonia, Hungary, Latvia, Lithuania, Poland, Slovenia and Slovakia had gained the right to live and work in any member state. Except, actually, they hadn't. Britain was almost alone in not imposing a temporary quota on migrants from the eight accession countries, and so it was that every aircraft and every bus bound for London from the new EU states had been booked up for weeks. Immigration officers were warned that coaches would be arriving from Eastern Europe at an unprecedented level, with the likelihood of chaotic disruption and delay for normal Bank Holiday travellers. The vast majority of the buses and bulging baby Fiats came from Poland, their occupants prepared to seek out work wherever their wheels might take them.

Previous government predictions as to how many Eastern Europeans would settle in the UK were based on the false assumption that most would head for Germany. Ministers had blithely talked about 5,000 a year. But, unlike Britain, the Germans had applied a quota and, in the first twelve months following accession, 70,000 of the new EU citizens made their way to the UK. As significant as the number of new arrivals was *where* they went. These migrants didn't behave like previous waves of foreign arrivals, trying to get a foothold in the poorer districts of big cities. They travelled everywhere.

There was not a postcode in the land that remained unaffected: from the tip of Cornwall to the most northerly parts of Shetland, Poles and Lithuanians, Latvians and Estonians became part of the local scene. What it meant was that millions of people in communities previously untouched by immigration overheard conversations at the bus stop conducted in a foreign tongue or saw

strange brands of beer, called 'Zywiec' or 'Tyskie', in the local supermarket. It certainly wasn't Theakston's Old Peculiar.

Although these new migrants were white Europeans, their
arrival proved quite unsettling for many voters and the issue of
immigration shot up the political agenda. 'Are you thinking what
I'm thinking?' Michael Howard asked during the 2005 election
campaign. 'It's not racist to talk about immigration,' he said. 'It's not
racist to want to limit the numbers.'

Anxiety about foreign migrants had shifted from colour to
scale. 'Over a hundred and fifty thousand people are now settling in
the UK every year – that's the equivalent of a city the size of
Peterborough,' the Conservative leader claimed. Bizarrely, Howard's
opponents accused him of dog-whistling to racists. Actually, in
comparison to most political discussion about immigration, he
could hardly have been more open. Howard was right: for the first
time since Enoch Powell's speech, mainstream politicians could
openly raise fears about immigration without being accused of
racism. But the political debate was no less dishonest than that
which had gone before.

Labour had been so timid about discussing immigration that
it almost forgot to mention how its open door policy had seen the
number of foreigners coming to live in the UK more than double
since it took office: from 224,000 in 1996 to 494,000 in 2004. Later,
government insider Andrew Neather would claim that there had
been a political purpose in using mass immigration to make the UK
multicultural. An advisor to the Prime Minister and Home
Secretary, Neather let slip how ministers understood the conservatism of their core voters and, while they might have been
passionately in favour of a more diverse society, 'it wasn't necessarily a debate they wanted to have in working men's clubs in Sheffield
or Sunderland.'

Labour's reluctance to talk about the record levels of immigration into Britain meant there was little public discussion about
the impact the new arrivals were having on communities and

resources. Having spent much of the twentieth century encouraging the often false perception that foreign migrants were putting a strain on public services, now that they really were pressurising parts of the system, ministers didn't want to talk about it.

In 2008, I made a report for the BBC's national television news, which revealed how maternity units in London and the South East had had to turn away pregnant mothers because they had not been properly resourced for the wave of immigration. When I rang the health department for comment, one official suggested my enquiries were racist. Another report I filed demonstrated how public services were spending more than £100 million on translation services, often undermining immigrants' attempts to integrate. Once again, when I called for a government response, a horrified press officer said she thought I worked for the BBC, not the far-right BNP.

The arrival of the Poles and other Eastern Europeans exposed some troubling truths about British society. Young, willing and able, they grabbed at the chance to fill many of the low-paid jobs that unemployed locals turned down as too much like hard work. Tourism, care of the elderly, and the building and agricultural sectors quickly came to depend on the foreign arrivals – not just filling existing jobs but creating new ones. Businesses started up or expanded because they had access to a new supply of enthusiastic labour. I remember going to Pitlochry, a Victorian tourist resort set amid the beautiful rolling countryside of central Scotland, and discovering how recent rapid growth of the local economy had been entirely down to what were called new workers. 'Your contribution to our communities is greatly valued and we wish you a safe and enjoyable time during your stay in Perth and Kinross,' the council said in a leaflet aimed at Poles, Lithuanians, Estonians and other foreign arrivals. A local hotel manager told me he was desperately worried the Eastern Europeans might go home at some point, depriving him of the cooks and chambermaids that kept his business going. Local farmers, shopkeepers, even the whisky distillery were reliant on immigrants.

Politically, success built upon foreign labour appeared to demonstrate a domestic failure. Why were these British jobs not going to British workers? The answer, in large part, was to be found in the shortcomings of policies on welfare, education, training and employment in the UK. Successive governments had failed to provide the skills and inspire the motivation needed for the local unemployed to compete with the new arrivals. But decades of disingenuous political rhetoric had encouraged people to see the issue in terms of illegal migrants, bogus asylum seekers or swarthy foreign infiltration. Politicians knew the reality was much more complicated, but in the run-up to the 2010 election, to engage with the detail was to risk appearing soft when every party needed to sound tough.

The truth was that immigration controls were irrelevant to the million Eastern Europeans who had settled in Britain – all the Polish plumbers and Latvian labourers were free to come and go as citizens of the European Union. Nevertheless, anxiety driven by EU arrivals, about which the major parties could do nothing, prompted promises to crack down on non-EU immigration, about which a good deal had already been done – it had been the case for a number of years that no unskilled or low-skilled workers could legally come to Britain from beyond the EU, and there was little evidence that significant numbers of illegal migrants were still sneaking into the UK. The only way left to allay the public's concerns, therefore, was to limit the arrival of those non-EU migrant groups that included people the country arguably needed and wanted – high-skilled workers and fee-paying students.

An attitudes survey conducted in 2011 for the Migration Observatory at Oxford University found close to two thirds of British people wanted to restrict low-skilled immigration in the UK, but less than a third were concerned about students or high-skilled workers coming. As the accompanying report noted, this has important implications for public policy debates because effectively all low-skilled labour migration to the UK comes from within the EU, over which the government has no control.

Political debate about immigration has always been about balancing principle and popular prejudice – realpolitik some might say. But history shows us that it has often been the opposite of 'real'. The way the debate has been framed has sometimes been plain fraudulent, a conjuring trick exploiting our most atavistic fears.

J IS FOR JUSTICE

The British suffer from an obsessive-compulsive disorder when it comes to crime and justice. No other country counts it, categorises it, debates it and worries about it quite as much as we do. It is not that we are a particularly lawless nation, but rather that the fight against crime has become a channel for anxiety about the state of our society. We probe and poke and pick away at every arcane detail, believing that within the piles of data, painstakingly collected and compiled, are the clues to understanding and solving our community's ills.

The figures actually demonstrate that the risk of being a victim of crime is at its lowest level for at least thirty years, and offences have been falling consistently since the mid-1990s. But Britain doesn't believe it. Most people are convinced the country is becoming a more frightening and dangerous place.

This unease translates into a demand for the state to 'do something' about crime and, typically, the answer from government ministers is to pass yet more laws and promise to get tough. The criminal justice system has come to be regarded as the mechanism for sorting out our social problems. If only police and probation officers, magistrates and judges did their job, we complain, all would be well.

One could argue that this is a thoroughly un-British attitude. The principles of our liberty and justice were founded upon an accepted community responsibility for keeping 'The King's Peace' that has its origins in Anglo-Saxon days. People didn't look to the authorities for answers – crime was a matter for local citizens to deal with themselves.

From the fourteenth century, it was the obligation and privilege of unpaid Justices of the Peace, selected from the local gentry, to direct the parish constables and watchmen in a system dating back to 1285 and the Statute of Winchester. For more than 500 years, the streets and gates of walled British towns were patrolled and guarded by a 'watch' of men from a roster of volunteers. Their main role was to arrest strangers when they found cause for suspicion and deliver the accused to the parish constable in the morning.

If a stranger resisted capture, then a 'hue and cry' was made, and the entire town was required to help apprehend the villain. Every man between the ages of fifteen and sixty had to keep in his house 'harness to keep the peace'. For men of superior rank that meant 'a hauberke and helm of iron, a sword, a knife and a horse'. The poor were obliged to have bows and arrows to hand. A person accused of stealing would be privately arrested, privately prosecuted and, if found guilty, would pay compensation and the costs of the case. Crimes were local, civil matters to be resolved by local civilians.

Gradually, over time and in the face of fierce resistance, some offences became 'crimes against the King' as English monarchs asserted state power over their subjects. But it was not until the huge social and economic changes that swept across Britain with the Industrial Revolution that security and justice were effectively nationalised and the criminal justice system as we now know it was created.

Capitalism and urbanisation together changed the dynamics of social behaviour. The 'watch and ward' system of security broke down in rapidly expanding cities, and both personal and property crime soared. Activities that were once accepted or tolerated became criminal as the rich and powerful sought to protect their wealth and influence by means of state intervention.

For example, in the early eighteenth century it was common practice for workers in a range of industries to take the scraps from manufacturing processes. These were the original 'perks' or perquisites of the job. However, a series of new laws was introduced criminalising this activity – the Clicking Act of 1723 made it illegal for shoemakers to take scraps of leather; the Worsted Act of 1777 turned mill workers into potential criminals if they took home snipped weft-ends or fragments of yarn. During the eighteenth century, Parliament enacted fourteen statutes relating to fifteen industries which turned previously lawful 'gleaning' into unlawful 'embezzlement'. Some academics have gone so far as to argue that our concept of 'crime' dates from this period, a state-fabricated illusion that justified the capitalist exploitation of the lower orders.

When wealthy Scottish merchant Patrick Colquhoun became anxious about the large amounts of valuable cargo being pinched from the Pool of London in 1795, he published a book entitled *A Treatise on the Police of the Metropolis* designed to convince his readers that the capital needed a regular, organised, paid police force to deal with a mighty tide of immorality, crime and disorder. Colquhoun was an early advocate of what we might now call evidence-based policy and used some suspiciously detailed numbers and tables to make his case.

He calculated that there were 115,000 people within what he identified as London's 'criminal class'. This population was then divided into twenty-four subgroups beginning with 'Professed Thieves, Burglars, Highway Robbers, Pick-pockets, & River Pirates' and concluding with 'Gin-drinking dissolute Women, & destitute Boys & Girls, wandering & prowling about in the streets & by-places after Chips, Nails, Old Metals, Broken Glass, Paper Twine, etc. etc.' The cause of the crime wave, he suggested, was that 'the morals and habits of the lower ranks in society are growing progressively worse'. Broken Britain, he might have said. It is a narrative that persists to this day – the idea of a distinct criminal minority threatening the law-abiding majority and requiring ever more authoritarian controls to protect the virtuous from the sinful. After the English riots in the summer of 2011, the Justice Secretary Kenneth Clarke wrote of a 'feral underclass', which needed to experience the 'cold, hard accountability of the dock'.

Colquhoun got his police force. The Thames River Police began operating in 1798 and two years later the Marine Police Bill transformed it from a private to public police agency. The legitimacy of this rapidly evolving criminal justice system – the enforcement of law, the application of justice and the management of sentence – was dependent upon the people. Unless the citizenry accepted the special powers conferred on state police, judges and gaolers, the whole edifice would have collapsed. Enter stage left: the gentlemen of the press.

The forces of law and order wooed the news media. Reporters were granted special status at trials; unlike those tucked away in the public gallery, they were free to chat to lawyers, to take notes and even ask questions of the judge. The courts were designed with a dedicated area for members of the press. They would get the best seats in the house to ensure that justice was 'seen to be done'.

The scribblers didn't take much wooing – the news media thrive on stories about crime and disorder. Journalists like to justify their fascination in terms of their responsibility as surrogate watchmen, metaphorically patrolling the city walls and ready to issue a hue and cry if they identify threats to individual or collective welfare. But crime's main attraction to the press is that it is a money-spinner. Like popular folk and fairy tales, the best crime stories reflect the endless struggle between good and evil and are cast with monsters, angels and heroes. We can't get enough of them.

Lawyers and journalists, wig and pen became partners in crime – neither could operate effectively without the other. Both feed on what Colquhoun dubbed the 'criminal classes' living outside 'civilised society': the greater the apparent external threat, the better for business. This symbiotic relationship is not unique to Britain, but the nature and intensity of the relationship here has had a powerful effect on public attitudes. As a result, huge amounts of research have been conducted into the impact of crime news. From the early 1980s, academics began producing evidence to suggest that the more crime stories people consume, the more they fear crime and the greater the demand for more police, more prisons and more punitive responses to crime.

The number of crime stories appearing in the British media has risen markedly. Criminologists had a happy time examining random samples of *The Times* and the *Mirror* newspapers for each year between 1945 and 1991. Immediately following the Second World War, roughly one twelfth of news stories was about crime. By 1991, in both papers, the figure had risen to one fifth.

The type of crime being reported also changed. In the 1940s and 50s property crimes featured frequently in news stories, but since the mid-1960s they have become rarities unless there is some celebrity angle. What the British press has increasingly focused upon instead is violence. The British Crime Survey estimates that approximately 6 per cent of crimes reported by victims are characterised as violent. But that is not the impression given by the media. One study focusing on one month in 1989 found that 64 per cent of the crime stories in the national press related to violence. On local television news bulletins in 1987 it was found that violent crime stories accounted for 63 per cent of all crime news.

Since our sense of the criminal justice system is shaped largely by the media, we could be forgiven for thinking there is a lot more crime and most of it is violent.

But there has been another change to crime reporting that has supercharged its impact, transformed the politics of law and order and, according to some, threatened to subvert the justice system. Barely mentioned in the 1950s, now centre stage is the victim.

No big crime story is complete these days without the press conference at which the police display the injured and bereaved. The cameras flash at every hint of raw emotion. Suffering has become a key component of these contemporary morality tales. This changes the way we think of criminality – from an offence against wider society to a matter of one individual harming another. It is a reversion to the principles of the ancient manor courts. It personalises crime. One might say it consumerises criminal justice. Victims sell papers, and the most effective are those who can be described as incontrovertibly innocent. The 'blameless victim' has become the most influential voice in the national debate about law and order.

The disappearance and murder of 10-year-olds Holly Wells and Jessica Chapman in the village of Soham in 2002 resulted in deep political soul-searching and led to changes in the way the criminal justice system operates. The young girls' faces are seared upon the conscience of the nation. Few, however, will remember 13-year-old David Spencer and 11-year-old Patrick Warren from Chelmsley Wood in Birmingham, even though their story is eerily similar. They went missing on Boxing Day 1996 and the suggestion is that they, like Holly and Jessica, were abducted and killed by a paedophile.

David and Patrick's disappearance received a tiny fraction of the coverage that the Soham story did because they were not ideal victims. Both boys had been in trouble at school. One of them had been caught shop-lifting. On the day they went missing they had been scrounging biscuits from a local petrol station. They did not possess what has been described as 'the complete and legitimate status of being a victim'. David and Patrick's bodies have never been found.

Criminal reform in Britain has been driven by the emotional

power of victims. The murder of 2-year-old James Bulger was a seminal moment in the politics of crime in this country: the justification for New Labour's 'tough on crime' rhetoric and the inspiration for what's been described as the crime policy arms race of the mid-1990s. Madeleine McCann. Stephen Lawrence. Sarah Payne. Damilola Taylor. Jill Dando. All these tragedies have changed the debate about crime and criminal justice in this country. They also all have at their heart an unambiguous victim.

The terrible deaths of Robert Knox, Jimmy Mizen and Ben Kinsella became the catalyst for press and political demands for action to deal with knife crime. While the victims of stabbings were young black men from drug-riddled estates in the inner cities, the calls for a government response were barely heard. Robert, Jimmy and Ben were all white boys described as 'blameless' by the press: Robert – the grammar school pupil who had appeared in a *Harry Potter* film; 'Gentle giant' Jimmy, the Catholic altar-boy; Ben, the GCSE student whose sister was a former soap star.

The innocent faces of Holly and Jessica, Sarah Payne and Madeleine McCann ensured paedophilia was cast as the threat from the predator, the outsider, rather than the much more common but no less damaging abuse that occurs among families and close friends. The political response was inevitably shaped by the risk from the former rather than the latter. It is an important point: the focus on the innocent victim reinforces the concept of them and us. They are criminals. We are respectable. There is little room for ambiguity or nuance.

In 2002, the government announced that it intended to rebalance the criminal justice system to place victims at its heart. Ministers proposed a Victims' Advisory Panel for England and Wales, accountable to Parliament and headed by a Victims' Commissioner empowered to advise ministers on how to do things better. This alarmed senior figures within the legal world, who suggested it wasn't so much rebalancing as destabilisation. The criminal justice system, they pointed out, is sanctioned by the state to protect the state. Prosecutions are conducted on behalf of the Crown, not the victim.

Senior politicians agreed. A committee considering the government's proposals concluded that telling a victim their views were central, or that the prosecutor was their champion, amounted to a damaging misrepresentation of reality. 'The criminal justice system is set up to represent the public rather than individuals, and there are good reasons for this.' Ministers were accused of blurring the critical distinction between criminal (state) and civil (private) law. Putting crime victims 'at the heart of the process' implied a return to the days of the medieval feudal courts, when accuser and accused argued their case on equal terms. Such a move, it was argued, threatened the legitimacy of the justice system as protector of the wider public interest. It might also undermine the right to a trial based on objective testing of the evidence, rather than passion or sentiment.

Another consequence of putting the victim centre stage has been the rise of 'penal populism' – an increasingly punitive attitude to crime that has forced politicians and the judiciary into having to defend themselves against the accusation that they are 'soft on crime'. When the press covers a big trial, it is usual practice to ask the victim of the crime on the steps of the court what they thought of the sentence. It is entirely understandable that most would have wanted the judge to have been tougher. Should they actually say they thought the sentence was fair, we cast them as curiously forgiving. No victim is ever likely to say the sentence was too severe.

Penal populism is not driven only by the media. The criminal justice system itself is sometimes complicit. In 2007 the Ministry of Justice put out a press release under the headline 'Victims of crime want punishment'. It cited a survey which found that almost half (49 per cent) placed punishment as the most important part of an offender's sentence. But read on and one discovered that 81 per cent would prefer an offender to receive an effective sentence rather than a harsh one and that an overwhelming majority of respondents (94 per cent) said the most important thing to them was that the offender did not do it again.

Part of the reason that most people in Britain still believed crime was rising fifteen years after it began to fall is that government ministers, police chiefs and others did not seek to challenge that mistaken view too strongly. In political terms there was a perceived danger that they would appear complacent, but also, pragmatically, they knew that resources tend to follow the problem; if the public were to accept that their chances of being a victim of crime were lower than at any time since government first started measuring these things in 1981, budgets might well have been cut. In fact, in the decade from 1995 in which recorded crime levels halved, the budget of the police increased by 40 per cent in real terms.

There is another reason as to why people believed crime was rising when it was falling – their relationship with the world just beyond their front door. As I discuss elsewhere in this book, when local roads, alleys and parks were busy with people walking about, communities effectively operated a watch and ward scheme by default. But the retreat from the street, the move from the public to the private domain inspired by the motor car and the television set, left large areas of our towns and cities unsupervised. Into this vacuum have moved the twenty-first-century equivalent of the 'Boys & Girls, wandering & prowling about in the streets & by-places'. Loitering youth is, according to surveys, the single biggest source of community anxiety.

Just as Patrick Colquhoun looked to a police force to deal with 'pursuits either criminal, illegal or immoral' on the River Thames in 1795, so the public today look to the police to deal with antisocial behaviour in their neighbourhood. Britain's obsession with crime and disorder reflects anxiety about the state of our society and has little to do with the scale of the threat. The sadness is that the fear feeds on itself and eats away at our quality of life.

K IS FOR KNIVES

On my first day as a cub reporter on my local newspaper in the late 1970s, I held the naïve view that the press was there to oil the wheels of our precious democracy. With my humble pen I would expose falsehood, prick pomposity and counter ignorance. I was a force for truth: power to the people! Thirty years later I still strive to tell the truth. But I do so with the knowledge that daily news is a commodity, just like pork bellies, coffee beans or silicon chips. It is manufactured to be marketed, traded, bought and sold.

Of course knowledge of contemporary affairs is a force for good, but I am not so green as to imagine that the news industry is always governed by principle ahead of profit. Globalisation and consumerism has transformed the newsroom in the same way it has the high street. Just as I can now buy a soda or a sofa at three in the morning pretty much anywhere in the developed world, I can also get my fix of headlines.

Staying ahead is thought to rest on staying in touch, as if to avert one's eyes from the 24-hour news channels for more than a few moments would see competitors race past you. Vast news hypermarkets churn out stories around the clock – some of their output little more than cut-and-paste rehashes, but sold with the thin promise that customers will know what is going on.

Demand for high-quality news massively outstrips supply and outlets constantly struggle to fill the shelves. There isn't always enough important stuff happening to keep the presses continuously rolling and so the vacuum has been filled by thousands more news production lines: story factories run chiefly by those who wish to influence the news agenda for their own advantage.

This is not necessarily as sinister as it may sound – a charity's media team will work tirelessly to compile a 'news story' in order to highlight their cause; a pressure group researches and writes a report to promote an issue close to its heart. But, in Britain, the most powerful and influential of all the manufacturers are to be found in a small patch of London SW1. Indeed, a great deal of what we think of as 'the news' reflects the particular and current interests of those inhabiting the Westminster bubble: the politicians, lobbyists and journalists who ply their trade around Parliament.

Political salience dictates what is important. In the crowded middle ground where British politics is now conducted, arcane differences become front-page headlines, with the elbow jostling of the parties turned into a narrative of accusation and rebuttal, spin and smear. Weaknesses must be exploited, attacks must be neutralised. In such a fevered environment, there may be little time for sober reflection. When this happens, reality can easily get drowned out by the thunderous rattle of the Westminster story machine. Whisper it not, but our democracy sometimes manufactures myths.

This is the tale of one such fable: the knife crime epidemic that never was.

No one in Britain during the summer of 2008 could have been left in much doubt that the country was suffering from a wave of fatal teenage stabbings. The leader of the Conservative Party, David Cameron, attended a vigil for one victim and described knife crime as having reached 'epidemic' proportions. Each new tragedy, granted front-page status by the papers, added to the sense that a ghastly phenomenon was sweeping the streets of Britain. 'If we don't do something now, it will go on and on,' the leader of the opposition said.

The Tories knew that the horrible crimes, documented almost daily, played neatly into a broader narrative they were hoping would take hold. With the government suffering in the opinion polls, Mr Cameron was determined to ram home his advantage by painting Britain as a 'broken society'. The phrase had particular poignancy alongside the punctured corpses of young men.

That there was no hard evidence that knife crime was getting worse was irrelevant. As I was told by hardened hacks on my local paper thirty years ago: 'Never let the facts interfere with a good story.' Prime Minister Gordon Brown had no option but to respond to the rising sense of alarm. It was politically inconceivable to deny there was a problem – that would leave his party exposed to the charge that they were callous and complacent. So a knife-crime 'summit' was held at Number Ten Downing Street. There was the promise of a 'crackdown' and 'tough measures'. It was a classic sequence: moral panic, hurried political reaction, futile (probably counter-productive) response.

On this occasion, part of the response was the unveiling of a new acronym – TKAP. The Tackling Knives Action Programme demanded that police resources in high-crime areas across England and Wales should be targeted at young men who carried blades. However, among some senior police officers there was puzzlement and anxiety. Evidence that knife crime was getting worse was restricted to the number of stories in the newspapers. The official crime statistics did not include a category for knives and so it was difficult to know what was happening. The Home Office data suggested no obvious spike in serious violent crime overall. If anything, the figures appeared to show violence declining. Some thought TKAP had the smell of a short-term political fix.

As a rough average, two people are murdered every day in Britain. The most common weapon used is a blade or other sharp instrument. The most likely stab victim is a young man. It has been like that for decades (see 'M is for Murder'). So, after the Downing Street summit, as the months rolled by, there was no shortage of fresh tragedy, further fatal stabbings to advance the knife crime fable. From this raw material, news organisations were able to fashion other stories: tales of human interest, political intrigue and passionate polemic in abundance. Editors knew that these accounts played to a common fear: that the security of traditional community values was being usurped by the brutal individualism of blade and bullet.

Inside Number Ten there was a different anxiety: that the government would seem powerless against a tide of viciousness on the nation's streets. Gordon Brown – portrayed by his opponents as a ditherer unable to repair a broken Britain – needed to appear decisive and in control.

In late 2008, the Prime Minister attempted to seize the initiative. It was decided that the 11th of December would be the day he would go to a community centre in south London to launch a new 'No to Knives' campaign, endorsed and supported by a host of celebrities from sport, music and television. But a foray across the river, even with soap stars and a couple of Premier League footballers, would not be enough to convince the public that the government was making a difference. Mr Brown needed some facts.

The problem for the advisors looking to prove the success of government activity was that there were very few hard facts to exploit. The Home Office held no statistics to show that knife crimes had been rising, never mind data to show that it was now going down. Still, Number Ten was determined to demonstrate progress and so they scoured Whitehall for evidence. The search led them to the Department of Health, which counted patients discharged from hospital after being admitted with stab wounds. The NHS stats people were contacted and the latest provisional figures were sent to London.

It looked as though Brown's team had found what they were looking for: the statistics showed a 27 per cent fall in the number of stab victims admitted to hospital in those English areas targeted by the government's action programme. Here was the 'proof' that the PM's decisive plan on knives had worked.

A press release was put together, trumpeting the success of TKAP. But with just hours to go before the Prime Minister's glorious announcement, the NHS stats team got wind of what Number Ten was planning – and they were not happy. The figures had only been sent to Downing Street on the understanding that they would not be published. It is standard procedure that ministers may look at statistics before formal publication only if they promise not to release the figures. On this occasion there was very good reason not to publish them: the hospitals hadn't finished counting stab victims and so the figure was likely to give a misleadingly rosy picture.

The chief statistician in the NHS wrote to one of Gordon Brown's inner circle, to assert that the data should not be released because 'they are potentially inaccurate and may give the wrong impression.'

This was the last thing Number Ten wanted to hear. The whole knife crime strategy – the PM's date with soap and soccer stars; the photo opportunity; the launch of No to Knives; the chance to get some positive publicity on a story that had been causing immense damage to the government – all of it was now jeopardised by some jumped-up data wonks in Leeds arguing that the figures were 'provisional' and might 'give the wrong impression'.

The Home Office had pulled together some other numbers but these, frankly, were pretty thin, if not outright dodgy. 'Number Ten are adamant about the need to publish this statistic,' the NHS team were told in an email. Even a desperate call from the National Statistician herself would not get Mr Brown's team to budge.

The following morning the Home Office released their knife crime 'fact sheet', with an accompanying press release proclaiming the 27 per cent fall in stab victims. The government news machine had effectively decided that the only way to counter an unhelpful myth was to manufacture another.

Over the next few months, official figures were released which offered a clearer idea of what had really been happening with knives on Britain's streets in 2008. In London, where many of the high-profile stabbings had taken place, police had been keeping records of knife crime, even though it was not required by the Home Office. When they compared what had happened during the 'epidemic' with the same period a year earlier they found that crimes involving knives had actually fallen 14 per cent. When the hospital admission figures were finalised they showed that, while Britain was in the middle of its knife crime panic, the numbers of people admitted to hospital with stab wounds was 8 per cent lower than it had been the year before. In the areas targeted by the government's programme, the number of stab victims taken to hospital didn't fall 27 per cent. No, it also fell 8 per cent – a slower reduction, it might be noted, than had been recorded in the months before TKAP.

The Tackling Knives Action Programme kept its name but, less than a year after its launch, it was quietly broadened to cover all violence, whatever the weapon. In other words, police went back to doing what they had always done.

Every stabbing represents an individual tragedy. But there was no knife crime epidemic in Britain in 2008. What we actually saw was an exercise in urban myth-making that may well have left Britain's communities more anxious, more suspicious and more vulnerable. Far from helping to counter ignorance and expose false-hood, the media became an accessory in undermining the truth.

L IS FOR LEARNING

The youth of today! What are they like? Can't sit still for a minute: constantly clicking and flicking channels on the TV; tapping and typing three simultaneous conversations on Facebook, text and Twitter; chit-chatting incessantly on their mobile while managing to listen to some new dance track they are downloading onto their iPod; one wonders that the computer's processors don't explode, such is the speed and ferocity with which they career about the Internet, like psychotic honey bees buzzing from bloom to bloom with no time to dwell. Why can't they just sit quietly and read a book, for goodness sake?

OK. I have got that off my chest. Now let us address the title at the top of this page – learning.

My point is, of course, that the way we access, absorb and use information has changed radically within a generation. Growing up in the 1950s, 60s or 70s, the era of the baby-boomer, was to inhabit a linear world where we read a book from cover to cover, we watched a television programme from beginning to end, a film from title to credits.

The new Internet generation, the so-called 'NetGen', inhabit a hypermedia world with fewer straight lines. Rather than reading, listening or watching in a pre-ordained order, my children and their peers routinely engage with information interactively. At the touch of a button they create their own TV schedules; on the Internet they are free to roam – picking up an idea here, researching it there, road-testing it somewhere else and, if they wish, publishing their conclusions too. All text can be processed, all sound can be sampled, all images can be formatted and manipulated.

It is not the end of narrative, thank goodness. Members of the Internet generation, like those from every generation before them, make sense of their lives through stories. They still go to movies, listen to music and read books from start to finish. But new technology has allowed the NetGen consumer to use knowledge in ways my generation, at their age, could not even imagine.

That is what is going on when I see my teenage daughter surfing and texting and listening and reading and chatting, all at the same time. She is participating in a hypermedia world, which has a different relationship with knowledge to the one I recognise. Or at least that is what I suspect my children will now say to me when I find them downloading YouTube clips when they should be revising their French verbs. It is understanding that changed relationship with knowledge that will be key to deciding how the British NetGen fares in an increasingly globalised world.

We talk about globalisation as though it is something new. One could argue that the process began some 5,000 years ago when trade links were forged between Sumerian and Harappan civilisations in Mesopotamia and the Indus Valley. But one has to turn the clock back less than two centuries to see new technology transforming the global market: the steam engine was shrinking the planet. The railways revolutionised domestic communication and the development of steam-powered ocean-going ships dramatically accelerated business in the expanding worldwide web of trade. Farmers who would once have taken their crops to market on the back of a cart were able to sell goods around the planet. Huge quantities of agricultural products from as far afield as New Zealand,

Australia and the United States were shipped to Europe to feed the hungry masses driving the industrial revolution. The cargo vessels then turned around, packed with new technology, consumer goods and ideas.

'Glory to God in the highest; on earth, peace and goodwill toward men': the first message sent across the transatlantic telegraph cable by Queen Victoria on 16 August 1858 to US President James Buchanan. 'May the Atlantic telegraph, under the blessing of heaven, prove to be a bond of perpetual peace and friendship between the kindred nations, and an instrument destined by Divine Providence to diffuse religion, civilisation, liberty, and law throughout the world,' he replied. The following morning, there was a grand salute of one hundred guns in New York as the church bells rang.

Unfortunately, the bond of perpetual peace literally snapped a few weeks later and it wasn't until 1866, thanks to the engineering genius of Isambard Kingdom Brunel and the doggedness of the crew of the SS *Great Eastern*, that a lasting connection was eventually made. But connect we had.

This communications revolution allowed for the integration of financial markets and provided a massive impetus for the expansion of international business. While the profits from global trading accounted for just 2 per cent of the world's wealth in 1800, by 1913 it was 21 per cent. Not only a global market, but also a global consciousness had arrived.

The UK, of course, fared very well during this round of globalisation. The invention and innovation of Britain's educated elite provided the cutting edge that saw it become the richest nation on earth. But British success was also built on harnessing the labour of millions of unskilled workers, people with often little or no education, who were moved from the fields to the factories. This was the formula upon which an empire was created, and it worked a treat in the nineteenth century. In the twentieth century a different formula was required: innovation and invention, yes, but in the new era, industrial development would be founded upon technically skilled workers.

The UK did not find it easy to adapt. Britain's sense of its own social architecture was essentially bipolar: gentlemen versus players, bosses and workers, upstairs-downstairs. The rivalry and tension that flowed along the divide hindered travel between the two distinct camps and prevented development of a respected technocratic class.

When in 1944 a tripartite system of education was proposed for England and Wales, the vision was at odds with the simple adversarial structures that had defined the country's politics, justice and commerce for centuries. The Education Act introduced three types of state secondaries: grammar schools for the intellectual and academic, technical schools for engineers and scientists, and modern schools to give less-gifted children practical skills for manual labour and home management. It was recognition that twentieth-century development required specific investment in technical and vocational skills. But Britain fluffed it.

Such was the lack of priority and money given to technical schools that very few were ever opened. Instead, state education reinforced the divide between the educated elite and the rest, helping create a schools system in Britain that still produces greater levels of educational inequality than almost any other in the developed world.

Vocational and technical training was usually left to private firms that often resented investing in young workers who might take their skills elsewhere or use their expertise to increase the bargaining power of the unions. Other industrialised nations, meanwhile, were spending heavily in the skills training of their workforces. By 1975, only 0.5 per cent of British secondary school pupils were in technical schools, compared to 66 per cent of German youngsters.

Britain experienced dramatic industrial decline and much bickering about what had gone wrong. Right-wing analysts tended to blame the bloody-mindedness of British unions. Left-wing analysts tended to blame the class structure and a poor education system. In truth, they were two sides of the same inflexible coin.

As the American historian and economist David Landes wrote of Britain: 'For every idealist or visionary who saw in education ... an enlightened citizenry, there were several "practical" men who felt that instruction was a superfluous baggage for farm labourers and industrial workers. These people, after all, had been ploughing fields or weaving cloth for time out of mind without knowing how to read or write ... All they would learn in school was discontent.' Even today you hear the same arguments. Britain clung to a belief that its traditional approach had won it an empire, and if only we could be true to those principles we would be great again. One consequence of this conviction was that the UK found itself with a higher proportion of low-skilled and unskilled workers than most other developed countries.

In 2006, a government review reported that 'as a result of low skills, the UK risks increasing inequality, deprivation and child poverty, and risks a generation cut off permanently from labour market opportunity.' More than a third (35 per cent) of adults were found to have low or no skills, double the proportion in competitors such as the US, Canada, Germany and Sweden.

That 35 per cent represented tens of millions of people whose livelihoods were increasingly threatened by higher-skilled and more motivated migrants or whose jobs would simply disappear when companies shifted manufacturing operations to countries with cheaper labour. Consider what happened to that most iconic example of British manufacturing greatness – the Cadbury's Creme Egg. Despite assurances that the factory in Somerset where these eggs were laid would stay open, when Kraft took over Cadbury's in 2010, they announced production would indeed switch to a new factory in Poland with a loss of 400 British jobs.

Tempting though it is to believe that a manufacturing nation like Britain should stick to what it knows, the numbers suggest this is a doomed strategy. The proportion of people employed in making stuff has fallen dramatically in virtually every developed nation since the 1970s. In 1978, almost 30 per cent of UK jobs were in the manufacturing sector. By 2012 it was less than 8 per cent, the lowest proportion since records began. There may be profit in making niche, high-tech or patented products, but churning out widgets or Wispa bars is not the way to go.

So, we prospered when the rules changed in the nineteenth century. We failed to adapt when the rule book was revised in the twentieth century. But we do have a chance to redeem ourselves in the twenty-first century. The rules are changing again.

Just as James Watt was critical in developing the technology for Britain's success in the industrial revolution, another Briton, Tim Berners-Lee is credited with the invention that is transforming the global economy today. The World Wide Web has powered a new period of globalisation. In the nineteenth century, it was about access to and the effective use of industrial machines. In the twenty-first century, it is about access to and the effective use of knowledge. As the Economic and Social Research Council puts it: 'Economic success is increasingly based upon the effective utilisation of intangible assets such as knowledge, skills and innovative potential as the key resource for competitive advantage.'

What do people mean by knowledge? A century ago knowledge was a tool. If you knew stuff you could use that to sell other tangible stuff. Now knowledge is increasingly the product in its own right. It is reckoned that within a few years, selling know-how will generate more than half of total GDP and account for half of total employment in advanced industrial economies like Britain. Business services, financial services, computer services, communications, media – these are the areas where developed countries may be able to maintain a competitive advantage.

Knowledge is providing the new jobs too. Go back to the early 1980s and almost half of UK jobs were unskilled or low-skilled jobs. Now it is about a quarter. People working in the knowledge industries accounted for a third of jobs in the early 1980s. Now it is closer to half. Knowledge services now account for more than two thirds of what Britain sells to the world. With low-skilled jobs disappearing and knowledge jobs expanding, it is obvious that the UK needs to invest in knowledge, to educate and train its workforce. Britain has a high proportion of NEETs – young people not in education, employment or training – twice the level of the Netherlands, Denmark, Austria, Sweden and Switzerland.

The credit crunch only served to magnify the point. Unemployment figures in the depths of the recession showed that among those working in the knowledge economy – financial consultants, business managers, lawyers – the proportion claiming jobseeker's allowance was 1 per cent. Among those who usually worked in unskilled admin jobs, the figure was 37 per cent. And for those without skills, matters are only going to get worse. Much worse.

Globalisation doesn't just open up new markets; it is bringing an estimated 42 million new people into the international jobs market every year – and most of those are unskilled. What's more, the process is accelerating as the population of the developing world soars. The celebrated Harvard economics professor Richard Freeman warns that this rapidly rising pool of labour will 'swamp' developed countries. 'The world has entered onto a long and epochal transition towards a single global economy and labour market,' he argues, a process which poses massive challenges for countries like Britain.

And it is not just a challenge for NEETs. It is a challenge for nerds too. According to forecasts by the World Bank, the global supply of skilled workers is likely to grow more quickly than that of unskilled workers. Emerging economies are educating their people faster than developed economies, albeit from a lower base. But in simple number terms, the challenge is obvious. For each Briton who graduates there are at least twenty Chinese and Indian graduates jostling for work in the global marketplace. Not every Indian degree is equivalent to a degree from Oxford or Cambridge. But then not every British degree is either.

The noisy arguments over higher university tuition fees in England have tended to drown out the really critical point: higher education is a product in the global knowledge economy and price is a factor of supply and demand. Domestic students still get a sub-sidised rate, albeit not quite as generous a subsidy as previously, but the real revolution has been that UK institutions have begun directly competing with each other to sell their courses. At the same time, their student customers have been encouraged to become increasingly canny shoppers.

A glance at the fees charged to overseas students has become a quick way of judging whether British undergraduates are getting a bargain or not. At Imperial College, for example, international fees can be three times what a domestic student is expected to pay. The Chinese and Indian youngsters who fork out that kind of money do so because they see it, not as debt, but as an investment in their future. They recognise the challenges of a single global economy and are prepared to spend to get the qualifications that help them stand out from the international crowd. To the business recruitment teams searching for talent, quality matters.

I have met senior Indian executives who now argue that the quality of degrees at their top domestic universities rivals Oxford and Cambridge. Certainly, since the Indian government launched the National Knowledge Commission in 2005, there has been a determination to develop an internationally competitive educa-tional infrastructure. The commission recently reported to the Prime Minister on its objective of how to meet the 'knowledge challenges' of the twenty-first century and increase India's com-petitive advantage.

The United Kingdom has in-built advantages as the global economy takes shape: an historic tradition of academic excellence with some genuinely world-class universities; the language of international trade still tends to be English; Britain has an unrivalled financial and business services sector. But does the UK have a fraction of India's determination to shape its workforce so it is best placed to grab the opportunities of globalisation? Can its students match the work ethic of the students in developing countries?

A few years ago, my family was lucky enough to have two Chinese students stay with us on an exchange. They explained how they started school at 6am and were often still there studying at 9pm. They rarely got to bed, they said, before eleven because they had so much homework they wanted to do. And, much to the horror of my children, they went to school on Saturdays. 'All work and no play makes Jack a dull boy' perhaps, but there is a Chinese proverb that warns: 'Be afraid only of standing still.'

The top universities in the developed world are targets for the brightest and most highly motivated young people from the developing world. Go to many British institutions and you will find that, during the lunch hour, the lecture rooms are filled with Chinese, Korean and Indian students doing extra revision and having group discussion around their topics. Domestic undergraduates tend to be relaxing.

One measure of a society's ability to 'meet the knowledge challenges of the twenty-first century' is the proportion of young people with a degree. Figures published by the OECD in 2012 show that while 36 per cent of British students end up graduating, it is over 40 per cent in Australia, Norway, Japan, Netherlands, New Zealand, Finland, and Denmark, and over 50 per cent in Poland, Russia and Iceland. Since the mid-1990s, many European countries have seen their graduation rates overtake the UK.

Just processing lots of people through often meaningless degrees is not enough, of course. If Britain is going to do well in the twenty-first century, it needs to produce the right kind of knowledge workers, to recognise the skills and abilities that will be most sought after by the global economy.

'Knowledge' is a misunderstood word, perhaps. Being able to learn and recall bits of information is important but there is no shortage of people who can do that. And in our Google age, knowing facts may become less critical.

The Canadian author of the book *Wikinomics*, business strategist Don Tapscott, recently argued that what he called 'the old-fashioned model' of education, involving remembering facts 'off pat', was designed for the industrial age. 'Teachers are no longer the fountain of knowledge; the Internet is,' he said. 'Children are going to have to reinvent their knowledge base multiple times. So for them memorising facts and figures is a waste of time.' It is important to have a solid foundation of facts one can call on without relying upon Wikipedia or Yahoo. But it is only the foundation. Knowledge is a hierarchy with memorising facts at the bottom.

In 1956, American University examiner Dr Benjamin Bloom published a book entitled *Taxonomy of Educational Objectives, Handbook 1: Cognitive Domain*. It was not the snappiest title, but the book was seized upon for its ideas on how to compare achievements in learning and is still used in teacher training today.

So 'knowing the facts' is the first step on the knowledge ladder. Then comes 'comprehension': understanding or interpreting the meaning of instructions and problems. These are still rudimentary knowledge skills. Next is 'application': taking that knowledge and comprehension and using it in a new situation. After that we have 'analysis': understanding what it is about the material or concepts that works so we might reproduce it in new situations. We are approaching the summit of the cognitive pyramid now, and educationalists differ on the description of the final steps. Bloom puts 'evaluation' at the very top – the ability to present and defend opinions about information based on evidence, the bedrock of academia. But his model has been revised in recent years, taking into account the most valued knowledge skills. The new taxonomy has at its peak 'synthesis': the ability to take elements of the previous steps and use them to create new knowledge.

Synthesis is the pinnacle – people who can synthesise are virtual gods in the knowledge economy, the most sought after talents in the globalised twenty-first century. British success in the new age is going to depend on workers who have knowledge and understanding, but also the ability to analyse and evaluate and synthesise information and ideas from multiple sources all at the same time. They will be individuals unrestricted by a single narrative.

And what do such people look like? They are eclectics, curious magpies taking intriguing shiny bits of knowledge into their nest and shaping them into something new. They are probably doing their homework while conducting three keyboard conversations and surfing the web and listening to music and switching between obscure television channels and chatting on the mobile. They are members of the NetGen. They could be our children.

M IS FOR MURDER

*Morse stood for a few minutes, gazing down at the ugly scene
at his feet. The murdered girl wore a minimum of clothing –
a pair of wedge-heeled shoes, a very brief dark-blue mini-
skirt and a white blouse. Nothing else.*

The first time we meet Chief Inspector Morse, in the murder mystery novel *Last Bus to Woodstock*, he is investigating the brutal
killing of a hitchhiker, Sylvia Kaye, whose body is found 'cruelly
streaked with blood' in an Oxford car park. Thirteen novels and
thirty-three television programmes later, it becomes clear that
Matthew Arnold's sweet city with her dreaming spires is Colin
Dexter's malevolent city with her shocking murders. Through the
books and episodes the corpses pile up, scores of gruesome deaths
suggesting a propensity for lethal violence in Oxford at odds with
its international reputation for civilised and genteel scholarship.

The city, though, does have a murderous past. In the 1340s,
immediately before the Black Death visited its own fatal curse upon
Oxford's population, records suggest that for every 900 inhabitants,
one would be bumped off during the course of the year. If the same
homicide rate were applied to the citizenry today, Morse would
have at least three bodies each week to gaze upon. However, figures

for contemporary Oxford show that an ambitious detective these days might only get the chance to solve a murder once or possibly twice a year.

Murder exerts a primal fascination upon us. Such is society's obsessive interest in the grisly, macabre and distressing details of what happens when one human being deliberately takes the life of another that our folklore, our culture and our daily routines are smeared with the blood of crime victims: the whodunnit on the bedside table, the psycho-noir flick at the local cinema, the front-page splash of the paper on the doormat.

Shortly after I first joined the BBC in the mid-1980s, the new head of current affairs John Birt expressed concern that the corporation's news bulletins were overdosing on murder in the search for ratings. Editors were urged to reduce the body count. His argument was that the preoccupation with untimely and violent death painted an inaccurate portrait of British society and risked unnecessarily alarming our viewers.

> *The death of Sylvia Kaye had figured dramatically in Thursday afternoon's edition of the Oxford Mail, and prominently in the national press on Friday morning. On Friday evening the news bulletins on both BBC and ITV carried an interview with Chief Inspector Morse ...*

So what clues can we muster to solve the mysteries of murder? Let us begin by asking whether a murder has actually been committed. We may, like Morse, have a body with a smashed skull and a bloodied tyre-spanner nearby, but classifying such crimes is rarely straightforward.

Murder has a strict legal definition that concerns the slayer not the slain. In England and Wales 'the crime of murder is committed, where a person: of sound mind and discretion (i.e. sane); unlawfully kills (i.e. not self-defence or other justified killing); any reasonable creature (human being); in being (born alive and breathing through its own lungs); under the Queen's Peace; with intent to kill or cause grievous bodily harm. In Scottish law, murder is defined as 'the unlawful killing of another with intent to kill, or with wicked recklessness to life'. One may be able to prove that Colonel Mustard killed Professor Plum in the Billiard Room with the candlestick – but was it murder? Within the prerequisites, caveats and legal arguments, there lies opportunity to demonstrate that no such crime has taken place. In England and Wales, for example, only 30 per cent of homicide prosecutions result in a conviction for murder. Detectives may launch a great many murder investigations, but until such time as one has nailed the murderer, no murder has been committed.

As a result, although this chapter is entitled 'M is for Murder', our inquiries will require us to keep an open mind on motive and offence – assembling clues that relate to killings of all kinds. What is beyond debate is that we are investigating a crime that has, at its core, a corpse.

Let us examine the body.

How old is the victim? The most likely age for a person to be unlawfully killed is, actually, in the first year of life. In England and Wales, infants under twelve months face around four times the average risk of becoming a victim of homicide. The offender is most likely to be one of the baby's parents – mothers and fathers are equally likely to kill their infant. Mothers, however, are offered special legal protection from a murder charge. Since the Infanticide Acts of 1922 and 1938, English law has recognised that the death may be the result of her mind being 'disturbed by reason of her not having fully recovered from the effect of giving birth'. However, less than a quarter of women accused of such crimes are convicted of infanticide – a significant proportion are sentenced to life imprisonment for murder.

The risk of being murdered falls sharply over the first two years of life and, although the press often dwell on the violent deaths of children, the chances of becoming a homicide victim during childhood are described by the Home Office as exceptionally low. The dangers do start to rise sharply, though, when we enter the teenage years, peaking and plateauing in our twenties and early thirties. During this period, homicide is the third most common cause of death but, should we survive until our thirty-fifth birthday, the risks start to tail off. By the time we collect our bus pass, the Grim Reaper has probably got other plans for our demise.

The typical homicide victim, then, is relatively young and probably male: seven out of ten of those killed at another's hands are men.

What can we surmise about the background of the deceased? Well, chances are that he or she will not be wearing a business suit. Less than 7 per cent of homicide victims had a professional, managerial or skilled occupation. Twice that proportion (14 per cent) will have had a manual job. But by far the most likely status is that they didn't have a job at all – 53 per cent of victims had 'no current occupation', with one in four classed as unemployed. If they did work, there are a few occupations that appear to be associated with above average risk of being murdered: security staff, medical staff, social workers and, often overlooked in the official statistics, prostitutes.

> The spanner and the solitary white button lay where Morse had seen them earlier. There was nothing much to see but for the trail of dried blood that led almost from one end of the back wall to the other.

We know something of the victim but what of the cause of death? In Britain, more than a third of homicides involve the deceased, whether male or female, having been stabbed. The weapon is likely to be a knife but may be one of many sharp instruments, including broken bottles. Beyond that, the modus operandi alters depending on whether the victim is a man or a woman.

The next most common implement for a male death is a fist or a foot – about a quarter are hit or kicked to death. For women it is strangulation, accounting for roughly one in five female victims. A blunt instrument (such as a tyre spanner) is used only rarely – in about 7 per cent of homicides of either sex. Although popular culture might suggest murderers often shoot people, in the UK this is described as relatively unusual. Around 7 per cent of male victims and 2 per cent of women are shot. It is a different story in the United States, however, where the gun is by far the most commonly used weapon in murders. At the height of the 'murder boom' in New York in the late 1980s and early 90s, almost 80 per cent of homicides involved firearms.

Around 60 per cent of homicides take place between 8pm and 4am. More than twice as many homicides occur on a Saturday as a Monday. (There is more than a whiff of alcohol in the figures, as we shall find out.) April and October are the most common months to be bumped off, February and November the least likely.

> 'I can only repeat to you that I am formulating a hypothesis, that is, a supposition, a proposition however wild, assumed for the sake of argument; a theory to be proved (or disproved – yes, we must concede that) by reference to facts, and it is with facts and not with airy-fairy fancies that I shall endeavour to bolster my hypothesis.'

Having identified the victim, the cause and the time of death, it is high time to begin tracking down the killer. If our murderer conforms to type, what kind of person will he or she be? Well, the odds are overwhelmingly in favour of the killer being a man. Around 90 per cent of offenders are male, and they are likely to be a similar age to their victims – between eighteen and thirty-five.

What about a description? Does a murderer have a distinctive look? Eyebrows too close together, an evil stare? According to Italian criminologist Cesare Lombroso's influential 1876 work *L'Uomo*

Delinquente, there is a direct relationship between physical appearance and murderous tendencies. Lombroso spent years conducting post-mortem examinations and anthropometric studies on criminals and concluded that the skulls of born killers exhibited a deficiency in their frontal curve, a projecting occiput and receding forehead.

Warming to his theme, the scientist applied his theory to the skull of Charlotte Corday, the young woman who famously and fatally stabbed Jean-Paul Marat in his bath during the French revolution. 'Not even the purest political crime, that which springs from passion, is exempt from the law which we have laid down,' he claimed. A statue of Valeria Messalina, the Roman empress who plotted to assassinate her husband Claudius, was also employed to support his argument. He sees in her effigy a heavy jaw, a low forehead and wavy hair – the marks of a killer!

However absurd these ideas may seem today, such was their currency that in June 1902 Sir Bryan Donkin and Sir Herbert Smalley, the senior medical staff of the English prison system, agreed to test them out. The heads of thousands of inmates incarcerated in Parkhurst, Portland, Dartmoor and Borstal gaols were measured, including those of convicted murderers who had been spared the death sentence.

In 1913 Charles Goring, the Deputy Medical Director at Parkhurst, published *The English Convict: A Statistical Study.* When the measurements had been tabulated and cross-referenced, the conclusion was that murderers and other criminals 'possess no characteristics, physical or mental, which are not shared by all people'. Tracking down a killer could not be achieved with a simple tape measure.

A century later and researchers were again inside prisons trying to spot the common factors among murderers. In 2000, David Freedman and David Hemenway published the results of long and detailed interviews with sixteen men on death row in the United States. As the stories of the condemned men unfolded, remarkable similarities emerged. All sixteen had experienced family violence; fourteen of the men had been severely physically abused as children by a family member. Three of them had been beaten unconscious. Twelve of the death row inmates had been diagnosed with traumatic brain injury.

Psychiatrist James Gilligan, while director of the Bridgewater State Hospital for the criminally insane in Massachusetts, also explored the life histories of incarcerated killers. Violent men, he concluded, have often been the victims of extreme physical and psychological violence during childhood. They have feelings of worthlessness, failure, embarrassment, weakness and powerlessness.

Research by the World Health Organization in Europe found a similar link: 'Exposure to violence and mental trauma in childhood is associated with atypical neurodevelopment and subsequent information-processing biases, leading to poor attachment, aggression and violent behaviour. Children who experience neglect and maltreatment from parents are at greater risk for aggressive and antisocial behaviour and violent offending in later life.'

> *He pondered the case, at first with a slow, methodical analysis of the facts known hitherto and then with what, if he had been wider awake, he would wish to have called a series of swift, intuitive leaps, all of which landed him in areas of twilight and darkness.*

The profile of our typical killer, then, may involve an abusive childhood. We can also make a guess as to where he or she lives: offenders tend to come from poorer neighbourhoods. Research on English murders in the 1980s by the social anthropologist Elliott Leyton concluded: 'It is clear that nine out of ten homicides, perhaps more, are now committed by members of [the] underclass – persons with little education and no professional qualifications, chronically unemployed and on welfare.'

However, assuming that poverty alone explains higher murder rates might prove a red herring. The link between homicide and deprivation is not as strong as its link with income inequality: several studies have demonstrated that murder rates go up as differences in wealth increase. An examination of violent crime rates in 125 of the largest cities in the US concluded that it wasn't objective poverty that could be linked to violence, but relative deprivation. The World Health Organization came to a similar conclusion, reporting that rising income inequality in Europe had resulted in an increase in homicide.

> For the first time Morse seemed oddly hesitant. 'He could have done it, of course.'
>   'But I just don't see a motive, do you sir?'
>   'No,' said Morse flatly, 'I don't.'
>   He looked around the room dejectedly.

We have a body and we have a description of the suspect. What we do not have yet is a motive. To help complete the picture, our detective will want to know the probable relationship between the murder victim and the killer. Are they strangers, acquaintances, friends or family? The answer is likely to depend on whether our murderer is a man or a woman.

According to UK government research, one in four of the victims of male killers will probably be a stranger to their assailant. Among those killed by women, one in twenty-three is likely to be a stranger. In fact, female killers often know their victims intimately – in half of cases research suggests it will be their husband or partner, an ex-partner or a relative. For male perpetrators, the proportion of their victims who are likely to be close family members is a quarter.

Although the average age of a killer is almost identical for men and women, at around thirty-two years old, the average disguises an important clue. If a man is going to murder he is most likely to do it in his early twenties, with probability dropping as the years pass and maturity increases. Women, however, kill with almost consistent regularity from their twenties through to their mid-forties. The motives for women tend to be buried in the chronic tensions of domestic life. For men, the causes are more likely to be found in the conflicts of their social or work lives.

Most homicides, around 60 per cent, are 'male on male', often categorised as either 'confrontational' or 'grudge/revenge' killings. Analysis by the criminologist Dr Fiona Brookman demonstrated how confrontational homicides 'generally arose from "honour contests" in response to relatively trivial disagreements'. Typically, we are talking about two booze-fuelled lads attempting to knock lumps out of each other over some perceived slight with neither intending, at least at the outset, to kill the other.

I think we get the picture when Dr Brookman writes, 'The violence tends to occur in more public settings where an audience, often comprising other males, prevails and where alcohol is a characteristic feature of the social context.' A cocktail of bravado and beer all too often results in another young man's corpse in the mortuary and another miserable statistic in the official record (See 'A is for Alcohol').

As Michael Gottfredson and Travis Hirschi described it in their book *A General Theory of Crime*: 'The difference between homicide and assault may simply be the intervention of a bystander, the accuracy of a gun, the weight of a frying pan, the speed of an ambulance or the availability of a trauma centre.'

Grudge/revenge killings, on the other hand, are premeditated and purposeful. While the weapon in a confrontational murder is likely to be a fist, a boot or a bottle, in a grudge murder it is likely to have been pre-selected and carried to the scene – a gun, a knife or an iron bar. These homicides are often linked to gangs: a UK study of 10- to 19-year-olds found that 44 per cent of those who said they were in a gang had committed violence and 13 per cent had carried a knife in the previous twelve months. Among non-gang members of the same age the figures were 17 per cent and 4 per cent respectively.

James Gilligan's studies inside the Massachusetts asylum attempted to unpick the psychological conditions that turn a young man into a cold-eyed gang killer. His conclusion was that for poor and often black American kids on the street, 'nothing is more shameful than to feel ashamed.' It is about a loss of self-respect – Gilligan describes it as the opposite of self-pride – which can only be restored through violent retribution.

Gang culture is founded on ideas of status and control. Rival gangs in the UK often ape their US peers and, employing Jamaican vernacular, choose 'diss' names for each other – alternative tags designed to disrespect or disparage. Many of the male on male homicides in British inner cities will have their origins in some incident deemed to have displayed impertinence or contempt.

> *'You're not being very fair to me are you, sir?' Lewis seemed downcast and annoyed.*
> *'What do you mean?' asked Morse.*
> *'You said the case was nearly over.'*
> *'It is over,' said Morse.*

It is time to gather in the library, to review the evidence and attempt to wrap up the case. The murder rate, it can be argued, offers a measure of the health or sickness of a civilised society. Most countries keep official homicide statistics, sometimes stretching back centuries into their past. To academics, such data are like a patient's records clipped to the end of the hospital bed. Let us trace the line along Britain's murder chart.

The first and most obvious point is that Britain's homicide rate is a great deal healthier than it used to be. Back in the Middle Ages, according to analysis of English coroners' records and 'eyre rolls' (accounts of visits by justice officials), the rate was around

35/100,000. This is equivalent to the homicide level in contemporary Colombia or the Congo.

From the middle of the sixteenth century, the homicide rate started to fall steeply, a dramatic reduction in risk that was maintained for two hundred years. Plenty has been written about why the situation improved so radically during this period – the development of a statutory justice system (see 'J is for Justice') is often cited – but it was also a period in which the aristocracy and professional class found alternative ways of dealing with dispute and discontent. The duel emerged as a controlled and respectable way of responding to an insult against one's honour. Spontaneous violence became disreputable for gentlemen of standing, while personal discipline and restraint were seen as the marks of a civilised individual. This was, of course, in contrast to the vulgar and uncultured ways of the lower orders.

The murder rate continued to fall, if less steeply, during the nineteenth and twentieth centuries, as state control and social policies increased. It was also partly a consequence of young men being given a substitute for interpersonal violence to demonstrate their masculinity: organised sport. Boxing, for example, developed from bare-knuckled no-holds-barred brawls to disciplined contests governed by a strict code and overseen by a referee. The Queensbury Rules, introduced into British boxing in 1867, became shorthand for sportsmanship and fair play. Society at all levels increasingly valued the virtue of self-control.

Close study of the vital signs of British society reveal a slight rise in the homicide rate over the past fifty years, but in historical terms the figures are still so low that a single appalling occurrence – a terrorist attack or the murderous activity of a serial killer like Dr Harold Shipman – can skew the data. In international terms, the UK is among the less likely spots to be murdered: our homicide rate is broadly in line with other European nations (a little higher than Germany but slightly lower than France) and roughly a quarter of the level in the United States. Home Office figures for

England and Wales published in 2012 show the lowest rate since the mid-1980s.

So how to solve this crime? Since the homicide rate is largely driven by the activities of relatively poor, frustrated young men, it is no surprise that this is the group upon which much attention has focused. When the World Health Organization looked at youth violence in Europe they found that 15,000 young people die from interpersonal violence in the region each year. (Britain, incidentally, had one of the lowest death rates for this age group – twenty-seven times lower than Russia and three times lower than Belgium, Ireland or Iceland.) 'The mass media and society are quick to demonise violent young people,' their report noted, pointing an accusatory finger at those who inspire juvenile aggression by their abuse or neglect of children and adolescents (see 'Y is for Youth'). 'Overall, good evidence indicates that violence among young people can be prevented through the organised efforts of society,' they said. 'The evidence base is much stronger for interventions that adopt a public health rather than criminal justice approach, and for those that reduce risk factors and strengthen protective factors among young people early in life than for measures that seek to reduce violent behaviour once it has already emerged.'

We cannot hope to solve all murders: killers are driven by a multitude of motives and inspired by countless causes. But the clues and the evidence add up to suggest that a great many of these tragedies stem from threads of intolerance and indifference that run through the fabric of our society. The true culprit is . . . all of us.

Morse turned off the light, locked his office door, and walked back along the darkened corridor. The last piece had clicked into place. The jigsaw was complete.

N IS FOR NUMBERS

When I was at school in the late 1960s, I remember my maths teacher standing proudly behind a very large cardboard box placed upon his desk. Slowly and with reverence, the box was opened and an extraordinary apparatus lifted into view. 'Boys,' he began, 'this is . . . a calculator.' A what? The word was new to us, but we instantly fell in love with the shiny, metal contraption – a cross between a giant typewriter and an arcade slot-machine. There was magic in the box of tricks on the teacher's desk.

My children laugh when I tell them this story. To me, as a youngster, the complexity and scale of mathematical problems were reflected in the complexity and scale of the device needed to solve them. Today, the most challenging calculations can be handled by a puny, mundane slice of plastic.

Technology has transformed our relationship with numbers. Where once we were in thrall to their mystique, we are now blasé. Common computer programs allow us to manipulate numerical data with ease: to sort, to rank, to engineer, to plot and to conclude. Statistical analysis used to be the province of the expert mathematical mind; now any fool thinks he can do it. Billions of numbers whizzing at light speed around cyberspace are routinely trapped, dissected and displayed as 'proof' of some theory or another. A political researcher with a bit of wit and a laptop can find and manoeuvre the figures to back up the policy idea.

In one sense, technology has democratised data. Statistics are now the potential servants of us all rather than the powerful allies of a few. But one consequence is that we respect them less and distrust them more: familiarity has bred a contempt that risks undermining reason and promoting prejudice. In Britain, a decisive battle has been raging for control of statistics, a clash with profound implications for our governance and our society.

The outbreak of the War of Numbers can be traced back to the early nineteenth century. Before that, there was a benign discipline, quaintly christened 'political arithmetic', which offered some scant numerical evidence about population, life expectancy and finance. But the novel idea that the state should routinely collect and publish 'statistics' blossomed in the Victorian spring and sparked a furious and protracted struggle for domination over data that continues to this day.

One of the forefathers of statistical science, Sir Francis Galton, regarded statistics as beautiful but combustible, warning that they should not be brutalised but delicately handled and warily interpreted. Benjamin Disraeli, however, was less enamoured. In 1847 he wrote of how delightful it would be to suppress their use and sack the imbecile who ran the Board of Trade's statistical department. It is doubtful that Disraeli ever did use the phrase 'lies, damned lies and statistics', but what is certain is that there were those who wished to smother the infant science in its cradle. Nevertheless, guided by the principles of the Enlightenment and inspired by the belief that the solution to society's problems lay in the hands of men, reformers saw statistics as the instrument for creating a better world. Britain witnessed a fevered, almost obsessive period of counting and categorising (see 'J is for Justice').

The Statistical Society of London, founded in 1834 and later becoming the Royal Statistical Society, had as its first emblem a wheat sheaf, representing a bundle of facts, bound by a ribbon with the motto 'to be threshed by others'. Members were told to confine their attention rigorously to facts stated numerically and arranged in tables, carefully excluding all opinions. But it quickly became obvious that total immersion in the pure waters of numbers was an untenable position. The motto and the prohibition were dropped in 1857.

From this flowed a rather unseemly free-for-all in Whitehall, with statistical squabbles over methodology, accuracy and interpretation spreading between departments and across generations. It took a real war and a fat cigar to instil some order onto this bureaucratic chaos. In 1941, Sir Winston Churchill demanded a Central Statistical Office 'to consolidate and make sure that agreed figures only are used'. Consolidation and agreement, however, would remain in short supply as the various departmental statistical branches competed to produce numerical justification for the experimental ideas that would shape post-war Britain.

Often their data proved to be unhelpful in justifying government's policy ambitions. The 'facts' had an irritating habit of getting in the way of the 'good stories' ministers wanted to tell. It was Churchill again who famously told a prospective parliamentary candidate: 'When I call for statistics about the rate of infant mortality, what I want is proof that fewer babies died when I was Prime Minister than when anyone else was Prime Minister. That is a political statistic.'

Harold Wilson had respect for data and those who assembled it. He had spent the war working as a statistician for the coal industry but, as Prime Minister, he too recognised the tension between statistics and politics. In a speech to the Royal Statistical Society in 1973 he said he had learned that, 'while you can always get someone to find the answers to the questions, what you need in government is the man who knows the questions to the answers.'

The balance of power between elected ministers and qualified statisticians, between politicians and scientists, shifted palpably with the arrival of Margaret Thatcher. She wanted all her numbers to be political and invited an ideological soulmate, Sir Derek Rayner, the man from Marks & Spencer, to conduct a value-for-money review of the Central Statistical Office. He helpfully concluded that it was 'too heavily committed to serving the public at large'. In Sir Derek's view, 'information should not be collected primarily for publication [but] primarily because government needs it for its own business.' Overnight, troublesome number crunchers were stripped of their public responsibilities. Many lost their jobs as the government wiped out a quarter of its statistical service. Instead of providing ammo for voters, Whitehall stats departments would do what they were told by ministers. If this was a key battle in the War of Numbers, it was one which saw the boffins crushed.

At 4.30 on the afternoon of Wednesday, 10 June 1981, more than 200 statisticians gathered at the London School of Hygiene and Tropical Medicine to lick their wounds and vent their frustrations. The discussion was described as forceful, the atmosphere electric. The collective noun for statisticians is 'a variance', but on this issue they were united and determined. The long fight back would be conducted neither in Whitehall nor Westminster. The statisticians would go global.

The collapse of the Soviet empire in the early 1990s had created newly independent states which, it was hoped, would abandon the corrupt centralised systems of the Communist era, including the control and manipulation of official numbers. Here was an opportunity for the statistical profession to regroup on the moral high ground. Under the auspices of the United Nations in Geneva, plans were set in motion for renegotiating the balance of power.

In 1994, the UN published what were called the *Fundamental Principles of Official Statistics*. Principle Number One was that official data were not the playthings of politicians. No, they were 'an indispensable element in the information system of a democratic society', to be 'compiled and made available on an impartial basis by official statistical agencies to honour citizens' entitlement to public information'. Other principles further empowered the statisticians. In order to retain public trust, the scientists would control everything and, should some uppity politician try to interfere, the agencies would have authority to comment on erroneous interpretation and misuse of statistics.

The UN statement was a direct challenge to governments. Statistics were too important to be left open to the potential abuses of elected representatives. A year later, at the headquarters of the Royal Statistical Society in north London, the shadow Home Secretary Jack Straw admitted that political control of numbers had deeply damaged the relationship between the governed and the governing class. 'There can come a point where the cynicism goes so deep that it corrodes the foundations of our political system, leading to a wholesale lack of confidence in the system,' he warned. 'I believe that we are dangerously close to that position today.'

The Labour Party, frustrated particularly by the way unemployment figures had been 'massaged', was promising a new independence for those compiling government data. Statistics had become 'the hard and brittle currency of politics,' Straw conceded. Controlling the numbers had become key to the partisan battle for the hearts and minds of the electorate.

When Tony Blair and Gordon Brown moved into Downing Street in 1997, their luggage contained a promise of evidence-based policy. The idea that cold facts rather than hot passions should lead government was further encouragement for statisticians who looked forward to seeing their work and their influence increase. A year after entering office, the new Labour government published *Statistics: A Matter of Trust*, which admitted what the public had long assumed – politicians cannot be trusted with the data. 'It is seldom suggested that ministers actively change the numbers, rather that there remains scope for statistics to be subjected to political influence in more subtle ways,' the report acknowledged. However, New Labour was determined to control its message, and that meant they needed to control the numbers too. For all the rhetoric, ministers were very reluctant to allow some unelected swot to prize their sticky fingers from the official figures.

A decade later, in 2008, the rather toothless watchdog created ostensibly to restore faith in government data, The Statistics Commission, had to admit that the use of official numbers 'continued to be driven largely by departmental requirements'. It also noted that government was able to spin the statistics because it often controlled both the release of the data and the ministerial reaction to it.

I witnessed the game being played at the Home Office when the crime figures were published. Journalists would be invited to a 'lock-in' at the department, quite literally. The press would be ushered into a windowless room and instructed to turn off all telephones. The doors would be shut as a news release was thrust into our hands, proclaiming the good news of falling crime and delighted ministers. Then the assembled hacks would thumb through the 'official' stats, searching for what they regarded as the real story. Buried in the pages of numbers and charts would be some narrow category of crime which was still increasing, evidence that equated with voters' settled view: crime was out of control and politicians were deceitful toads. Upon being freed from our enforced purdah, that is the story we would tell. The more ministers struggled to convince the public that overall crime was falling, the less the electorate trusted them. In seeking to spin the numbers, they destroyed the reputation of government statistics and themselves. What was particularly galling for both politicians and statisticians in the Home Office was that the figures really did show that crime was falling. Quite a lot. And in almost every category.

However, the real damage to government credibility was being felt at the Treasury, where the Chancellor Gordon Brown was increasingly concerned that trust in economic statistics was denting international confidence. In a brief statement in Parliament towards the end of 2005, Mr Brown announced he would make 'the governance and publication of official statistics the responsibility of a wholly separate body at arm's length from government and fully independent of it'. A new statistical watchdog would be created whose responsibility, enshrined in statute, would be to protect the statistical system's integrity.

The news was afforded little more than a weary shrug, but the Statistics and Registration Service Act 2007 amounted to a rare but decisive victory for science over politics. The United Kingdom Statistics Authority (UKSA) was given the job of 'promoting and safeguarding' official statistics, including their impartiality, accuracy and relevance. It placed a duty on ministers and officials to comply with a code of practice drawn up by the authority, although the legislation specifically states that 'no action shall lie in relation to any such failure'. Offending spin doctors would not be dragged off to the Tower.

Nevertheless, under the chairmanship of Sir Michael Scholar, a Whitehall mandarin who had been Margaret Thatcher's Private Secretary when she emasculated the statisticians, the authority opened for business in April 2008. Any questions as to where Sir Michael's loyalties lay, however, were quickly dispelled when he sent a public and censorious letter to Number Ten following the government's use of 'unchecked' figures on knife crime (See 'K is for Knives'). He called the affair 'corrosive of public trust in official statistics, and incompatible with the high standards which we are all seeking to establish'. There was a sharp intake of breath across Whitehall. How would ministers and the civil service react to being openly ticked off by the anoraks in the stats department?

The reply from Gordon Brown, now at Number Ten, was revealing. His Private Secretary Jeremy Heywood wrote of how 'the Prime Minister remains strongly committed to building public trust in official statistics and to the new measures he has put in place to safeguard their independence.' Following the letter, the head of the home civil service, Sir Gus O'Donnell, reminded all his staff of the need to protect the integrity of official statistics.

The War of Numbers was not over, however. When the coalition government came to power, determined to reduce Britain's budget deficit, conservative instinct and economic adversity led one Cabinet minister to suggest statisticians were an unnecessary luxury. 'The money being spent on form fillers and bean counters could be far better spent helping elderly people to stay in their homes,' Communities Secretary Eric Pickles argued, before adding, 'or almost anything, in fact.' True to his word, he then scrapped a number of statistical surveys in the face of vehement opposition from Sir Michael Scholar and the National Statistician Jil Matheson. 'We are keen to move away from costly top-down monitoring and measurement of local policies,' Mr Pickles said. 'These surveys are a cosmetic exercise which never change anything,' his ministerial colleague Grant Shapps explained. To many of the so-called bean counters, it was as if the ghost of Sir Derek Rayner was haunting Whitehall once more.

Shortly before his departure from the UKSA in 2011, Sir Michael Scholar responded to what many statisticians feared was a new attack upon their profession. 'There are strong forces at work,' he warned, 'to demote rationality, analysis and the pursuit of knowledge within government.' He spoke of Whitehall's diminishing interest in neutral information and a growing interest in the persuasive press release, with its careful selection of facts and numbers, designed to communicate as effectively as possible some predetermined message.

Only one in six people in Britain thinks the government doesn't manipulate official numbers. In a recent survey of public trust in official statistics across the twenty-seven member states of the European Union, the UK came twenty-seventh. 'Right at the bottom of the class,' Sir Michael said.

The War of Numbers grinds on. But what is becoming clearer to protagonists on all sides is that, when they lack credibility, all numbers add up to zero.

O IS FOR OPIUM

Cultural orthodoxies are like piles of sandbags – resistant walls of principle and prejudice built up over time, which shape our democracy. Argument hits these solid barriers and is stopped stone dead. Further discussion is futile. Debate has reached society's buffers.

Our leaders know the lie of the land, where Britain's invisible ideological boundaries are placed. There is little point in entering territory upon which the court of public opinion has a settled view; indeed, to stray into such minefields may be regarded as political suicide. What actually tends to happen is that elected representatives, often aided and abetted by the popular press, add further layers to the existing bulwarks, reinforcing the external margins of conventional thought as they play to public opinion.

Our national conversation is conducted according to this geography, a narrative fixed by the co-ordinates of accepted wisdom. The mysteries of the news agenda are understood by those who can read the map. However, it is not entirely a one-way process. Gradually but inexorably, quietly but determinedly, non-conformist ideas can work away at the foundations of orthodoxy. New voices and ideas, with enough force, can start to undermine the status quo. The first objective is to open debate as to whether the wall should exist; once that has been achieved, and with often shocking speed, the whole edifice may collapse, the sandbags carted off to be piled up somewhere else.

When it comes to Britain's relationship with opium and other recreational drugs, the walls of the debate have not shifted for half a century. A towering cultural orthodoxy has been constructed around an accepted view that such substances are evil, a malevolent force that must be eradicated by uncompromising use of the criminal justice system.

But it seems to me that we are witnessing an increasingly powerful challenge to this philosophy. Former Cabinet ministers and police constables, peers of the realm, academics, senior journalists, business leaders and celebrities – mainstream establishment voices from all quarters – are asking whether we need to test conventional thinking.

Recent governments have seen what is happening but dared not engage. A parliamentary exchange between a former Home Office minister and a Lib Dem backbencher in 2010 indicates the nervousness that has existed. Tom Brake asked Labour's drugs spokesman Alan Campbell if 'when sound, factual evidence is produced to show what is effective in tackling drug crime and addressing health issues, the hon. gentleman will sign up to that?' Mr Campbell thought he detected a trap: 'I cannot give the hon. gentleman the assurance he seeks because he is sending me along a route he knows I cannot go down.' The route, of course, would have required the Labour spokesman to consider decriminalisation or legalisation of what were prohibited drugs. He could hear the sound of Joshua's trumpets: the walls of conventional debate were threatened and chaos lay beyond.

I do not propose to debate the wisdom of legalising drugs on these pages; readers will have no trouble finding proponents on all sides of what is an increasingly noisy discussion (albeit conducted outside the Palace of Westminster). But I did want to offer an historical perspective to explain how we got here.

Taking the long view, a slogan to describe Britain's attitude to recreational drugs would be 'Just Say Maybe'. The United Kingdom has been a reluctant prohibitionist and, one hundred years after the original international drugs control treaty was signed, it should not come as any surprise that this country's liberal and practical instincts are rising to the surface once again.

The first gangsters to use extreme violence and intimidation to control the supply of illegal drugs were associates of the British government. In the eighteenth century, the state-regulated East India Company secured a monopoly of opium production in India and, despite China's determination to ban the highly addictive drug from its soil, smuggled hundreds of tonnes a year into the country. When the Chinese authorities tried to clamp down on the foreign traffickers, the United Kingdom's Prime Minister Lord Palmerston sent in the gunboats. Royal Navy cannons ensured a swift victory for the British smugglers and dealers.

The consequence of the Opium Wars was that the drug became one of the most valuable commodities in the world and the British Empire took full advantage. By the 1880s, the Indian opium fields produced enough to satisfy the daily needs of around 14 million consumers in China and South East Asia, and the British Raj was reliant on feeding the addiction it had helped create.

Quantities of the drug arrived back in Britain. Mrs Beeton recommended readers of her *Book of Household Management* to keep their cupboards stocked with 'opium, powdered, and laudanum [opium mixed with alcohol]'; '*Vivat* opium!' the poet Elizabeth Barrett Browning reportedly told a friend; Prime Minister Gladstone put it in his coffee to steady his nerves. To some well-connected Victorians, opium was the opium of the people.

Domestic condemnation from religious groups grew, but the sparkle from 93 million silver rupees in annual Indian revenues prompted a more pragmatic than principled response. Gladstone, once a severe critic of the narcotics trade, appointed a Royal Commission on Opium which helpfully concluded in 1895 that the evil of the drug had been exaggerated and there was no association with any significant moral or physical health problems. Hurrah! The British government had scientific justification for a fruitful policy of zero intolerance, which was to last another seventeen years.

When in 1912 the Americans eventually cajoled Britain into signing an international agreement limiting the opium and cocaine trades, the UK did so half-heartedly and with ministerial fingers secretly crossed. After all, it had sustained an empire by selling narcotics. If one had popped into Harrods at that time looking to purchase something 'for when the nose is stuffed up, red and sore', the assistant would probably have suggested Ryno's Hay Fever and Catarrh Remedy. It consisted of almost pure cocaine. How about chocolate cocaine tablets for customers with a sweet but aching tooth? And what better way to support the boys at the front during the First World War than Harrods gift packs, containing morphine and cocaine?

It wasn't until 1916 that the British government was convinced to take firm action. Ministers were worried that the use of drugs might be undermining the war effort, so the Defence of the Realm Act brought in Home Office controls on the unauthorised possession of opium and cocaine. It was Britain's first embrace with prohibition, but this country did not share the passion for proscription that gripped the United States.

From among the federal agents recruited for America's moral crusade against the evil drink in the 1920s emerged a man whose enormous enthusiasm for prohibition would go on to influence global drugs policy for the next forty years. His name was Harry J. Anslinger. Anslinger regarded the opium poppy as 'the instrument of unprincipled men who by it satisfied their lust for wealth and power, of nations who used it for amoral reasons and as potent weapon of aggression'. He saw himself at the centre of an international struggle against 'the narcotics evil'.

Under diplomatic pressure from the Americans to honour its obligations and toughen up its drug laws, the UK government decided to play for time by setting up a committee under the chairmanship of Sir Humphrey Rolleston, an eminent physician. The medical men around the table took a very medical view of the drugs problem, concluding after two years' deliberation that addiction was a disease and an addict was ill. It was, therefore, the right of the medical practitioner to use his discretion in the choice of treatment in this, as in other illnesses. The pharmaceutical companies that manufactured prescription opium offered a silent prayer.

The US saw drug abuse as a sin; the UK had decided it was a sickness. Harry believed the answer was global prohibition; Sir Humphrey concluded the cure lay in the hands of doctors. What became known as the 'British System' was seen as a direct challenge to the prohibitionists on the other side of the Atlantic. There was due to be a showdown in Geneva in 1936; the Americans, with Anslinger in determined mood, demanded a new international convention that would oblige nations to introduce laws for severely punishing every aspect of the non-scientific drugs trade – from cultivation through production, manufacture, distribution and consumption. Anslinger's philosophy had a totalitarian simplicity: 'We intend to get the killer-pushers and their willing customers out of buying and selling drugs. The answer to the problem is simple – get rid of drugs, pushers and users. Period.'

When other delegates successfully argued that the proposed new sanctions should not apply to manufacturers or users, the United States went into a huff and refused to sign. The treaty was never implemented, but it was a turning point. The prohibitionists had changed the language of the debate.

Not that the Brits were particularly bothered. Drug abuse, they believed, was largely restricted to medics who had been trusted with the keys to the pharmacy, some wealthy bohemians, and a few foreigners with exotic habits. But after the Second World War, with more pressing matters on its mind and reliant on American aid to rebuild its battered economy, Britain was not looking for a fight over narcotics. Anslinger took his chance, incorporating prohibitionist steel into the structure of the new United Nations. When it came to international drugs policy, there would be a reduced role for doctors and greater influence for law enforcement officials.

Police in Britain took their cue amid post-war anxiety that 'alien' influences were contaminating the minds of the country's young men. On the night of 15 April 1950, officers from Scotland Yard raided a nightclub on London's Carnaby Street, looking for drugs. Club Eleven, now regarded as the crucible of modern British jazz, made headlines because the men found in possession of cannabis and cocaine were predominantly white, young and UK-born.

Six musicians spent the night in Savile Row police station before appearing at Marlborough Street Magistrates Court the next morning, among them future jazz legends Ronnie Scott and Denis Rose. Scott failed to convince the authorities that his cocaine was treatment for toothache, later recalling how one police officer told the court the arrests had taken place at a bebop club. 'What,' asked the judge gravely, 'is bebop?'

'A queer form of modern dancing – a Negro jive,' came the answer.

The event helped confirm a growing establishment suspicion that illicit drugs were a cause of the impertinence seen in an increasingly disrespectful youth. Britain was struggling to understand the changes that were transforming the social landscape. Many old orthodoxies were being challenged, the sandbagged bulwarks of conformity in danger of collapse.

In the Home Office, officials were instructed to monitor the spread of heroin and in particular a new group of young users in London's West End. Their dealer, a man called 'Mark', was arrested in September 1951 for theft from a hospital pharmacy. But what particularly concerned the drugs inspectorate was how this one pusher's activities could be traced through to a wave of new addicts spreading across the capital. Heroin abuse was likened to a contagious disease infecting the young. By the time the 1950s careered into the 60s, Whitehall had become convinced that the use of dangerous narcotics was threatening the established order. The papers were filled with scandalised commentaries on the craze for 'purple hearts' (pills containing a mixture of amphetamines and barbiturates) said to be sweeping Soho dance clubs.

It wasn't just a challenge for Britain. At the United Nations, attitudes were hardening and Harry Anslinger was on hand to encourage the worldwide community to sign the 1961 Single Convention on Narcotic Drugs, which described addiction as a 'serious evil'. It was an important victory for the prohibitionists, confirming in an international treaty that addicts were sinners rather than sick; drug abuse was a moral rather than medical problem. The British System now seemed quite at odds with the UK's global obligations.

However, in London, a few so-called 'junkie doctors' were continuing to supply the vast majority of heroin users, their activities reported to and neatly recorded inside the Home Office. The drugs inspectorate noted that numbers, although still only in the hundreds, were rising fast and they were terrified at the prospect of criminal gangs muscling in on the growing drugs trade. One senior Home Office staffer, Bing Spear, took it upon himself to stand outside Boots the chemist on Piccadilly Circus at midnight as addicts picked up their prescriptions. If a user didn't have a 'script', Bing would point them in the direction of a helpful doctor. Far better that, it was felt, than lining the pocket of some underworld pusher.

When a Whitehall committee investigated the escalating use of narcotics, they interviewed a psychiatrist who was known to prescribe heroin to some of her patients. After listening to her evidence, the chairman, Lord Brain, turned to the Home Office inspectors and said: 'Well gentlemen, I think your problem can be summed up in two words – Lady Frankau.'

Lady Isabella Frankau, wife of the venerated consultant

surgeon Sir Claude, is said to have almost single-handedly sparked the 1960s heroin epidemic in Britain. Records confirm that in 1962 alone she prescribed more than 600,000 heroin tablets to hundreds of users who flocked to her Wimpole Street consulting rooms.

Her patient list read like a *Who's Who* of 1960s bohemian cool. Poets, actors, musicians, writers and refugees from the strict drug laws in the US and Canada knew that Lady F would not ask too many questions and, if you were a bit short of readies, might even waive her consultancy fee. American jazz trumpeter Chet Baker was among those who turned up at her door, later recalling how 'she simply asked my name, my address and how much cocaine and heroin I wanted per day.'

Lady Frankau's motivation was to heal, but what was later described as her 'lunatic generosity' saw the end of the British System. As prescribing rules were tightened up, black-market Chinese heroin and other narcotics flooded in. Our relationship with drugs would never be the same again.

The 1960s throbbed with social upheaval and inter-generational tension. The Establishment was alarmed by the confidence and rebelliousness of the young – attitudes towards drugs became a divide and a battleground. In 1967, Marianne Faithfull was famously found under a fur rug, wearing nothing but a spacey smile, as the drugs squad busted a party and dragged Rolling Stones Keith Richards and Mick Jagger off to court. When The Beatles paid for an advertisement in *The Times* declaring that 'the law against marijuana is immoral in principle and unworkable in practice', there was angry condemnation in Parliament.

Home Office Minister Alice Bacon told the Commons of her horror at reading the views of Paul McCartney as she was having a shampoo and set. 'Paul McCartney says among other things: "God is in everything. God is in the space between us. God is in that table in front of you. God is everything and everywhere and everyone. It just happens that I realised all this through acid but it could have been through anything."'

'Is the right honourable lady quoting prominent people in favour of drug taking?' a shocked backbencher interrupted. 'It is terribly dangerous to quote people like that when we are against drug taking.'

Over the course of a few years, the British Establishment had lost control of the drugs problem. Between 1964 and 1968 the number of known teenage heroin addicts in Britain had risen from forty to 785. As health professionals were forced out, criminal gangs had moved in to supply all manner of new substances to young thrill-seekers with money to burn.

The Home Secretary James Callaghan told Parliament how Britain faced a pharmaceutical revolution presenting such risks that, if the country was 'supine in the face of them', it would quickly lead to 'grave dangers to the whole structure of our society'.

'Stimulants, depressants, tranquillisers, hallucinogens have all been developed during the last ten years, and our society has not yet come to terms with the circumstances in which they should properly be used or in which they are regarded as being socially an evil,' he explained, adding that 'the government intends to give full support to the endeavours to get international agreement on these problems.' It was the beginning of the global War on Drugs.

In 1971, US President Richard Nixon described drug abuse as 'public enemy number one', as the United Nations passed a new convention on psychotropic substances, which widened international controls to almost any mind-altering substance imaginable. The same year, the British Parliament passed the Misuse of Drugs Act, giving the Home Secretary direct authority to ban new drugs and increase the penalties associated with them. Political debate about prohibition was being closed down; the criminal justice system would be the main tool to fight drug abuse.

The War on Drugs pitted Establishment authority against defiant and disrespectful youth; the old order against the dangerous young generation. In the mid-1970s, Britain's punk movement coincided with an outbreak of glue sniffing because, it has been suggested, teenagers wanted to use the most visibly distasteful substance they could find. Illegal drugs were part of the armoury of rebellion, so when huge quantities of cheap, smokeable heroin flooded into Britain in 1979, punks were among the first in line.

The government was slow to realise what was happening. Amid the social turbulence and industrial unrest of the early 1980s, the Home Office was a department with other matters on its mind. Underworld drug syndicates quietly exploited the weakness of communities ravaged by unemployment and dripped low-quality heroin into the veins of a generation. The gangs targeted the poorest estates in the urban conurbations of Liverpool, Manchester, Glasgow, Edinburgh, Bristol and parts of London. They set up highly resilient distribution networks in which thousands of jobless, marginalised young men were recruited as street salespeople, running the gauntlet of an increasingly aggressive law enforcement system in return for a bit of low-grade smack and the thin promise of fabulous wealth.

At the beginning of the 1980s there were almost no heroin users in the Merseyside borough of Wirral. Six years later there were known to be about 4,000 addicts. As users searched for cash to support their habit, the impact of the crisis began to be felt in wealthier neighbourhoods. Burglary rates soared and what had been an issue of the underclass became a middle-class and, consequently, ministerial anxiety. 'Heroin outbreaks', as they were described by Home Office experts, spread down the west side of the Pennine hills, bringing a wave of crime and misery to each community they touched.

The irony was probably lost on government ministers, but a significant proportion of the heroin was coming from the Golden Triangle of South East Asia where, a century earlier, Britain had made a fortune from selling illicit opiates. As though reaping the consequences of some long-forgotten Chinese curse, Britain found itself with a drugs problem it could not control. To add to the bewilderment and helplessness felt in Whitehall, it emerged that the metaphorical heroin 'epidemic' had a real and potentially cata-strophic viral element: HIV/AIDS.

With the police and prison systems straining to cope with the explosion in crime fuelled by drugs, and a major health disaster on the cards, the British government was in pragmatic mood. While Ronald Reagan was going around his Cabinet table demanding to know what his team was 'doing for the War on Drugs', Margaret Thatcher was seeking practical solutions to the crisis. For all the front-of-house anti-drugs rhetoric, behind the scenes the Prime Minister gave approval for the introduction of community drug teams and needle exchanges, handing out clean equipment and health advice to heroin injectors. The philosophy was one of harm reduction rather than moral crusade; echoes of the British System could still be heard in parts of Whitehall.

For some, this shift in approach amounted to capitulation, but illegal drugs had become so intermeshed with mainstream youth culture in Britain that policy was aimed at damage limita-tion. The Home Office ostensibly led on government drugs strategy, but the initiative increasingly rested with the Department of Health, creating departmental tensions that mirrored the old argu-ments over whether illicit drug use should be regarded as sin or sickness.

For hundreds of thousands of British teenagers it was nei-ther. Popping pills or smoking dope was a bit of fun and just part of growing up. Towards the end of the 1980s, a new designer drug started appearing in clubs. Within five years, shocked ministers were told that a million and a half ecstasy tablets were being consumed every weekend. Three million people had used cannabis in the previous twelve months. In 1996, parliamentary advisors reported that almost half of Britain's 16- to 24-year-olds had tried drugs and a fifth were regular users. The prisons system was overwhelmed as the courts dealt with 8,000 drug offenders each month, while drug-related crime accounted for much of the rest of its workload. Coroners were recording more than a hundred drug-related deaths each month. Police were seizing record amounts of narcotics but reporting that global supply to the UK was still going up.

When Tony Blair arrived in Downing Street he swiftly appointed a 'drugs tsar', the former police chief Keith Hellawell, to try and bring some order to the chaos. But what the government called its vision for the future was fuzzy and contradictory. The rhetoric was punitive but the huge cost to the criminal justice system demanded a more pragmatic response. It was bound to end in tears.

Towards the end of 2001, a parliamentary committee of MPs from across the political spectrum began investigating whether the government's drugs strategy was working. By May the following year it had made up its mind. 'If there is any single lesson from the experience of the last thirty years, it is that policies based wholly or mainly on enforcement are destined to fail,' it unanimously concluded. 'It remains an unhappy fact that the best efforts of police and Customs have had little, if any, impact on the availability of illegal drugs.'

Among those who put their name to the document was the future Prime Minister David Cameron. He supported a recommendation that Britain should initiate a discussion at the United Nations on 'alternative ways – including the possibility of legalisation and regulation – to tackle the global drugs dilemma'. Shortly afterwards, the Home Secretary David Blunkett signalled that he didn't want police in England and Wales to continue arresting people for possession of small amounts of cannabis by ordering that it be reclassified as a less dangerous drug. He said he wanted an 'adult and mature debate' and a focus on the 'drugs that kill'. Mr Hellawell, whose prohibitionist instincts had seen him increasingly sidelined, resigned, asking: 'How on earth can you justify messages which appear to soften the approach?'

In June 2003, senior Cabinet ministers arrived in Downing Street for a presentation on the drugs situation from government advisors. The lights were dimmed as a series of slides were displayed. It was a sobering event. The annual cost to Britain from illegal drugs, they were told, stood at £24 billion, a figure equivalent to the entire spending budget for the country's armed forces.

So were they winning the War on Drugs? 'The drugs supply market is highly sophisticated,' ministers were advised, 'and attempts to intervene have not resulted in sustainable disruption to the market at any level.' From a sea of graphs and tables, the horrible truth emerged. 'The drugs supply business is large, highly flexible and very adaptable; over time the industry has seen consumption grow and prices reduce,' the advisors warned. 'Even if supply-side interventions were more effective, it is not clear that the impact on the harms caused by serious drug users would be reduced.'

The Generals in Iraq might have been claiming victory over Saddam, but the campaign against illegal drugs was going very badly indeed. British ministers attempted to hush up the gloomy news, but governments across the world were getting similar reports and responding. The Portuguese decreed that the purchase, possession and use of any previously illegal drug would no longer be considered a criminal offence. The Russians made possession for personal use a civil matter. The Spanish moved drugs policy from criminal justice to health.

In Britain, there were calls for the expansion of pilot schemes allowing GPs to prescribe heroin once again. Billions were pumped into drug treatment programmes as police drugs officers were quietly told their principal aim was now harm reduction rather than strict law enforcement. But the politics of drugs proved almost as toxic as the narcotics themselves.

In 2008, with the government deeply unpopular in the polls, ministers launched a new and 'relentless drive' against the drugs menace. Rejecting the advice of official experts, the Home Secretary announced the criminal sanction for possessing cannabis would be increased to a maximum of five years in prison. The move was welcomed in the tabloid press, but set government on a collision course with its own scientific advisors.

The following year, the Advisory Council on the Misuse of Drugs said the harms associated with ecstasy did not justify its Class A status; the committee chairman, Professor David Nutt, argued that the dangers were equivalent to the risks from horse riding. Again, the government rejected the committee's evidence because of concerns about 'public perception'.

In October 2009, following the publication of a paper that suggested harsher penalties for cannabis possession might cause more harm than good, Professor Nutt was fired by the Home Secretary. His dismissal led to numerous resignations by government scientists who accused ministers of putting politics before evidence.

Ironically, as the professor was clearing his desk, the previously hawkish UN drugs chief Antonio Maria Costa also published a paper. 'Punishment is not the appropriate response to persons who are dependent on drugs,' it read. 'Indeed, imprisonment can be counter-productive.' Within the once prohibitionist microclimate of the UN Office on Drugs and Crime, the weather was changing. 'I appeal to the heroic partisans of the human rights cause worldwide,' Mr Maria Costa wrote, 'to help UNODC promote the right to health of drug addicts: they must be assisted and reintegrated into society.' The United Nations appeared to be nudging the international drugs debate towards something that looked a bit like the long-forgotten British System.

Despite a broad political consensus in Britain against moving an inch from the approach of strict prohibition, the towering cultural orthodoxy around drugs is weakening. Policy makers are unsure where the co-ordinates of accepted wisdom currently lie. They must act as though the map remains as it was, but a fog has descended. When it lifts again, I expect the walls of principle and prejudice to have shifted.

P IS FOR POVERTY

... but public attitudes towards poverty in Britain mean that debate almost inevitably shifts to P for Plasma screen televisions, Packets of twenty, Pints of lager and Punts on the 3.30 at Chepstow. 'Poverty' is an explosive term in the UK, exposing a deep fault line in our understanding of what it means, what – if anything – should be done about it, and whether it even exists at all. Our response to poverty, therefore, reveals something of the disposition of the British people – our values, our heritage and our morality.

In the mid-1970s, a survey across the European Economic Community asked people in different countries why they thought there were people in need. Was it inevitable, bad luck, injustice or was it because poor people were lazy? In Britain, 43 per cent of respondents said the primary cause of poverty was laziness or lack of willpower – the most judgemental attitude of any country in the EEC.

Although subsequent polling in the 1980s and 90s showed the proportion blaming poverty on idleness going down as unemployment went up, over 60 per cent of the UK population continues to assert it is either unavoidable or the fault of the poor themselves.

There is much to suggest that the UK is a generous and compassionate nation. Analysis of charitable giving habits around the world following the South East Asian tsunami and other natural disasters in 2004–5 found that two thirds of Britons had each donated more than $100 to good causes that year, compared to 21 per cent in Germany, 30 per cent in Spain and Italy, and 34 per cent in France. But such levels of empathy do not appear to extend to the domestic poor, with campaigners complaining of harshly judgemental attitudes and government research suggesting that public sympathy for the poor in Britain has actually declined in the last decade.

Attitudes appear to be shaped by the use of the word 'poverty' itself. A significant proportion of the population simply does not believe it can exist in a country like Britain, with its wealth and welfare system. Around 40 per cent of people think there is very little poverty in the UK and, where families are in need, it is their own fault.

The research company Ipsos MORI conducted a series of focus groups on poverty in 2007 and concluded that the British public generally thought there was no excuse for poverty – it was down to bad choices and wrong priorities and therefore not a subject for public help. People, they found, had a mental model of 'people like us', the strivers, versus 'freeloaders' or the skivers. This image of strivers versus skivers chimes precisely with the familiar political rhetoric of 'hard-working families' as opposed to 'welfare scroungers and benefit cheats', a contrast that has its origins in the historical notion of the 'deserving' and 'undeserving poor'.

The Reformation marked a fundamental shift in attitudes to poverty in Britain. Before the dissolution of the monasteries in the mid-sixteenth century, close-knit devout communities would have looked to the Bible and religious orders for guidance on moral expectations in responding to the poor and needy. Instructions were set out in the Book of Matthew, Chapter 25: 'Feed the hungry, give drink to the thirsty, welcome the stranger, clothe the naked, visit the sick, visit the prisoner, bury the dead.' Being poor was to be closer to God: monks, nuns and friars swore an oath of poverty, that material concerns might not distract them from seeking salvation.

However, the collapse of the feudal system, the enclosure of common land and Henry VIII's suppression of monasteries and convents prompted a profound change in the country's relationship with the poor. Neither the church almshouses and hospitals nor the philanthropic traditions of Lords of the Manor were able to provide for the needy in the way they once had: begging, destitution and starvation stalked the kingdom, with tens of thousands of peasants deprived of land, work and succour. Amid fears of widespread civil disorder, the state was eventually obliged to take responsibility. Parliament required that assigned parish officials should collect charity for the relief of the poor. Those who refused to donate voluntarily might be taxed and ultimately imprisoned.

The move from charitable donation to enforced taxation, from the personal and moral to the bureaucratic and rational, effectively marked the conception of the welfare state and changed the relationship between wider society and its poorest members. The Poor Laws attempted to mitigate resentment at the new tax by spelling out who was entitled and who was not entitled to state aid – enshrining in statute the concept of deserving and undeserving poor. The former included 'the impotent poor', those deemed too old, too sick or too young to work. They might receive 'indoor relief' – lodging in almshouses, orphanages, workhouses or hospitals. The deserving category also included those who wanted to work but couldn't find a job. These strivers, as pollsters might categorise them today, were entitled to 'outdoor relief' – clothes, food or perhaps some money.

The undeserving poor were the equivalent of today's 'skivers': people deemed able to work but who chose not to. Rather than blaming poor policies for extra taxes and social strife, citizens were encouraged to blame poor people. The Poor Law of 1572, for instance, justified itself by stating that 'all parts of this Realm of England and Wales be presently with rogues, vagabonds and sturdy beggars exceedingly pestered.'

Cast as enemies of the state, they were accused of 'horrible murders, thefts, and other great outrages, to the high displeasure of Almighty God, and to the great annoy of the common weal'. For this group, therefore, poverty was not a grace but a sin requiring punishment. Those convicted of a roguish or vagabond trade of life were liable to be 'grievously whipped and burnt through the gristle of the right ear with a hot iron', branded as identifiable scapegoats for what were arguably the political and economic failings of others.

This was the birth of the underclass, the detached and dangerous group the Victorians referred to as the 'residuum', whose fecklessness and criminality threatened the law-abiding and hardworking majority. Culpability for every social ill would be routinely pinned upon this subset of humanity, a cultural group whose pathological behaviour was said to pass down through the generations.

For centuries, politicians would argue they were supporting the impotent and deserving in society while pointing an accusatory finger into the shadows. The outbreaks of looting and arson across parts of urban England in the summer of 2011 were widely blamed on an idle and immoral 'underclass'. The warnings going back to the Poor Laws of how the undeserving might rise up in a tempest of flame and greed appeared to have come to pass.

It is this historical narrative that has shaped our attitudes to the poor, framing the debate in terms of 'them' and 'us'. As Britain got richer in the late twentieth century, so the argument shifted: from deserving and undeserving poor as to whether true poverty even existed at all. On 11 May 1989, John Moore, then Secretary of State for Social Security, stood up to make a speech in the refined opulence of a Conservative private members' club in Westminster. 'We reject their claims about poverty in the UK,' he said of his government's critics, arguing that the word was being used to describe what was in reality simply inequality. His sentiments echoed the words of a senior civil servant who had told a parliamentary committee the previous year: 'The word "poor" is one the government actually disputes.'

With campaigners claiming that a third of the British population were living on or under the breadline, the definition of the word 'poverty' had become the subject of intense political debate. It was obvious that the UK did not suffer from the squalor and starvation associated with poverty in previous centuries or less developed countries. Absolute poverty in Britain was rare. But the demands for social reform had seen the development of the concept of relative poverty.

One of the loudest voices in the movement to redefine the word for the twentieth century was Professor Peter Townsend, a left-wing academic who founded the Child Poverty Action Group in 1965. He argued that people were in poverty when they were excluded from the ordinary living patterns, customs and activities of the average family. To Conservative thinkers including John Moore, the true motive for redefining poverty was 'so they can call Western capitalism a failure'. However, the idea that poverty was a measure of social exclusion had been taking hold.

In 1975, the Council of Europe had described the poor as those 'whose resources (material, cultural and social) are so small as to exclude them from the minimum acceptable way of life of the Member State in which they live'. Eight years later, with UK unemployment approaching 3 million for the first time for half a century, London Weekend Television commissioned a survey to test public opinion on what a minimum acceptable standard of living looked like.

Entitled *Breadline Britain*, the researchers asked what items people regarded as essential for an acceptable living standard in 1983. Almost everyone agreed that 'heating to warm the living areas of the home' was a necessity, two thirds regarded a washing machine as essential, half the population thought a television was an essential item, while less than a quarter included a car on the list. The survey also asked respondents whether they lacked these items, allowing the programme to manufacture some shocking headlines. Applying the findings to the whole population, *Breadline Britain* claimed that approximately 3 million people in Britain today couldn't afford to heat the living areas of their homes and around 6 million people went without some essential aspect of clothing – such as a warm waterproof coat – because of lack of money.

What the programme makers inadvertently did, however, was reveal that while nearly 3.5 million people didn't have consumer durables such as carpets, a washing machine or a fridge, virtually no one lacked a television. *Breadline Britain* stoked the debate as to whether the poor themselves, through misplaced priorities, were to blame for their own misfortune.

Shortly after the programme was aired, a letter appeared in *The Sunday Times* from S. Turner of Wolverhampton: 'Anyone who visits low-income families has experience of homes which are lacking in carpets, furniture, or decent clothing for children, but contain a large colour TV.' If they can afford a telly, beer and fags, the cry went up, they are not poor – they are taking the rest of society for a ride. The undeserving poor were at it again!

In 1997, two sociologists working at Bristol University – David Gordon and Christina Pantazis – decided to challenge this folk wisdom. They looked for the evidence of an 'underclass' blighted by some pathological culture of poverty. They went back to the Pauper Pedigree Project of the Eugenics Society, which ran from 1910 to 1933. They scoured the pages of the Problem Families Project of 1947. They looked at the multi-million-pound government funded Transmitted Deprivation Programme of the 1970s. The conclusion: 'Despite 150 years of scientific investigation, often by extremely partisan investigators, not a single study has ever found any large group of people/households with any behaviours that could be ascribed to a culture or genetics of poverty.'

The idea of an impoverished underclass feeding on wider society implied a distinct and stable group, culturally at odds with mainstream values. What the evidence actually showed was that most people had experienced at least a brief spell of living in poverty, but there were only a very few 'whose poverty could be ascribed to fecklessness'. Official figures from the Department for Work and Pensions would later estimate that about three in five British households experienced income poverty for at least one year during the 1990s and the early years of the new millennium.

What about the packets of twenty and the pints of lager? Gordon and Pantazis found that in 1992, for example, the least well-off families spent £3.00 a week on alcohol (3.2 per cent of total expenditure), compared to the average family, which spent £11.06 (4.1 per cent). Poorer families spent £3.51 a week on tobacco, compared to an average spend of £5.38. 'This is unsurprising,' Gordon and Pantazis pointed out. 'The poorest households spend less on everything than all other households as they have less money to spend.'

The politics of poverty have moved markedly in the past fifteen years, with both Labour and the Conservatives now considering it a real and debilitating consequence of social inequality. Tony Blair walked into Number Ten in 1997 promising to eliminate child poverty by 2020. David Cameron walked into Number Ten in 2010 promising his party was 'best placed to fight poverty in our country'. Gone are the days when senior British politicians argue whether relative poverty exists.

Public attitudes, however, remain deeply sceptical. An Ipsos MORI focus group in 2007 was presented with evidence of severe deprivation in some of Britain's poorest communities. 'They probably don't wear coats because it's fashionable not to', was one participant's explanation. 'People in Cornwall don't need so much money – they can go out and cut trees down for fuel', said another. The researchers concluded that people were reaching for outlandish explanations as to why the evidence didn't match their opinions.

Poverty denial remains a significant barrier for those organisations campaigning on behalf of the poorest in Britain. Numerous academic papers have been written, trying to explain why people simply refuse to believe there is real deprivation in the UK – research which has led some back to a book written in 1980 by the American social psychologist Melvin Lerner. *The Belief in a Just World: A Fundamental Delusion* identified a relatively common tendency to assume that people get what they deserve and deserve what they get: that the good get rewarded and the bad get punished. Professor Lerner argued that 'people are very reluctant to give up this belief, and they can be greatly troubled if they encounter evidence that suggests that the world is not really just or orderly after all.'

Since the book's publication researchers have tried to see whether those who have a belief in a just world (BJW) react differently to poverty than those who don't. In one experiment conducted at Columbia University in 2003, volunteers were asked how strongly they agreed or disagreed with a long list of statements, including: people who get 'lucky breaks' have usually earned their good fortune; careful drivers are just as likely to get hurt in traffic accidents as careless ones; in almost any business or profession, people who do their job well rise to the top; the political candidate who sticks up for his principles rarely gets elected.

The answers allowed the researchers to divide the group into *strong* BJW and *weak* BJW. Then all the volunteers were presented with the story of Lisa, a mother of two children having a difficult time making ends meet. More information about her circumstances was then given, and participants were asked whether they thought she was deserving of welfare or not. For example, they might be told that 'Lisa was working last year and is still working at the same job', or that 'Lisa sometimes skips meals so that her children can eat', 'Lisa is going to school to improve her job skills' or 'Lisa is looking for a better job'. The difference between the two groups could hardly have been more marked.

Among those with a strong BJW, Lisa's efforts to cope with her poverty made her *less* deserving of aid. The other group, with a weak BJW, saw Lisa's actions as evidence that she was *more* deserving. Indeed, 'the more indications given that Lisa was acting responsibly or making an effort to improve her situation, the more likely respondents with a strong general belief in a just world were to find her undeserving. Conversely, the more of these characteristics that Lisa possessed, the more likely respondents with a weak general belief in a just world were to find her deserving.' To those with a strong BJW, the mythical Lisa's struggles against poverty demonstrated she had the capacity to improve herself and was not, by definition, a member of the impotent (and therefore deserving) poor.

There is now a substantial body of evidence about the kind of people most likely to be found among the strong BJW group. According to research by Zick Rubin of Harvard University and Letitia Anne Peplau of UCLA, they tend to be 'more religious, more authoritarian, more conservative, more likely to admire political leaders and existing social institutions, and more likely to have negative attitudes toward underprivileged groups'.

There are obvious links between the belief in a just world hypothesis and the German sociologist Max Weber's concept of the Protestant work ethic (PWE). This defines the view of those who believe that hard work pays off and, unsurprisingly perhaps, such people tend to be highly judgemental of the poor. Recent research into British attitudes involved an experiment in which 109 working adults were divided up into those with high and low PWE. Volunteers were asked how much they agreed or disagreed with statements that included: 'Most people who don't succeed in life are just plain lazy', 'Life would have very little meaning if we never had to suffer', and 'I feel uneasy when there is little work for me to do'.

The psychologist behind the experiment, Professor Adrian Furnham at University College London, concluded that 'a high

PWE scorer is likely to explain poverty in terms of idleness and poor money management; wealth in terms of hard work, honesty and saving; unemployment in terms of laziness and lack of effort; and he or she is likely to be opposed to both taxation and social security.' Max Weber's influential ideas suggest the Reformation did not simply trigger an economic and political shift in attitudes to poverty and wealth – it also inspired a psychological change.

Catholic tradition stressed that individual thought, deviation from the status quo, might amount to heresy with all its unpleasant and painful consequences. Salvation was assured by the dutiful acceptance of church teaching and authority. Protestantism was based on the idea that each faithful Christian was responsible directly and immediately to God. It was a philosophy founded on individualism; no longer did the church determine piety – the decision lay with the common man or woman. They were free to judge the poor.

The difference in approach can still be seen today in people's attitudes to begging. In Catholic countries, beggars are more likely to be tolerated, if not pitied and supported. In Protestant countries, begging is often an offence. In England and Wales, the Vagrancy Act of 1824 still applies: sleeping on the streets and begging is a criminal offence. By contrast, until recently there was no law against beggars in Italy. Venice became the first Italian city to make begging illegal in 2008, a response to the attitudes of tourists rather than Venetians. Ireland only introduced laws against aggressive begging in 2011 after its High Court had ruled that old British vagrancy laws were unconstitutional, conflicting with enshrined Irish rights on freedom of expression and communication.

British attitudes to poverty, shaped by our religious, political and economic history, appear paradoxical. Around 70 per cent of people think the gap between rich and poor in Britain is too wide, but there is no corresponding support for redistributive measures by government to reduce it. The British have led the way in ambitious campaigns to 'Make Poverty History' and to 'Feed the World', but government research recently found the public to be a long way from supporting an anti-poverty agenda in the UK.

When it comes to domestic poverty, the country is almost exactly split down the middle between the 'liberal' and the 'sceptical'. Five hundred years of argument and uncertainty as to the duties of the state and the individual in supporting the needy still rage across Britain to this day.

Q IS FOR QUEEN

My grubby taxi bounced through the streets of Old Tallinn, squeaking and complaining as its driver attempted to avoid puddles that might have hidden an axle-breaking pothole. The shower had cleared the air and a triumphant sun beamed onto the shiny cobbles, onyx-black stones twinkling as though encrusted with diamonds. It all made sense. I was on my way to meet a queen.

It was 1992 and I was indeed destined to shake hands with royalty – an assignment for BBC *Newsnight* had taken me to the Estonian capital, where we had arranged to interview Her Majesty Queen Margrethe II of Denmark. It seemed odd to have ended up on what was technically foreign soil for both of us, but while Tallinn would subsequently be invaded by countless British stag parties, my interviewee could claim that her ancestor had got the beers in first: King Valdemar II of Denmark had captured the place at the Battle of Lyndanisse in 1219. Indeed, it transpired the city's very name meant Danish castle.

The cab door announced my arrival with a pained creak. Although I liked to imagine myself as a hard-bitten hack, blasé about rank, unimpressed by pomp and immune to institutional sycophancy, I couldn't prevent my heart missing a beat as I stepped from the taxi. It is not every day that one is introduced to a real live queen.

Back home in the UK, the British Royal Family appeared to be in turmoil: the tabloids were gorging on courtly scandal as princes and princesses queued up to heap humiliation and disgrace upon the House of Windsor. 'Squidgygate', 'Camillagate', 'Fergiegate' – the Palace walls had been multiply breached and squalid, intimate details of collapsing marriages and suspect morals were tumbling out into the public domain. Rumblings of republicanism were encouraging some to believe the kingdom itself was threatened, that we were witnessing something akin to the final chapter in the *Wizard of Oz*: the terriers of the British press pack had managed to enter the inner sanctum, rip the curtain aside and reveal the monarchy to be mundane.

The Danish queen breezed towards me with a matter-of-factness to her stride. She proffered a gloved hand, which I shook, grateful that I had not needed to commit myself to complying with deferential protocol. 'Good morning,' she said, in business-like tones.

The queen was charming and intelligent: her answers to my questions diplomatic and assured. Given the travails of her blood cousins in Britain and her own apparently unassailable popularity in Denmark, I asked what words of advice she had for her relatives. Her gracious reply revealed nothing unexpected, but the scoop was that she had agreed to be interrogated at all.

Something about the experience had left me troubled, though, and I couldn't quite work out what. The interview had been fine, we had more than enough interesting material for our needs, but I was discomforted nevertheless. It was only as I sat back in London reviewing the tapes and writing my script that it dawned on me what was wrong.

In January 1776, a pamphlet simply signed 'Written by an Englishman' began to be passed around among the population of the colonies of the New World. Entitled *Common Sense*, the article's radical ideas enjoyed an enthusiastic welcome: the paper sold more than 500,000 copies and was read aloud in taverns. The author, it emerged, was Thomas Paine, a former English taxman, tobacconist and radical who became, of course, one of the Founding Fathers of the United States of America.

As well as being a manifesto for independence from Britain, the pamphlet also offered a devastating critique of the English monarchy. 'There is something exceedingly ridiculous in the composition of Monarchy,' Paine declared, arguing that nature frequently ridicules royal succession by 'giving mankind an ass for a lion'. He contrasted the common sense of his pamphlet's title with the absurdity and superstition that inspired the English prejudice for monarchy, arising 'as much or more from national pride than reason'.

Logic and proof were guiding principles of republican philosophy, a political theory that prided itself on its rationality. Paine was a child of the Enlightenment, inspired by the scientists and thinkers of what he would later describe as the Age of Reason. Monarchy just didn't stack up: not only was it contrary to the laws of natural justice, he argued, it consistently failed to work that well. 'Did it ensure a race of good and wise men it would have the seal of divine authority, but as it opens a door to the foolish, the wicked and the improper, it hath in it the nature of oppression.' To this day, British republicans refer to Paine's *Common Sense* almost as their sacred text. Its direct, accessible and witty prose was as powerful in its day as a thousand editions of the *Sun* packed with exclusive Squidgygate revelations.

But monarchists have their own sacred text. Written almost exactly a century afterwards, Walter Bagehot's *English Constitution* was a belated but stirring response to the revolutionary arguments of a Founding Father. 'In the American mind and in the colonial mind there is, as contrasted with the old English mind, a literalness, a tendency to say, "The facts are so-and-so, whatever may be thought or fancied about them."' Bagehot had decided not to fight reason with reason – but with magic. 'We catch the Americans smiling at our Queen with her secret mystery,' he wrote. There is a sneer in Bagehot's prose. He presents Americans as shallow, worshipers of the visible and the obvious. They can't help it, poor things. The colonists' struggle with the wilderness marked their minds so that when they come to choose a government, 'they must choose one in which all the institutions are of an obvious evident utility.'

Bagehot employs the trickery of the illusionist. He accepts, even builds upon, many of Paine's criticisms: 'An hereditary king is but an ordinary person, upon an average, at best'; 'hereditary royal families gather from the repeated influence of their corrupting situation some dark taint in the blood, some transmitted and growing poison which hurts their judgements'; 'For the most part, a constitutional king is a damaged common man'. Then, just as you imagine Bagehot will crush himself with his own rationality, he vanishes in a puff of smoke, only to reappear a moment later in the front row of the Royal Circle. 'This illusion has been and still is of incalculable benefit to the human race,' he announces to the startled auditorium.

In a magic act, it is the inexplicable that matters. Superstition, Bagehot conceded, is of no use in electing rulers, but it renders possible the existence of unelected rulers. The rationalists and empiricists must have been shaking their heads at such mystical mumbo-jumbo, but the showman had more tricks up his sleeve. 'English people yield a deference,' he continued, 'to what we may call the theatrical show of society.' With a flourish of his rhetorical wand Bagehot added: 'The climax of the play is the Queen.'

It was a breathtakingly bold argument. An old and complicated society like England required something more than mundane, dreary logic. It deserved a true monarchy, sparkling with mystic reverence and religious allegiance, imaginative sentiments that no legislature could manufacture. 'You might as well adopt a father as make a monarchy.'

Bagehot had identified and exploited a developing national characteristic. As colonial power and the riches of empire declined, there was a desire to define greatness as more than wealth and territory. Britain wanted to believe in magic. As J. M. Barrie put it in *Peter Pan*: 'All you need is trust and a little bit of pixie dust!'

A conjuror knows that convincing your audience to suspend its disbelief requires a balance of flamboyance and mystery. The committee that convened to organise the 1953 Coronation of Queen Elizabeth II took a full year to finalise the details amid argument as to how to maximise its impact. The Prime Minister Winston Churchill was reportedly horrified at the idea that 'modern mechanical arrangements' (television) should be used to broadcast from inside Westminster Abbey. He told the House of Commons: 'It would be unfitting that the whole ceremony, not only in its secular but also in its religious and spiritual aspects, should be presented as if it were a theatrical performance.' Perhaps Churchill recalled Bagehot's advice: 'We must not let in daylight upon magic.' But the Queen and her advisors decided the cameras should be allowed to relay every moment of the meticulously planned ceremony – with one exception.

The television audience missed nothing of the pomp and pageantry, feathers and fur, golden spurs, jewel-encrusted orb, bracelets of sincerity and wisdom, ritual swords, anthems and trumpets. From the quiet of a choir softly singing 'Come Holy Ghost, Our Souls Inspire', to the shouts, bells and cannons that greeted the crowning moment, the organisers didn't miss an emotional trick in trying to inspire the tens of millions crowded around small black and white TV sets. But, in the middle of it all, a section of the service was conducted in secrecy.

The Act of Consecration is the most magical aspect of an English coronation, so extraordinary that history (and the 1953 Coronation Committee) decreed it must remain out of sight. In preparation, the Queen was disrobed of her crimson cloak, her jewellery was removed and the young Elizabeth was seated in King

Edward's chair, an ancient and simple throne, clothed in a dress of purest white. It was a moment of high theatre. A golden canopy held by four Knights of the Garter was suspended above and around the monarch, a grander version of the cloth cabinet a conjuror might wheel onto stage before making his glamorous assistant disappear.

With the Abbey almost silent, the Archbishop of Canterbury was handed the Holy Ampulla, a flask in the shape of an eagle, wrought in solid gold. Legend had it that the vessel had been given to St Thomas à Becket by the Virgin Mary in a vision while travelling in France, was lost and later recovered by the Black Prince at the Battle of Poitiers in 1356. A more credible version has it that the object was crafted in 1661 for the coronation of Charles II. A spoon was also passed to the Archbishop, a relic that had survived the civil war and was probably made for Henry II or Richard I. The props dripped with provenance: antique, sacred, mythical.

From the flask, the Archbishop poured some 'blessed oil' of orange, roses, cinnamon, musk and ambergris, and anointed the Queen in the form of a cross, on the palms of her hand, on the breast and on the crown of her head. As he did so, he whispered these words: 'Be thy Head anointed with Holy Oil: as Kings, Priests, and Prophets were anointed. And as Solomon was anointed King by Zadok the priest and Nathan the prophet, so be you anointed, blessed and consecrated Queen over the Peoples, whom the Lord thy God hath given thee to rule and govern.'

In that instant, the viewing public were meant to believe that their queen was transformed. As a newsreel commentator put it: 'The hallowing: a moment so old history can barely go deep enough to contain it.' When the golden pall was removed and the cameras rolled on the monarch once more, hey presto and hallelujah, Elizabeth had become associated with the divine.

A few days later, two sociologists began writing an academic essay on how all this had gone down with the wider audience. Englishman Michael Young and American Ed Shils had joined the crowds in the East End of London, dropping in on street parties and chatting to local people. Grappling with the challenges of post-war rationing and austerity, how had the masses responded to the extravagant and elaborate show in the Abbey? 'The Coronation provided at one time and for practically the entire society such an intensive contact with the sacred that we believe we are justified in interpreting it as we have done in this essay, as a great act of national communion,' they wrote.

Their thesis, entitled 'The Meaning of the Coronation', admitted that some had dismissed the whole affair as the product of commercial exploitation, media manipulation, hysteria, obsession with tradition, or just an excuse for a knees-up. Such hecklers, Young and Shils argued, 'all overlook the element of communion with the sacred, in which the commitment to values is reaffirmed and fortified'.

The idea of a communion with the sacred was at odds with what modern historians have painted as a period of increasing secularisation in post-war Britain. Church attendances were falling: on Easter Sunday 1953 there were 14 per cent fewer people in Anglican congregations than the equivalent service in 1939. And yet the country did appear to have relished the quasi-religious ritual of the Coronation.

In trying to understand this paradox, some sociologists suggested the phenomenon had its origins in the state-run festivals of ancient Athens. The French philosopher Jean-Jacques Rousseau had developed the theory, coining the term 'civil religion' to describe the way that societies unified themselves by weaving a sacred authority into the calendar and symbols of a nation. We see it in the reverence afforded to flag, anthem, patriotic ceremony and historical monument. Each may be invested with mystical or religious significance.

In Britain, the monarch is the constitutional, religious and symbolic core of the nation: the Central Office of Information once described the Queen as 'the living symbol of national unity'. Her routine marks out the rhythm of the country. Among the spring daffodils of Royal Maundy at Easter, Trooping the Colour in high summer, the autumnal solemnity of the Festival of Remembrance and the Christmas Broadcast, the crown is placed at the centre of seasonal ritual. From stamps and coins to warships and pots of marmalade, the Queen's head and coat of arms are imprinted upon national life so that British identity becomes almost indivisible from monarchical tradition. The American sociologist Peter Berger described a 'sacred canopy' of civil religion that is able to unify the disparate elements of a modern society. It was a phrase, of course, which echoed the golden pall used to such great effect in the Abbey on 2 June 1953.

Affection for the Queen has remained high and virtually constant since she acceded to the throne sixty years ago. The pollsters MORI reported in 2002 that support for the monarchy was probably the most stable trend they had ever measured, consistently around 72 per cent over three decades of opinion surveys. Despite scandal, misjudgement and tragedy, a significant majority of the British people have remained loyal to a family whose privileged position and power is quite at odds with a meritocratic democracy.

As a suitably rebellious teenager in 1977, I worried my mum and dad by purchasing a copy of 'God Save The Queen', a punk anthem by the Sex Pistols. The song, with its nihilistic anti-Establishment message, was banned by the BBC and thus guaranteed widespread attention. Even without airplay it reached number two in the charts, and there were reports (never denied) that the singles chart was fixed to keep it from reaching number one.

But the Queen needn't have worried about a sweeping mood of republicanism. Within days of buying my copy of the record, I joined in the Silver Jubilee celebrations marking the Queen's twenty-fifth year on the throne. My local village in Hampshire was bedecked with red, white and blue bunting. The parish had spent months organising parades and parties and I remember my own father, a church warden, having some important role in lighting one of the hill-top beacons that formed a visible network around Britain. I am sure I gave a cynical teenage shrug at much of it, but the national enthusiasm for the event and its ritual appeared to transcend the ephemeral appeal of popular culture. It wasn't cool but it felt important: I participated in the same way I would have done at a family christening or funeral.

The largely deferential and respectful response to the jubilee was in contrast to the toxic politics of the time: social tensions were spilling into the streets, sparking belligerent challenge to the established order. It was a divisive time and Britain was a troubled and anxious place: when the Sex Pistols screamed that the country had no future there were many who feared they might be right. But, if anything, the strife of the 1970s and 80s saw the public take refuge in the reassuring familiarity and constancy of the Queen and royal ritual. Republicanism remained an intellectual fashion statement rather than a political force.

The historian Sir David Cannadine wrote that 'kings may no longer rule by divine right; but the divine rites of kings continue to beguile and enchant.' There had been an assumption that, as the British population became better educated, royal ritual would be dismissed as little more than primitive magic, conjuring tricks to distract from the iniquities of hereditary privilege and the class system. It didn't happen.

In the 1990s, the Queen faced a different challenge: a confident and expanding media profiting from the consumerism of the age. Celebrity culture, popular fascination with fame and fortune, saw the telephoto lenses trained upon the Royal Family, unconstrained by traditional protocol or deference. Blurred images of human frailty brought questions about the legitimacy of monarchy into sharp focus: what proved to be a long-running soap opera of disintegrating marriages and bitter public recrimination did not square with the 'ideal family'.

There was much public discussion about whether the monarchy provided value for money – a pocket-book calculation of income and expenditure that led to debate about the tax affairs and perks of the Queen and her family. Consultancies wrote detailed analyses of the Royal Family as a brand, equating the 'authenticity' and 'saliency' of the Crown with that of Toilet Duck. Thomas Paine would have been delighted.

The death of Diana, Princess of Wales, was the tragic climax of this chapter. At the time, I recall, editors were thrown by the paradox of the extraordinary public response. On the one hand, the country appeared to be turning on the Queen for her perceived failure to emote. On the other, the outpouring of sentiment and devotion in the days running up to the funeral suggested a profound need to embrace royal ritual and hold tradition close. Commentators marvelled at the irrationality of the response. I remember standing at night among the banks of flowers laid outside Kensington Palace, a thousand candles glowing as crowds of silent mourners walked slowly by. It was a spiritual scene. The public believed in the magic.

There was a moment in those frantic days when pollsters suggested support for the monarchy had fallen from 72 per cent to 66 per cent – hardly a constitutional crisis. In fact, the solemnity of the occasion played to its strengths. The Crown has seen its place in national life consolidated; the Queen's Diamond Jubilee in 2012 saw public backing for the monarchy at 80 per cent, its highest ever level.

Sitting in my edit suite twenty years ago, it dawned on me what had troubled me about that meeting with the Queen of Denmark. Her polished replies to my questions, the rehearsed arguments and sound bites were exemplary. It was a brilliantly staged public relations exercise in which a 'spokesperson' for European monarchy had put forward the corporate line. And that was the problem. There was no magic in Tallinn that day. The cobbles were just cobbles.

R IS FOR REGIONS

Bubbling beneath the surface of England's green and pleasant land is a thick soup of confusion, foaming with indignation and threatening at moments to erupt in volcanic anger: road signs have been ripped from the ground; whitewash has been splattered; civil disobedience campaigns staged; public officials unceremoniously ousted. It is a quiet fury borne of an ancient conflict between personal identity and public administration. As one Member of Parliament recently described the situation for some of his constituents: 'To them, it is a mystery where they actually live. That is an extraordinary thing.'

It was a Friday in the House of Commons, the day of the week when MPs are traditionally able to discuss matters that do not fall under the definition of mainstream politics. On this particular Friday in 2007 the issue was local government boundaries, a subject that might have led even the most avid watchers of the parliamentary TV channel to reach for the remote. If viewers had slipped off to sort out their sock drawer or polish the brass, they would have missed a wonderfully stirring debate that revealed something of the identity crisis afflicting the English personality.

'One of the most tragic cases is in the west of my county where a small number of people find themselves, for administrative purposes, in Lancashire,' an MP complained. 'Can anyone imagine anything worse for a Yorkshireman than being told that he now lives in Lancashire?' Well, no. Another Yorkshire voice spoke up. 'I represent the beautiful East Riding,' he told the House. 'For a time, that area was told, against its will, that it was no longer the East Riding ... but part of Humberside!' 'There was local civil disobedience,' a man from Bridlington reminded everyone. 'Signs were not just whitewashed over but physically removed by Yorkshiremen who regretted having that name attached to the county that they loved,' the representative from Scarborough explained. 'It is said that one can always tell a Yorkshireman, but one cannot tell him much. Telling a Yorkshireman that he lived in Cleveland or Humberside did not go down well.'

It wasn't just a re-run of the Wars of the Roses. Members from all over England were roused from the green benches of the House of Commons to explain how history and geography were being disrespected. The natives were restless. 'There is confusion about exactly where Cleethorpes is,' one Lincolnshire MP complained. A political opponent sympathised, revealing that some of his constituents 'think that they live in Dorset. They do not know that they live in Somerset.' The situation in Essex was, apparently, just as baffling. Proud residents were said to be deeply offended by misplaced county signs. An accusatory finger was pointed at 'those who sit in Whitehall', at the administrators who think they know better than ordinary folk and 'suddenly decide to rename things'.

It is an argument that has been running since the Romans first divided Britain into regions, trying to impose some kind of order on the warring tribes that squabbled over territory. They built walls, laid roads and drew maps, but locals regarded them as bossy European bureaucrats. The Roman historian Tacitus recorded one native moaning at how 'a single king once ruled us; now two are set over us; a legate to tyrannise over our lives, a procurator to tyrannise over our property.'

When the legions departed, the neatly defined *civitates* quickly frayed as rivalries resurfaced. The arrival of Angles, Saxons and Jutes, formidable warriors from Germany, intensified the struggle and added to the general confusion. As the immigrants fought each other over territory, the older Celtic tribes were absorbed or restricted to the margins and classed as aliens in their own land. The Anglo-Saxon word for foreign was *Waelisc* and foreign territory was *Wealas*. Thus the Brythonic (British) Celts were Welsh and lived in Wales. Those who occupied the south-western peninsula (*cern* in Celtic or *cornu* in Latin) lived in Corn-wall – the foreign land on England's horn. The Pictish and Gaelic Celts of Scotland and Ireland –Tacitus described them with their 'red hair and large limbs' – were too belligerent for even the Romans to manage and so the extremities of the British Isles were excluded from the partitioning of England in the Dark Ages. Left to their own devices, they wrote their own story.

Public administration is a struggle between the tidiness of maps and the fuzziness of real life. History books often describe Anglo-Saxon England neatly divided into seven kingdoms: Northumbria, Mercia, East Anglia, Essex, Kent, Sussex and Wessex. But for centuries after the Romans left, the regions were disputed territories, their boundaries shifting and twisting as battles raged. In the end, bloody territorial skirmishing between the kingdoms proved an irrelevance in the face of a far greater external threat: the arrival of the Vikings.

It was 8 June AD 793 when Norsemen destroyed the abbey on the island of Lindisfarne, Northumbria's Holy Island, an attack that shook Britain in much the same way as Pearl Harbour affected America more than a thousand years later. 'Never before has such an atrocity been seen,' a Northumbrian scholar observed. After seventy years and innumerable raids, the Danes mounted a full-scale invasion. Within a decade the heptarchy was no more: their royal families scattered or dead; their property destroyed. Only the kingdom of Wessex held firm, from where King Alfred began assembling an army of his own.

England's destiny was decided in early May AD 878, upon blood-soaked turf close to a settlement called Ethandun. Alfred was victorious and upon that grim battlefield England was born. But where is Ethandun? It wouldn't be England if there wasn't a dispute as to which county has the honour. Ethandun, or Edington as it became, is the name of villages in both Wiltshire and Somerset. Of course, each has laid claim – and almost certainly blamed some faceless official for the confusion.

Alfred proclaimed himself King of the Anglo-Saxons and attempted to unite the people of the ancient kingdoms in a military network of forts and boroughs, roads and beacons designed to ensure that the Vikings could never again catch them by surprise. He was also responsible for spreading the West Saxon style of administration, dividing areas up into 'shires' or shares of land, each shire with a nominated 'reeve' responsible for keeping the peace – the title 'shire-reeve' becoming shortened over time to sheriff.

A shared terror of the Vikings just about held the nation together, but a far greater test of Englishness was imminent. Another army of heathen bureaucrats was on its way, an invasion of administrators, clerks, cartographers and planners with designs on the new kingdom. The Normans were coming.

If William the Conqueror had had access to clipboards and those pens you hang round your neck, he would have negotiated a bulk purchase. In 1085, hundreds of surveyors and auditors were recruited to get the lie of his new land, sent 'all over England into every shire [to] find out how many hides there were in the shire, what land and cattle the king had himself in the shire, what dues he ought to have in twelve months from the shire', as the Anglo-Saxon Chronicle put it. Having sized the place up, he then published the whole lot in the Domesday Book, introducing a bit of Norman styling to the process. The old shires were designated counties – the Saxon sheriff often replaced by a Norman count. Both names, however, survived – just one of a series of compromises that resulted in convoluted and often tautological names for large tracts of English countryside.

The County of Gloucestershire, for example, incorporates the Roman name for the main town (*Glevum*) attached to an ancient British fort (*ceaster*) then adding the Anglo-Saxon shire (*scir*) and capping the whole lot with a Norman count (*comte*). A thousand years of history is scrambled into names that often confound logic and sensible spelling, geographical relics that have come to be regarded as the essence of England. Devotion to such anachronism is soaked in nostalgia for a simpler, rural age; a time when people knew their place and lived their days on a scale where a close eye could be kept on strangers.

Industrialisation, when it came, was no respecter of ancient boundaries, disgorging giant smoking cities that squatted noisily across the countryside without a care for traditional county ways. In the century after 1750, Manchester was transformed from a market town of 18,000 inhabitants to a teeming metropolis of 300,000. It was a similar story in Bristol, Birmingham, Liverpool, Leeds and Newcastle: huge urban centres grew so rapidly that the mapmakers could barely keep up. By the beginning of the twentieth century some influential voices were asking whether the old counties, still obliged to nod their allegiance to the centralised powers in London, really made sense any more. With the Empire crumbling and the government considering Home Rule for Ireland, the question as to how the United Kingdom might best be administered was debated in Parliament.

In 1913 Winston Churchill wondered aloud about the idea of an American-style federal system in which Scotland, Ireland and Wales might each have separate legislative and parliamentary institutions, while England would be broken up into principalities or states. The great business and industrial centres of London, Lancashire, Yorkshire and the Midlands might 'develop, in their own way, their own life according to their own ideas and needs', he suggested. One of the great thinkers of the time, the Scottish evolutionist and sociologist Sir Patrick Geddes, was also an enthusiastic federalist, arguing that the new 'conurbations', as he coined them, should be allowed to break free from central control. He too envisaged a federal UK, with England divided into three regions: Industrial England in the Midlands and north; Metropolitan England incorporating London, the south and east; and south-west England including Wessex, Bristol, Cornwall and Devon.

But Parliament had other matters on its mind, not least the increasing Irish agitation for Home Rule, and the moment when English regionalism might have been seriously considered was lost. Unlike Scotland, Ireland and Wales, which revelled in their separateness, England's cultural identity was based on the opposite – its importance within the wider United Kingdom and empire. While the Scots, Irish and Welsh tended to look within their borders to describe themselves, the English looked beyond, identifying themselves, as often as not, as 'British' and lamenting the devolution which diminished their sense of imperial centrality.

After the Second World War, however, the landscape looked very different: Britain's global influence had declined and many of the industrial regions that had prospered in the nineteenth century were struggling in the twentieth. The sense of common purpose that had held England together since the Vikings was under pressure, with increasing resentment at the power and money residing in the capital. In the early 1960s, Prime Minister Harold Macmillan instructed the Conservative peer Viscount Hailsham to don a cloth cap and head for the North East with a promise of regional regeneration. But it was not enough to save the Conservatives.

Labour's Harold Wilson crept over the political finishing line first in 1964 with a commitment to help the industrial regions, whose voters had handed him the key to Number Ten. Within a year he had created eight Regional Economic Planning Boards to administer the regeneration strategy, but Wilson was an unenthusiastic federalist and the new bodies spread a message of avuncular benevolence rather than devolving any real power. However, he was persuaded something needed to be done about England's medieval local government structure, an historic system that appeared increasingly archaic in the technological age. Any answer was going to be controversial, so Wilson did what politicians in Britain traditionally do with a problem too toxic for elected Parliamentarians: he set up a Royal Commission, headed by a dependable member of the House of Lords.

Lord Redcliffe-Maud, a Whitehall mandarin known for his impressive intellect and safe hands, spent three years looking at England and its boundaries. But, despite such talents, his report could not help putting the reforming cat firmly among the old school pigeons. Instead of a system based on the ancient counties, he proposed new local councils based on major towns – so-called unitary authorities. It was a plan driven by urban realities rather than traditional loyalties and it was probably a century overdue.

The Rural District Councils Association (RCDA), however, was immediately opposed. Its members, the quintessence of grassroots Tories, were horrified at the idea that they would be subsumed into modern and soulless metropolitan inventions. The association's president, the 5th Earl of Gainsborough, was the largest landowner in England's smallest county, Rutland, and he was appalled at the prospect of being absorbed into neighbouring Leicestershire. 'We are looked upon as a nuisance and irrelevant. We are not going to lie down under that,' he proclaimed. 'The fight is to save local government for people in rural areas who do not want decisions made by people forty or fifty miles away in large towns.'

Rutland exemplified the political dilemma: an historical anachronism famous for the World Nurdling Championships (don't ask), its collection of horseshoes (many presented by royalty) and its splendid Ruddles bitter (now brewed in Suffolk), it made no sense to the prosaic minds of public administrators, but its very eccentricity played directly to rural England's sense of itself.

When the Tories came to power in 1970, they found themselves in something of a bind: they knew they needed to modernise local government in England but, politically, they could not afford to upset traditional Conservative voters. Their attempts to find a compromise proved tortuous, and ultimately it was a doomed process. The Local Government Bill was debated fifty-one times in four agonising months between November 1971 and March 1972, as MPs argued over boundaries, place names, geography and history. The result was an Act of Parliament that, in attempting to satisfy everyone, infuriated millions.

As the law was passed, a bonfire was lit at the site of the Uffington White Horse, a prehistoric carving on the Berkshire downs. Protestors claimed to have a petition of 10,000 demanding the new county boundary be amended to prevent the figure residing in Oxfordshire. The fact that the horse pre-dated England's historic counties by some two thousand years was not the point: the bureaucrats were fiddling with heritage.

The Local Government Act created metropolitan counties that trampled all over ancient allegiances. So it was that Greater Manchester included both parts of Lancashire and Yorkshire, while South Yorkshire included parts of Nottinghamshire. It also formed new non-metropolitan counties that twisted traditional county boundaries or, in some cases, abolished the original shire completely. Somerset and Gloucestershire became Avon, parts of Lincolnshire and Yorkshire were designated as Humberside, while bits of Cumberland, Westmorland, Lancashire and Yorkshire were cobbled into Cumbria. Bournemouth went to bed in Hampshire and woke up in Dorset. Rutland ceased to exist.

It had been such an exhausting experience for all concerned that there was little appetite for further review. As a trainee reporter, I attended classes on local government administration in the late 1970s, a topic so complex and confused that I sensed every twinge of political pain in the reforms. I swatted over single-tier and two-tier authorities, boroughs and districts, mets and non-mets, trying to fix in my mind the varied responsibilities and powers of each. Throughout my time in local newspapers and radio, I kept a dog-eared copy of my public administration textbook by my desk in case of emergency.

The social and political turmoil of the 1980s saw the invention of a new and unofficial English boundary – the North–South divide. The *Yorkshire Evening Post* newspaper is thought to have coined the phrase in an article in 1984 that contrasted the affluent south with the job-starved north, a line being drawn from the Severn to the Wash, separating the 'haves' from the 'have-nots'. Prime Minister Margaret Thatcher dismissed the divide as a myth, insisting there were 'simply areas of difficulty in all parts of the country'. She criticised the 'moaning minnies' of the struggling industrial regions as she killed off virtually all of the bodies offering regional assistance in a quango cull. Before she came to power, 47 per cent of the working population received some kind of regionally administered subsidy. Within five years the figure had fallen to 15 per cent.

There were two important political consequences: northern England became increasingly resentful at the London-based government, while the Labour opposition became more interested in regional devolution. The party's bookish leader Michael Foot asked an MP with impeccable northern working-class credentials, John Prescott, to produce an Alternative Regional Strategy, a task he undertook with enthusiasm.

Labour's interest in regional policy also coincided with important changes on the international stage: the European Community had told member states that huge sums in development aid, so-called Structural Funds, would be channelled directly to regional bodies. To many UK Tories, this looked like the slippery slope to Euro-federalism and a threat to British sovereignty. So the politics of English administration became sharply polarised between the traditionalist instincts of the Conservative Party and the devolutionary demands of the Labour heartlands.

When John Major arrived at Number Ten, struggling with trunk-loads of anti-European baggage, he sought to emphasise his love for Olde England, 'the country of long shadows on cricket grounds, warm beer, invincible green suburbs, dog lovers and pools fillers', as he later described it. It was vital he stressed his patriotic credentials as he negotiated Britain's place in Europe. So, just as he was signing the Maastricht Treaty, which gave English regions a voice within the new European Union, Major also set up a commission to review the controversial changes to county boundaries that had so angered his party's rural power base.

The chair of the commission, the business leader Sir John Banham, had been handed a poisoned chalice, of course. He said he hoped for some 'early wins' by abolishing the unloved new areas of Avon, Cleveland and Humberside, but he was quickly ensnared by the deep passions and ancient prejudices of local governance in England, as well as the complexities of Westminster politics.

The commission was unable to recruit enough willing staff, saw its funding squeezed, its terms of reference changed and its deadline brought forward. There was intense lobbying from MPs of all shades, trying to influence the new power structures within their constituencies, particularly the creation of authorities based around towns or smaller counties. Tempers became frayed and when Sir John Banham presented his plan in 1995, the government refused to accept all his recommendations. 'I well recognise that the commission has not done the bidding either of the government or of the parliamentary Labour Party,' Sir John wrote bitterly, as he cleared his desk.

From the tangled mess, the counties of Herefordshire and, yes, Rutland were awoken from their slumbers, restored as local government bodies. But Huntingdonshire was denied authority status because 'there was no exceptional county allegiance', Cumberland and Westmorland likewise. Lancashire and Derbyshire, fearing their abolition, went to the High Court and won a reprieve from total bureaucratic execution, but Somerset lost its case. Most of the historic counties saw chunks of their territory carved off or administered from town or city centres, a technocratic exercise based primarily on urban geography rather than English history.

The Conservatives attempted to defuse some of the simmering resentment in the Tory shires by quietly drawing up the Lieutenancies Act, legislation nodded through the House of Lords that consolidated the role of a county's Lord Lieutenant – an office dating back to Tudor times. In an appendix, the Act defined English counties by their historic boundaries, thus ensuring that the existence of the ancient shires was retained within the legislative structure. The presence of a uniformed Lord Lieutenant with his (or her) responsibilities for arranging visits of the Royal Family, presenting medals, advising on honours and liaising with the local military, played elegantly to the traditionalist cause. But it also added to the general confusion.

When New Labour bounded to power in 1997, Deputy Prime Minister John Prescott was rewarded with his own sprawling Whitehall empire, the Department of the Environment, Transport and the Regions. The letter 'R' in DETR gave him licence to dust off his Alternative Regional Strategy, creating nine agencies dotted around England to take control of billions in development funds.

By its second term, Tony Blair's government was suggesting it might go much further: there was talk of a 'regional renaissance', with proposals for English regions to be put at the heart of 'a modern and more prosperous society'. Prescott was the flag bearer of the plans for elected regional assemblies, but he faced some formidable obstacles. Not only did he have to convince the sceptical Tony Blair and Gordon Brown to relinquish some of their centrally based powers and resources; as he tried to draw the new regions, he re-awakened the traditionalists in the historic counties. 'Is it not the case that whenever a boundary is drawn around anything, people on the edge of it believe that they should be on the other side?' asked one MP. 'In the end, no one is ever happy,' advised another. 'The solution is not simply for a minister or a civil servant to sit in an office in Whitehall with a map of England and a blue pen.'

The Deputy Prime Minister pressed ahead but, without enthusiastic backing from Brown and Blair, he was obliged to reign in his ambition for a speedy devolution of power to the English regions. He agreed to test his plans on the area of England he thought would be most receptive to the idea of regional government, the north-east. On 4 November 2004, the Great North Vote was held. The referendum had seen two distinct strategies: the 'yes' campaign (Be Proud, Be Positive, Vote Yes) was filled with uplifting anthems, balloons and local celebrities; the 'no' campaign (Vote No to More Politicians, More Bureaucracy, Extra Taxes) consisted largely of an inflatable white elephant plonked unceremoniously in shopping centres. When the votes were counted, the result was decisive: overwhelming rejection by a ratio of almost four to one.

It was a massive blow to John Prescott and his supporters, some of whom turned their fire on what they called the 'Westminster class'. Kevin Meagher, a ministerial advisor and committed regionalist wrote: 'The civil service smirked. You could sense their *Schadenfreude* from 250 miles away. The Labour government never really believed in the policy; it's as simple as that.'

It may have been a lack of Cabinet support, but the clear-cut nature of the result suggested something more: a profound distrust of bureaucrats, administrators and their political masters. Even in the north-east, with its powerful regional identity, the simple message contained in a blow-up pachyderm was enough to get people registering their opposition to the idea of an elected assembly.

Around the same time, some particularly irked traditionalists in the shires were embarking upon a counter-offensive. A group calling itself CountyWatch was promising 'direct action' in its fight to 'keep alive and healthy the names and the real boundaries of our counties'. Television crews were on hand as members ripped out twelve signs that claimed to mark entry into 'County Durham: Land of the Prince Bishops', and then re-erected them along the historic border between Yorkshire and Durham, the River Tees. In another covert operation, a CountyWatch cell stole four 'Welcome to Bedfordshire' road signs from the edge of Luton (an independently administered town within the historic county) and re-erected them in front of 'Welcome to Luton' signs a few miles away. 'This is absolutely crazy,' a councillor complained.

Under the patronage of Count Nikolai Tolstoy, a colourful Anglo-Russian monarchist, CountyWatch claimed to have removed, re-sited or erected eighty county boundary signs in Dorset, County Durham, Greater Manchester, Hampshire, Lancashire, Lincolnshire, North Yorkshire, Somerset and Warwickshire. The campaign connected with a general anxiety that administrative change threatened to cut England off from its roots, and there was a series of parliamentary attempts to force local authorities and surveyors to respect historic boundaries when erecting traffic signs or drawing maps.

The member for the constituency of Romford was particularly exercised. 'As I travel back after a busy week at Westminster to my home town,' he said, 'I enter the boundaries of Essex and Romford, but nowhere do I see a road sign welcoming me to either place. They have been written off the map by a dreadful local government culture that seems to recognise only the often made-up and artificial names of administrative boroughs or districts.' An MP from Somerset blamed the 'successive waves' of local authority reformers: 'People are not defined by the authority that collects their rubbish, but by the place in which they grew up and live.'

Efforts to win government support for the Historic Counties, Towns and Villages (Traffic Signs and Mapping) Bill got nowhere – the Labour Cabinet Office minister Gillian Merron said proposals to freeze-frame history were neither appropriate nor practical and left the debating chamber. But the bigger argument about English governance would not go away.

The coalition government of 2010 sought to banish any thought of regionalism in England to the extent that civil servants resorted to the use of an acronym when discussing the issue: TAFKAR – the areas formerly known as regions. Its localism agenda promises power to the parishes, grass-roots influence which may well give voice to people who remain deeply aggrieved at the actions of anonymous planners.

What is revealed in all of this is an important facet of the English personality. After two thousand years of administrators trying to bully the population into neatly defined blocks, England has developed a natural distrust of straight lines on a map. They prefer the quirkiness of a complicated back story, they like things to be irregular and idiosyncratic, revel in the fact that Americans cannot pronounce, never mind spell, Worcestershire. As the nation's influence has diminished, people have wanted to reconnect with the past in all its obscurity and convolution. What's more, the English apparently delight in putting two old-fashioned fingers up at any official with a clipboard who gets in their way.

S is for Silly Hats

Ask a foreigner to describe Britain and the picture painted is likely to be of a nation obsessed with the trappings of its past. Millions come to gawp at earnest looking men with one-and-a-half pounds of Canadian bearskin perched on their heads, or strutting about in bright red stockings and Tudor-style gold-laced tunics. Feathers and fur, sequin and serge – the effect is of a people who like nothing better than to parade in kitsch fancy dress.

But such peculiarity is treated by most of this country's inhabitants with solemnity and profound respect. The hushed tones of a television commentator describing the State Opening of Parliament are a case in point. A bureaucratic state function that could be achieved with a simple press release is transformed into national spectacle with a bejewelled monarch, a golden carriage and a great deal of ermine. Doors are banged with sticks, men walk backwards, and ceremonial hostages are taken. No one is allowed to giggle.

Tradition is serious business. The hats are silly for a sensible reason. The homogenising force of globalisation risks turning every town into Anytown: from the architecture of a bank to the thread of a screw, standardisation and conformity drive towards a multinational, corporate modernity. So we decorate Britishness, our national identity, with strange, surprising and often plain daft souvenirs from a time gone by.

Many countries parade their identity with historical tradition that looks odd against the cellophane culture of the twenty-first century, but the British have turned anachronism into a distinguishing feature. Tourists flock to watch the Changing of the Guard because it reflects a typically British conceit – that nothing really changes at all. We present ourselves as a country steeped in the ancient and wonderful ways of our ancestors. Tradition, though, does not stand still. It is an evolving and adapting reflection of how a nation sees itself and how it wants others to see it.

The historian Eric Hobsbawm famously claimed that British traditions 'which appear or claim to be old are often quite recent in origin and sometimes invented'. A committed Marxist, his assertion that many of the ceremonial trappings of nationhood hailed from the late nineteenth and early twentieth centuries was dismissed as lefty propaganda by some conservatives. This scrutiny of tradition, holding it up in the light to check its provenance and authenticity, was condemned as thoroughly unpatriotic.

The Tory MP David Willetts gave a lecture at his party's conference in 1998, accusing Hobsbawm and others of mounting an attack on conventional national identities. 'They are quite right to show how traditions and cultural identities may emerge,' he said, but they were wrong to suggest 'there is some other authentic form of national identity'. In other words, the ostrich-plumed cocked hat may be a relatively recent addition to the ceremonial dress, but who cares? 'We should simply keep calm and refuse to be shocked by these so-called disclosures,' he told the Tory faithful.

A few years later, the Labour academic Anthony Giddens returned to the fray. In a Reith lecture for the BBC he described tradition as 'perhaps the most basic concept of conservatism', arguing that kings, emperors, priests and others invented rituals and ceremonies to legitimate their rule. The very term 'tradition', he said, was only a couple of centuries old. 'In medieval times there was no call for such a word, precisely because tradition and custom were everywhere.'

No one denies that cultural heritage has to start somewhere and, through adaptation and time, becomes part of the warp and weft of a nation's fabric. Take the tartan kilt. The iconic symbol of Scottish dress was almost certainly designed by an Englishman after the Act of Union in 1707. Clan tartans are thought to be an even later invention, many originating in the weaving rooms of one shop near Stirling. William Wilson & Sons of Bannockburn supplied 'authentic' clan patterns to tribal chieftains who wanted their names included in an historical collection being put together by the Highland Society of London in 1815.

The point, though, is not when and where the idea of men in patterned skirts first came from, but whether the tradition reflects the character and heritage of the nation. Wearing a kilt not only hints at the belted plaid worn by highlanders in the sixteenth century, but requires a degree of bravado and hardiness that chimes with our impression of Scottishness.

Born and raised in Glasgow until the age of ten, I regularly put on the kilt as a boy and would suggest there was something else about wearing it that reflected the character of Scotland. It was a bit of a laugh. There were inevitable comments about whether I was wearing underpants, about what I kept in my sporran and how I felt dressed like a girl. But I felt I was in on the joke – the gentle teasing only made me more proud. The Scots are masters of self-mockery, as demonstrated by the ridiculous ginger Jimmy wigs they wear when supporting the country's sports teams.

It is a similar story with English cricket fans. The self-styled Barmy Army have managed to invent a new tradition of their own: the Saturday of a domestic Test Match has become fancy dress day when supporters wear outrageous costumes and, inevitably, the silliest of hats. No other nation, I would suggest, attempts to conjure a sense of national pride by attending an international sports event dressed as Mr Blobby.

Britain's island status may help explain our sense of otherness, our need to define ourselves by nonconformity. We have always been good at eccentricity – our dislike of straight lines, perhaps, as the previous chapter identified. The 'crazy Brits' have something of a reputation for it. Being slightly dotty is not cause for concern but for celebration: 'You don't have to be mad to work here, but it helps!' The wildly eccentric nineteenth-century aristocrat Jack Mytton, for example, fed the favourites among his two thousand dogs on steak and champagne, and dressed his sixty cats in livery. His wardrobe contained one thousand hats, many of them remarkably silly. And we love him for it.

Our heroes, historical and fictional, tend to be blessed with odd mannerisms and idiosyncrasies. From Sir Winston Churchill to Dr Who, from William Blake to Sherlock Holmes – as John Timbs wrote in his nineteenth-century anthology, *English Eccentrics and Eccentricities*: 'They may be odd company: yet, how often do we find eccentricity in the minds of persons of good understanding.' We warm to those who choose to wear a deer-stalker in Baker Street or a Panama hat to go time travelling. From *The Goons*, through *Monty Python* to *Little Britain*, our comedic tradition also reflects a uniquely British sense of humour celebrating foible and quirk.

Perhaps post-colonial Britain feels the need to counter any suggestion of residual imperial arrogance by nurturing a reputation for modest self-deprecation. We define ourselves by our history, but to adapt a phrase from the US statesman Dean Acheson, maybe we have lost an empire and not yet found an identity. There is a tension between the blazered traditionalists in the cricket pavilion at Lord's and the raucous beery crowd in pantomime drag, but they are both patriotic faces of the same nation. We simultaneously tip our trade-mark bowler to a glorious past and lampoon such pomposity with the Ministry of Silly Walks. Britain has become the land of clowns as well as castles.

Some see this contradiction as dangerous, that we must either embrace our past or risk losing our very identity. Immigration and globalisation, it is argued, threaten our cultural integrity, and so there is a need to celebrate our history and heritage more enthusiastically than ever. Rituals and traditions should be moulded into a compelling island story, but they must be handled with care. 'Tradition that is drained of its content, and commercialised, becomes either heritage or kitsch – trinkets bought in the airport store,' Anthony Giddens warned. Well, maybe – but the New Labour project he helped design regarded heritage as a key to the future peace and security of the United Kingdom no less. The government-regulated lottery has diverted billions to heritage projects, which it says provide 'the foundation of a confident, modern society'. The old is seen as vital for the new.

But heritage has the power not only to define but to divide. One only has to go to Northern Ireland to see how traditions have evolved as expressions of separateness and sectarianism. During the late nineteenth century, Irish nationalists and British patriots manufactured customs to differentiate each from the other. Whether it was Gaelic League or Orange Lodge, communities on both sides sought ways to highlight cultural difference.

While Orangemen were parading their Protestantism in bowler hats and sashes, nationalists were seeking to establish an 'authentic' Irish cultural identity. The president of the Gaelic League Douglas Hyde called for the rejection of English colonial culture ('West Britonism', he called it) and encouraged his countrymen to recover Ireland's language, manners, customs, music, games, place names, personal names and literature. From these culture wars flowed the bigotry and hatred that contributed to decades of violence and unhappiness.

In the 1990s, European Union funds were spent trying to reverse the process. A grants scheme promoted the development of cultural traditions which would 'encourage cultural confidence and an acceptance of cultural diversity in Northern Ireland'. Effectively, this was cash for customs – money was on offer for those who could come up with new traditions that encouraged community cohesion.

'Identity', it has been said, 'is always a modern project: an attempt of differing political and economic interests to construct their historical pasts as the representation of the "truths" of their present day practices.'

The author of that, American sociologist Jonathan Church, spent time on the Shetland Islands investigating what he called 'confabulations of community'. Confabulation is a wonderful psychological term to describe the confusion of imagination with memory. But Dr Church used it to mean something altogether more sinister – the way in which invented traditions may be used to construct a false identity.

He had gone to Shetland to study the Hamefarin – a homecoming festival first held in 1960 and revived in 1985, which stressed the ancient Viking roots of the people of the islands. It seemed like innocent fun, but Dr Church was anxious this new tradition was closing down a more complex historical back story featuring Scottish kings, German merchants and American oil tycoons. 'A singular gaze has become appropriated and institutionalised in the power of official memory,' he concluded.

Traditional ritual possesses a magic, a powerful nostalgic force. Once it has entered the folklore, it is sacred – part of what is called the civil religion of a state (see 'Q is for Queen'). Revision, as with a bible, must be conducted with great care. But the transformation of Britain's ethnic and cultural make-up means revision is deemed necessary and urgent. In describing a modern national identity, tradition may be seen as an obstacle.

British pomp and pageantry were often created to remind people of their place – consolidating the feudal or hierarchical structures of British society. Everyone knows his or her position in the Lord Mayor's Parade. On inspection, ceremonial may have its origins in morally dubious military and political activity. Custom and tradition are sometimes criticised as sexist, elitist, racist and worse. Certainly, their impact can appear at odds with contemporary values and ambition. Great and ancient universities have been urged to give up the Latin ceremonial, gowns and processing which, it is argued, can appear elitist and act as a barrier to social mobility. In the dying days of the twentieth century, the first female members were welcomed into the Long Room at Lord's.

Social identities based on class, faith and politics may have been diluted, but the passions behind them cannot be dismissed. Enter the heritage industry to smooth out any dangers during transition, promoting a sanitised version of our past to encourage a placid future. I once walked through a miserably predictable shopping precinct in an old cotton town in Lancashire, where the only unexpected feature was a glass box set into the pedestrian paving. Inside was a shiny mill wheel turning very slowly. Britain's homogeneous high streets, illuminated by the same corporate shop windows, have left many towns exploring their past in the search for distinction. Derelict buildings are being restored, traditional activities revived and neglected customs embraced once again.

The problem with this strategy is that, like Lymeswold cheese (see 'C for Cheese'), it tends to be bland and a bit dull. Each quiet revolution of the gleaming mill wheel is a feeble nod to a real revolution, driven by invention and exploitation, struggle and greed. Authenticity would demand not polish on its bearings, but blood, sweat and tears. Such rose-tinted history is perfumed with sentimentality. But to engage with truth means accepting our past, warts and all. In celebrating ancient battles, we risk opening old wounds.

Government ministers have claimed that heritage-led regeneration can cut crime, improve public health and make communities function better. Slices of heritage can act as focal points 'around which communities will rally and revive their sense of civic pride', argues one regeneration agency. Most politicians would accept that passing laws isn't a terribly good way of achieving these vital social outcomes and, in the face of obvious community tension and disharmony, one can imagine the hope they have for a dose of heritage and tradition.

Success lies in finding and promoting aspects of our past which are non-divisive, but not so 'safe' as to render them inauthentic. Which is where the silly hats come in. Britain's straight-faced eccentricity is regarded as a national strength, a characteristic of self-confidence and independence. Absurd relics from our past can be shaped and embellished, buffed and displayed as symbols of British assurance and autonomy. Ridiculous customs, bizarre traditions, ludicrous dress and the silliest of hats: we know that it is harder for people to laugh at us if we know how to laugh at ourselves.

T IS FOR TOILET

I shuddered when writing the above. I was brought up to believe that 'toilet' was a term never *ever* to be uttered in company. Or even in private. More shameful than any curse (which merely revealed a foul mouth), use of the word was regarded as irredeemably 'common'. With its ooh-la-la continental pretentiousness, 'toilet' suggested the worst sort of proletarian social climber: someone lacking the necessary sophistication or breeding. My shudder was as much at its reminder of the middle-class snobbery incorporated into my toilet training as the word itself.

Almost any term associated with the disposal of human waste is loaded with social baggage in Britain. In asking for directions to the ... [insert euphemism of choice here], we probably reveal more about ourselves than if we were to squat in the gutter. My family, when absolutely required to describe the facility in question, would most probably plump for 'loo'. This three-lettered sobriquet of disputed derivation is now, apparently, the most popular choice of any, a timid little thing without hard consonants or even an ending to speak of, a word that barely whispers its presence in a sentence.

Contrast 'loo' (regularly used by 80 per cent of Brits) with 'bog' (a no-nonsense label employed by just 15 per cent) or khazi (less than 4 per cent of people utilise this Cockney slang); the latter are words with self-confidence, even attitude, and they are falling out of fashion. Four out of ten of us talk of 'going to the bathroom' when we have no intention of taking a bath. The 'little boy's/girl's room', 'powder room' or the 'restroom' (invasive Americanisms) are similarly coy descriptions for facilities that seem to require increasing amounts of demure disguise with each century that passes. Indeed, the start of the twenty-first was marked by the coining of a new British euphemism: the designers of the eco-friendly tepee-shaped public convenience in the Millennium Dome were moved to describe it as a 'beacon of relief'.

Britain's changing relationship with basic bodily functions reflects the evolution of its society. It is not just vocabulary: the toilet charts the boundaries of public responsibility and private life, of our relationship with each other and even with ourselves. The shiny porcelain of the bowl acts as a mirror to British values, identities and hang-ups.

The Slovenian writer Slavoj Žižek famously suggested that 'you go to the toilet and you sit on ideology.' In an article for the *London Review of Books* in 2004, Žižek compared the design of German, French and, what he called, Anglo-Saxon lavatories. 'In a traditional German toilet, the hole into which shit disappears after we flush is right at the front, so that shit is first laid out for us to sniff and inspect for traces of illness,' he wrote. 'In the typical French toilet, on the contrary, the hole is at the back, i.e. shit is supposed to disappear as quickly as possible.' The Anglo-Saxon version, he continued, 'presents a synthesis, a mediation between these opposites: the toilet basin is full of water, so that the shit floats in it, visible, but not to be inspected.'

The three designs, Žižek postulated, are an expression of a triad of national cultures first identified by the German philosopher Georg Hegel: 'Reflective thoroughness (German), revolutionary hastiness (French), utilitarian pragmatism (English).' Whether this academic contemplation upon the toilet bowl can withstand

Germanic levels of scrutiny is debatable, but what is undeniable are deep-seated cultural differences in the attitudes of societies towards excretion.

I recently took my children to the ancient Roman fort named Vindolanda, close to Hadrian's Wall in Northumberland. They dangled their legs over an excavated wall and tried to imagine what it must have been like on that spot almost two thousand years earlier, because what they sat upon was the remains of the sixteen-seater latrine. Here the soldiers would have occupied wooden seats, side by side, suspended above a channel of running water. In front of them a separate narrow channel, also flowing with water, which would be used to rinse the sponge-on-a-stick that served as lavatory paper. The detail of this scene that provoked most interest was not the expert plumbing of course. It was the impossible, appalling, disgusting thought of communal defecation. And yet public latrines, as against private 'closets', were the normal and often only form of provision for many British people until the nineteenth century.

In the Middle Ages, communal lavatories were a familiar feature of urban life. London's Lord Mayor Dick Whittington, pantomime's thigh-slapping ailurophile, left money in his will for the construction of a monster 128-seater – sixty-four each for men and women – overhanging a gully on the banks of the Thames. Emptied by the tide, 'Whittington's Longhouse' was still in operation in the seventeenth century. The self-cleaning design was a significant improvement upon numerous latrines that clogged up the city's waterways.

For centuries after the Roman garrisons left, British plumbing was a chaotic and unsanitary mess. Partly, this reflected a rejection of anything connected with Rome: pipes and drains from this period almost define the phrase 'bodged job', as if the engineers had deliberately constructed waste disposal systems to defy the laws of Caesar and physics. Cleanliness itself was rejected as a Roman indulgence by some early Christians: the English hermit St Godric walked to Jerusalem without washing, perhaps heeding the words of St Jerome, who declared that 'a clean body and a clean dress means an unclean soul.'

This denunciation of basic hygiene as un-British and un-Christian may have offered some cultural and theological justification for the stink and the filth. But it didn't make it any less unpleasant or dangerous. In 1326 tragic Richard the Raker fell into his cesspit and drowned 'monstrously in his own excrement' – possibly the worst accidental death imaginable. The great pits of human waste also contributed to the spread of diseases that could wipe out whole villages and decimate towns.

For all but the richest, the process and product of defecation remained a manifestly public business. There was no place for modesty. Even at Hampton Court Palace, Henry VIII built the Great House of Easement – a twin-level, twenty-eight-seater latrine suspended over the moat – for the use of his courtiers. He, meanwhile, would sit privately upon a luxurious 'close stool' with padded seat, trimmed with silk ribbons and studded with gold nails. Privilege and class increasingly defined the politics of the privy, a legacy still in evidence today.

In 1530, the Dutch humanist Desiderius Erasmus finished a book that instantly became a European blockbuster. *De Civilitate Morum Puerilium* ('A Handbook on Good Manners for Children') was the bestseller of the sixteenth century, translated into twenty-two languages and running into dozens of editions. Although it purported to offer thoughts on the moral and practical education of children, what it really amounted to was the first self-help book on how to be civilised. It became essential reading in the upper echelons of British society, not least for its thoughts on the manners of the toilet. 'It is impolite to greet someone who is urinating or defecating,' Erasmus wrote. 'A well-bred person should always avoid exposing without necessity the parts to which nature has attached modesty. If necessity compels this, it should be done with decency and reserve, even if no witness is present.'

Three decades later, the Italian cleric Giovanni della Casa took these ideas further. In his famous treatise on manners, *Il Galateo*, he wrote that 'it does not befit a modest, honourable man to prepare to relieve nature in the presence of other people.' The public latrine had been condemned. Britain's upper classes would look to privatise poo.

Modesty and affected repugnance at bodily functions became fashionable behaviour. Indeed, Queen Elizabeth I was something of a pioneer in the new manners, influenced by her 'saucy godson' and courtier, the poet Sir John Harington. In 1596 he published *A New Discourse of a Stale Subject, Called the Metamorphosis of Ajax*, a controversial tome that literally and satirically argued for the cleansing of the court. It ends with a two-line verse:

To keepe your houses sweete, clense privie vaultes.
To keepe your soules as sweete, mend privie faults.

It turned the teachings of St Jerome upside down and encouraged a return to Roman sanitation and hygiene methods. Harington's manor was close to the city of Bath and the book was evangelical in its praise for the waste disposal systems of the ancient emperors. It also included his own design of the first flushing toilet, the Ajax (a pun on 'a jakes', the colloquial word for a privy), which was installed in a number of the great houses of the time, including Richmond Palace.

Beyond the walls of such grand residences, however, the lack of even a rudimentary sewage system meant urban life remained contaminated by the odorous and potentially deadly consequences of human waste. The aristocracy turned their superior noses up at 'the great unwashed masses of humanity', as the political philosopher Edmund Burke described them. How you smelled defined your status.

The arrival of industrialisation only served to widen the gulf between the personal hygiene habits of the ruling classes and the common people, as rapidly expanding towns and cities were quite unable to cope with the sanitation demands placed upon them. Waves of cholera, influenza and typhoid in the 1830s brought a new urgency to matters, and with all social strata at risk from infection, Parliament asked the public health activist Edwin Chadwick to investigate. His *Report on the Sanitary Conditions of the Labouring Population* led to a raft of legislation attempting, in the course of a few years, to transform the practices and attitudes of centuries.

The Public Health Act of 1848, for instance, made it mandatory to have some sort of private lavatory in one's home – privy, ash pit or flushing WC. However, there was opposition to such ideas in working class areas. Many labourers and their families thought it unhygienic to have a lavatory inside the house and regarded the new laws as parliamentary interference with the most basic and domestic of human rights.

The aspirational middle classes, on the other hand, largely welcomed the privacy and modesty afforded by the new technology and increasingly associated personal hygiene with moral virtue. Public health reform was seen as the key to the spiritual regeneration of the urban poor and an army of propagandists, including many women, sought to save the working classes from the corruptive stench of human waste. The Ladies' National Association for the Diffusion of Sanitary Knowledge was founded in 1857 and published a series of penny tracts with titles such as *Hints to Working People about Personal Cleanliness* and *The Power of Soap and Water*. The Reverend Charles Girdlestone, a Black Country parson with fervent views on hygiene, claimed that the sanitary reform movement was 'pregnant with the most important advantages to the human race, in every point of view – social, moral and religious'. The toilet had become the measuring stick for a civilised society.

At the Great Exhibition at Hyde Park in 1851, the engineer George Jennings installed his Monkey Closets in the Retiring Rooms of Crystal Palace. More than 800,000 visitors spent a penny to use what were the first public conveniences. The price included a private cubicle, a clean seat, a towel, a comb and a shoeshine. As the sociologist Norbert Elias wrote later in his book *The Civilizing Process*, industrial societies like Britain had developed 'embarrassment at the mere sight of many bodily functions of others, and often at their mere mention, or as a feeling of shame when one's own functions are exposed to the gaze of others, and by no means only then'.

The novelist William Thackeray described the Victorian era as 'if not the most moral, certainly the most squeamish', and it was from that peculiarly British mixture of prudery, pride and invention that our contemporary attitudes to the lavatory have their roots. The development of vitreous china by Twyford, Wedgwood and Doulton; the flushable WC refined and mass-produced by Thomas Crapper; the opening (often with a fanfare) of public lavatories incorporating the very best in artistry and design – in the field of human waste disposal, Great Britain led the world in technology and magnificence.

To this day, the Isle of Bute council promotes its gentlemen's convenience in Rothesay as a tourist attraction:

> The interior is magnificent with walls entirely clad in decorative ceramic tiles, ornately patterned in rows. The floors are designed with ceramic mosaic, with the crest of the Royal Burgh of Rothesay at the entrance. Fourteen urinals stand like sentinels along two walls, another six surround a central stand – each a white enamel alcove topped with the legend 'Twyfords Ltd. Cliffe Vale Potteries, Hanley' and crowned with imitation dark green St Anne marble.

The cast-iron, oak and porcelain assurance of the Victorian convenience often echoes to this day in the domestic lavatories of Britain's professional middle class: a wooden seat, white tiling and a no-nonsense functionality. Conversely, apricot pedestal carpets, fluffy toilet-roll covers and potpourri fragrance are reflections of the continuing influence, perhaps, of the Ladies' National Association for the Diffusion of Sanitary Knowledge. The 'smallest room' may offer abundant clues as to how the owner sees themselves, their aspirations and self-confidence. My wife's grandmother, for example, used to have two supplies of lavatory paper in her highly scented bathroom: soft for the ladies and scratchy Izal for gentlemen callers (as well as her husband). From class values to sexual politics, one learned more about her character and background from a trip to the lavatory than anywhere else.

While Britain developed its own unique loo politics based on centuries of subtle toilet-training, elsewhere in Europe and around the world, different historical, religious and cultural forces have been at work. The French toilet remained a 'hole in the ground' long after the sit-down WC had won universal acceptance in the UK, and while many Brits might consider such basic provision as archaic and uncivilised, the international world of sanitary hygiene remains divided over the 'sit or squat' debate. Sharia law requires the use of running water for cleaning, and many Muslims regard sitting on the loo as un-Islamic. There are similar cleansing rituals and customs in Jewish and Far Eastern cultures that are at odds with sedentary British practices.

The Germans have a peculiar respect for human excreta, Sigmund Freud being one among those who have documented the country's association between *scheiss* and *geld* (excrement was once a valuable fertiliser). One consequence is a bluntness and honesty to bodily functions, in contrast to British coyness and modesty. While a UK advertisement for a laxative might hint at its purpose in achieving regularity, its German equivalent is likely to include a diagram and stress the product's effectiveness on the 'sluggish intestine'. While Britain's loo-roll commercials feature puppies, Germans get a drawing of buttocks with the legend: 'Velvety soft Servus turns a dissatisfied butt into a satisfied face.'

The Americans have been on a similar journey to their British cousins. Early settlers imported pre-Enlightenment attitudes to cleanliness, regarding excessive bathing as an indulgence, but with urbanisation came a moral propriety that went far beyond Victorian prudery. In the 1950s, Hollywood sensibility meant bathrooms featured in movies never contained anything as vulgar as a toilet.

The business of relieving oneself has become such a source of potential embarrassment and shame in both Britain and the US that it is cited as an explanation for widespread constipation and the prevalence of bowel cancer. Men in both countries are also said to suffer particularly from Shy Bladder Syndrome or 'paruresis' – the inability to pee in a public lavatory. This was famously (or infamously) revealed in a 1976 study of university students.

Psychologist R. D. Middlemist wanted to test the hypothesis that subjects would take longer to start urinating if someone was standing next to them. He initially tried to measure this by setting up an experiment involving three urinals, one of which was occupied by a 'confederate' and another marked 'Don't use, washing urinal' with a bucket of water and a sponge on top. The trouble was, as he explained in his report, it was tricky to know at exactly what time the subject starting peeing: 'The urinals were so silent that even the confederate standing adjacent to the subject could not hear the urine striking the urinal.' So, with the students oblivious to all of this, Middlemist opted for visual cues, embedding a periscopic prism in a stack of books lying on the floor to watch the stream of urine.

The American Psychological Association later said that the experiment was not only unethical but probably unlawful in many countries. That said, the results are still cited: with no one else in the lavatory the average student took 4.8 seconds to start urinating; with a confederate one urinal away the time rose to 6.2 seconds; if the accomplice was at the next urinal it took 8.4 seconds. Privacy and modesty have turned to embarrassment and shame. Doctors warn that our bodily functions are in danger of becoming almost dysfunctional.

However, the legacy of lavatorial innovation has now passed from British Victorian inventors to Japanese electronic giants, who promise a new generation of high-tech toilets protecting the delicacy and well-being of the user. Often designed as pre-fabricated toilet 'pods', the sophisticated machines include an array of photo-electric buttons and gizmos that preclude the need to touch anything or the risk of emotional distress. Some play music or the sound of running water to disguise more basic noises and computerised features allow consumers to personalise their toilet experience.

At the Ideal Home Show 2011 in London, visitors were told how technologically advanced toilets were set to dramatically change Britain's bathroom habits. The AquaClean, it was explained, would clean you with a gentle spray of water, the temperature adjusted to suit your requirements, leaving the user with a feeling of 'extreme cleanliness and a sense of well-being'.

What is happening is that market globalisation and industrial standardisation are driving the development of a corporate international lavatory culture. Designers and technicians are working to banish the anxiety of using a 'foreign loo', whether it be a Londoner in Lille or a Saudi in Salford. In Britain, though, I doubt that the expertise of the finest engineers in the world will be able to neutralise the whiffs of class and snobbery that have always pervaded the (shudder) toilet.

U IS FOR UMBRELLA

When the bid team for the 2012 Olympics put together their video to sell London to the world, they felt bound to include dark-suited, bowler-hatted City gents using their trademark black umbrellas like épées. It was a knowing nod to the way many people around the world think of Britain: sombre, reserved, slightly eccentric and wet.

Precisely rolled, with Malacca cane and gold-plated collar, the traditional umbrella has become global shorthand for a national cliché. It is both the ceremonial sword of the archetypal British gentleman and a symbol of a country where, as the Roman historian Tacitus declared in AD 94, 'the sky is overcast with continual rain and cloud.' Two thousand years later, and the American travel writer Bill Bryson made the same point: 'Sometimes it rained, but mostly it was just dull, a land without shadows. It was like living inside Tupperware.' Britain, with its moderate and unspectacular climate, is summed up by the benign brolly.

There could be worse associations: the umbrella is eminently practical and prudent, but it also has an ingenious trick up its sleeve. When required, a dull stick may transform itself into an exuberant canopy: first impressions belying a hidden and unexpectedly flamboyant face – rather like the British people themselves, some might suggest. The umbrella, I think, does tell us something important about Britain, but it is not what people imagine. So, let us consider this ingenious contraption.

In 1871, the Victorian writer William Sangster thought it unbelievable that a busy people like the English had 'ever been ignorant of the blessings bestowed on them by that dearest and truest friend in need and in deed, the umbrella'. The umbrella (or parasol) may have Chinese origins, it may have been familiar to the ancient Greeks, the technology may owe much to the ingenuity of German and French designers, but as a handy protection against a shower rather than the sun, it is widely regarded as a British accessory.

Women were the first to spot the potential of the umbrella, using it to keep off the English rain as early as 1705. Englishmen took a while to catch up, perhaps nervous of being seen as the wally with the brolly (as an England football manager would later be terminally lampooned). The eccentric philanthropist Jonas Hanway ostentatiously carried one in London from around 1750, enduring much derision for doing so. Hackney coachmen apparently saw its use as a threat to their business and would 'toot and hustle' Hanway into the kerb, attempting to splash him with 'guttersludge'. The cabbies needn't have worried; you can never find a taxi in the rain to this day, even though the umbrella has become a ubiquitous feature of national life.

It is an ancient and familiar notion, that people can be defined by their habitat. In about AD 7, the Greek historian and geographer Strabo hinted at an association between Britain's rainy and foggy weather and the locals' temperament, 'simple and barbaric – so much so that, on account of their inexperience, some of them although well supplied with milk, make no cheese'. (See 'C is for Cheese'.)

The suggestion was that the damp, gloomy climate had incubated an uncivilised, backward race.

Strabo was drawing upon accepted wisdom. Four centuries earlier, Hippocrates, the 'father of medicine', had drawn powerful links between climate and regional disposition, ideas that he used to explain the dominance of Greek culture. Asian peoples lacked courage, endurance, industry and high spirit, he argued, because the weather was too uniform and balanced. The Europeans on the other hand, stimulated by severe heatwaves, severe winters, droughts and copious rains, responded to such climatic 'jolts' with energy and bravery.

In 1733, the Scottish doctor and writer John Arbuthnot attempted to apply the theory to the British Isles. His *Essay Concerning the Effects of the Air on Human Bodies* built its central argument upon measurements obtained from his barometer, an invention that had found an energetic market among Britain's army of weather obsessives. He concluded that variations in atmospheric pressure found in cold northern climes meant citizens had 'greater activity and courage'. People in hot countries, by contrast, were free from such agitations and sensations, rendering them 'lazy and indolent'. In short, barometric readings explained why northern Europeans, notably the British, were more civilised than others.

The barometer helped inspire an extraordinary period of meteorological record-keeping in Britain, with enthusiasts and academics keeping detailed weather diaries in the belief that, through observation and measurement, science might render the country's capricious climate explainable and predictable. In the 1660s, members of the newly formed Royal Society encouraged data collection and research: Robert Hooke published a 'Method for Making a History of the Weather' and John Locke kept a weather diary for almost forty years.

The contemporary historian Jan Golinski, who studied many meticulous accounts, concluded 'the compilation of weather diaries can be understood as part of the large-scale enterprise of "civilising nature"'. It was as though the country wanted to demonstrate that its gentle, moderate climate was indicative of the self-control that made Britain great. By understanding our weather, we might understand ourselves.

Samuel Johnson, however, took a rather more dismissive view of the 'inspectors of barometers', whose confidence in their ability to predict the weather was, he thought, akin to believing in bugbears and goblins. 'The oraculous glasses have deceived their votaries; shower has succeeded shower, though they predicted sunshine and dry skies; and by fatal confidence in these fallacious promises, many coats have lost their gloss and many curls have been moistened to flaccidity.' Dr Johnson famously mocked this peculiar fixation with daily forecasting, observing that 'when two Englishmen meet, their first talk is of the weather. They are in haste to tell each other, what each must already know, that it is hot or cold, bright or cloudy, windy or calm.'

However, eighteenth-century science continued to challenge ancient superstition that rain-ruined harvests and drought-shrivelled crops signified divine vengeance or that the activities of the heavens were random, unfathomable phenomena. The daily tapping of barometers marked out a rhythmic determination to explain how mild British weather had sculpted the great British people.

The Scots philosopher David Hume was unconvinced. 'The only observation, with regard to the difference of men in different climates, on which we can rest any weight, is the vulgar one, that people in the northern regions have a greater inclination to strong liquors, and those in the southern to love and women,' he wrote. Even this association was doubtful, Hume felt, given the Greeks who 'seem much addicted to the bottle'.

The unpredictability and variety of the British weather, however, has always played powerfully upon this nation's sense of itself. Each morning, pulling back the curtains, the population prepares itself for what may be outside. A clear blue sky might lift the spirits; flat grey cloud may prompt correspondingly neutral shrugs; dreary drizzle is likely to be met by sinking hearts. How can one deny that sunshine or showers, convivial warmth or bitter cold, don't help set the mood and perhaps, over time, the personality of a people? It is a persuasive argument – but does it stack up?

During the last few decades, a significant amount of research has been conducted into the relationship between mood and weather, with scientists looking for a link between atmospheric condition and personal disposition. Do high temperatures make people passionate? Does precipitation dampen enthusiasm? Are people happier in summer than in winter?

Analysis in the 1970s and 80s variously suggested that high pressure, high temperature and low humidity were associated with positive emotions – basically, nice weather seemed to put people in a good mood. More recent research, however, has challenged this assertion with a number of studies suggesting the link is either very small or non-existent. One paper published in 2008 concluded that 'the idea that pleasant weather increases people's positive mood in general is not supported by the findings of this study'.

The author of that research, Jaap Denissen, accepted that his conclusions apparently contradicted common sense, but insisted that there could be a number of factors to explain the discrepancy between empirical results and widely held beliefs. For example, it may be that historical associations between good weather and having enough food and shelter have been culturally transmitted down the ages. He also suggested that the discrepancy might be down to the impact of a small number of extreme cases in which people's mental health is genuinely affected by the weather.

Seasonal Affective Disorder, or SAD, was first described and named by the South African psychiatrist Norman Rosenthal in 1984, who noticed that after his move from sub-tropical Johannesburg to seasonal New York he was less energetic and productive in the winter months. Often described as 'winter blues', Rosenthal found the condition was more prevalent in northern latitudes: virtually no one in sunny Florida was diagnosed with the condition, while almost one in ten of the population further north in New Hampshire was said to suffer from SAD.

In Britain, the disorder is thought to affect around 7 per cent of people. Most of them suffer during the winter months, but it applies to people who become depressed at the change of any season. The *Observer* newspaper columnist Barbara Ellen has written about her experience of what is sometimes called reverse-SAD: 'With me, SAD hits when the days get longer and brighter,' she revealed. 'I know when summer is coming because suddenly I feel wrong. I don't make sense in the summer, everything is too hot, too hopeless, too bewildering. I always feel I'm half a beat behind the world, playing an eternal game of catch-up.'

Science is still trying to make sense of what is going on. The link between cold, dark climates and depression seems so plausible and yet Icelanders exhibit remarkably low levels of SAD. Some suggest this might be down to a genetic factor (Canadians of Icelandic origin also appear to have lower levels of SAD), while others think they may be protected by eating lots of fish, a diet high in Vitamin D.

The British public, it seems, remains largely committed to the view that if it lived in a warm, sunny environment instead of enduring waves of Atlantic cloud and rain, everyone would be a lot happier. For proof, people confidently assert that suicide rates are higher in countries straddling the Arctic Circle. But are they?

Proportionately, far more people kill themselves in the warmth of South Korea than in the chill of Scandinavia. Finland, which has the highest suicide rate of the Nordic nations, has a similar level to France and Belgium. The Swedes have long tried to explode the myth that their climate makes them a depressive bunch, blaming a speech by President Eisenhower in 1960 for an association between European socialism and suicide. World Health Organization data suggest Sweden's rate is roughly in line with South Africa, Hong Kong and New Zealand.

The idea that a warm, sunny climate makes us happier doesn't hold up. The countries with the highest levels of reported well-being, the places where people themselves say their lives are great, tend to be those experiencing long, cold winters: Canada, Sweden, Finland and Norway regularly feature in the top positions. If climate is having an effect, it is more than offset by other factors.

And yet. And yet. And yet. I *know* that I feel chirpier when the gloomy days of a British winter give way to spring, when the clouds break and sunshine strokes my face, when the interminable flatness of creamy skies is replaced by sharp contrasts of light and shade. Immediately following a rain shower, when the sun bursts out and sparkles on puddles through clean, fresh air, colours are brighter and senses somehow keener, as if a divine technician had cranked up the chroma and the brightness – those moments are profoundly exhilarating. Don't tell me that is not real.

Perhaps the explanation is hidden in a newspaper article from New Delhi in India a couple of years ago. 'A sudden spell of drizzle in some parts of the national capital lifted the mood of its residents, as many people took time off from work to enjoy the pleasant weather,' it read. One city dweller apparently decided to stay indoors and watch the rain through his window. 'It's beautiful weather and I was dying to get back home fast and curl up with a book and a cup of coffee while hearing the light pitter-patter of the rain on the roof,' Rashmi Jain was quoted as saying.

The story suggests that it is not the type of weather that is as important for our mood as the change from one meteorological condition to another. While an English tourist in New Delhi might have cursed the damp, cloudy conditions so similar to what he'd left at home, locals who had endured weeks of dry heat were reportedly delighted by the break in the weather. In Britain in 1976, after weeks of boiling weather and drought conditions, the Prime Minister Harold Wilson instructed one of his ministers to do a rain dance. When the heavens did indeed open a few days later, the nation rejoiced.

There is evidence that people become habituated to the weather, that the thrill felt on the first beautiful summer's day is less on the second and virtually non-existent after a month of such conditions. In 1998, David Schkade and Daniel Kahneman published a paper entitled, 'Does Living in California Make People Happy?' The two professors had noticed what they described as 'a stereotyped perception that people are happier in California ... anchored in the perceived superiority of the California climate'. Two interesting conclusions emerged from their research: firstly, tanned Californians were no happier than people from the Midwest, with its wind and rain; second, of all the factors that affected people's life satisfaction, weather was listed at the bottom. Midwesterners moaned about the weather more than Californians, but that didn't appear to make much difference to their overall contentment.

If change in the weather is more important than the weather itself, then perhaps (as Hippocrates suggested) it is the very unpredictability and variable nature of the British experience that shapes the national character. Tupperware skies are always promising or threatening something else. Our caution and conservatism may be the product of countless daily reactions to the cheery weather girl with her symbols, the newspaper weather map with its swirling isobars, or the view from the window at breakfast.

To put it another way, it is less the umbrella that defines us, as the fact that we feel the need to carry one.

V IS FOR VEGETABLES

The Battle of Rawmarsh School was a skirmish in a feudal food fight that has been rumbling along for centuries. On one side, the professional classes – teachers and nutritionists led by celebrity chef Jamie Oliver, determined to improve the quality of school meals eaten by pupils at a Rotherham comp. On the other, working-class mothers equally determined that their children should not be forced to eat rabbit food, the salads and vegetables which had replaced burgers and, famously, deep-fried turkey twizzlers on the menu.

The press chronicled how, one afternoon in 2006, three mums posted buns and chips to their children through the school railings 'like day trippers feeding animals at the zoo'. The story encapsulated the ancient link between class and diet in Britain – more particularly on this occasion, the changing standing of vegetables. From peasant fodder to superfood, from working-class staple to middle-class statement, from the humble turnip to the flowering baby courgette, our relationship with veg has been turned on its head.

For King Henry VIII to have been seen eating a carrot stick would have been to betray England's social order; as shocking today as a YouTube clip of the Queen secretly guzzling a monster chicken bargain bucket. Vegetables were the food of the poor and their place at the Tudor top table was restricted to a few small 'sallets' and garnishes surrounded by colossal quantities of expensive meat. If a vegetable did make an appearance at the feast, it was presented in an almost ironic way, like mini fish 'n' chip canapés at a corporate networking function. One recipe for 'an Excellent Sallet ... usual at great Feasts, and upon Princes' Tables' consisted of a spoonful of herbs, fruit and nuts smothered in sugar.

The French penchant for fresh green vegetables was regarded with suspicion in Britain where, from the Middle Ages, the veggie option had consisted largely of onions, leeks, turnips and garlic, the occasional cucumber and a handful of dried peas or beans.

For peasants, food was fuel. The daily challenge was to consume enough calories to survive a life of toil and poverty. The question 'what's for dinner?' would almost invariably be answered the same way: pottage. A glamorous definition of the dish might be a rustic stew of meat or fish with grains, herbs and vegetables. In reality it was oats and water with the odd turnip, a bone or two, apple cores and some dandelion leaves chucked in for flavour. The cooking process – boil for hours over a fire until all ingredients have been absorbed into a homogenous gloop – was designed to minimise the significant health risk from the fertiliser often spread on the fields: human excrement. Vegetables were consumed because they were available, not as a good source of sustenance. For a landless rural worker and his family, they might be a last resort as hunger closed in; gathered from the wild, rustled from private gardens or pilfered from stores of animal feed.

The nobility, meanwhile, used the dining table to display their social status, measured by the range and sheer quantity of dead birds and animals on offer. So unhealthy was this carnivorous bingeing that the wealthiest Tudors were the first group to suffer the obesity and other health problems associated these days with poverty and deprivation. A refusal to eat their greens meant noblemen were prone to mild forms of scurvy, bladder and kidney problems. Gout, a painful arthritic condition often caused by too much meat and drink, was regarded as the disease of kings.

As Western explorers returned from their adventures, new exotic vegetables were introduced to Britain; the tomato from Mexico and the potato from Peru in the sixteenth century. While other European cultures embraced and adopted the new arrivals, Britain's suspicion of strange alien produce delayed their introduction into the nation's diet. Potatoes were said to cause leprosy and flatulence. Tomatoes, a relative of the deadly nightshade, were thought to be poisonous. In March 1669, the diarist Samuel Pepys reflected the caution with which foreign fruit and veg were met in Britain, when presented with a glass of fresh orange juice. 'I was doubtful whether it might not do me hurt,' he wrote.

Vegetables won an improved status in the rural economy when it was realised that including legumes like beans and peas in crop rotation dramatically improved soil fertility and yields. During the British agricultural revolution in the eighteenth century, the Whig Parliamentarian Lord Charles Townshend became convinced of the central role for the turnip in this new agricultural system, earning both the inevitable nickname Turnip Townshend and a reputation for boring the pants off anyone who engaged with him on the subject.

The British have always tended to regard vegetables as objects of ridicule, particularly root crops. The very words mangelwurzel and turnip are used to mock unsophisticated rural life. The peasant Baldrick in the comedy series *Blackadder* is asked by Lord Edmund: 'Tell me, Baldrick, do your life's ambitions go anywhere beyond the acquisition of turnips?'

'Er, no,' Baldrick replies simply.

TV consumer champion Esther Rantzen may be best remembered for the section on her show devoted to misshapen vegetables resembling genitalia, national mirth derived from our slightly dysfunctional relationship with root crops and sex organs.

While the Germans venerated the cabbage and the Italians gave the tomato a place of honour in their national cuisine, the British treated vegetables as lowly ingredients, fit for livestock and rabbits. The potato did win popularity right across the Western world, chiefly because it provided shovel-loads of energy from small amounts of land and could be stored for long periods or left underground. It proved a wonderfully versatile crop and became so central to the working-class diet in the United Kingdom that it replaced almost everything else. It certainly had greater appeal than yet another bowl of pottage.

But our love affair with spuds aside, the British relationship with vegetables remained unconsummated. In the nineteenth century, as workers migrated from farms to the factories, the industrial revolution helped bring food prices down. Suddenly people had a choice, and for the population setting up home in the new towns and cities, the opportunity to reject the unfashionable elements of the rural diet – the reviled vegetables. In what became known as the nutrition transition, Britain's working class shunned their carrots, cabbage, watercress and beetroot (extolled as superfoods today, of course) in favour of aspiration foods: white bread, the ubiquitous potato, meat and dripping. Vegetables were unloved and unappreciated, their value placed so low that even those catering for patients in many hospitals served none at all.

When the social reformer Seebohm Rowntree investigated the diet of the urban poor in York in 1901, his report revealed a class prejudice against fruit and vegetables. The British Medical Journal asked: 'Who is responsible for the conditions which lead to the state of poverty and the bad nutrition disclosed by this report? Lies the fault with the poor themselves – is it because they are thriftless, because they lack training in cooking and in the economical spending of such income as they possess? Or is it that the actual wages which they can command are so low that it is impossible for them to purchase the actual necessities of life?' Britain's professional elite had initiated a critique of working-class diet that continues to this day. Vegetables, it was being discovered, were key to the nation's security and so it was that, just as the urban working classes were giving up on veg, British officialdom was offering a lingering glance to the greengrocer's barrow.

The government and the military had been shocked by the poor physical health of young men they wanted to recruit for the Boer War, and suddenly nutrition became a national concern. A parliamentary committee was assembled and experts recruited to try to explain what was missing from the diet of the working classes. An answer was discovered in a laboratory at Cambridge University by biochemist Sir Frederick Gowland Hopkins: vitamins. In what became known as the Golden Age of Nutrition, scientists across the developed world were demonstrating that there was much more to food than a source of energy and flavour. Fresh fruit and vegetables, it was realised, were a vital part of a balanced diet and consumption rose dramatically, particularly among the educated and better off. Britain's working class, however, did not share the newfound respect and enthusiasm for carrots and beans.

With the Great Depression in the 1930s, millions were once again forced to swallow their greens and their pride. Some well-meaning authorities encouraged unemployed workers to grow-their-own in temporary allotments. Others set up soup kitchens where the hungry would stand in humiliating lines for a bowl of thin vegetable stock. In 1934, 68 million free school meals were doled out to poor pupils in elementary schools as the League of Nations published official guidelines suggesting children should consume at least 100g of green leafy vegetables every day. For a generation of working-class youngsters, the shame of being marked out as a classroom charity case would always be associated with the slop of overcooked veg hitting a dinner plate.

With the outbreak of war, among the few food items not rationed or in short supply were carrots, swede and potatoes, and so government hatched a plan to rehabilitate vegetables, to rid them of their lowly status. The maître-chef de cuisine at the Savoy, François

Latry, and a peer of the realm, Food Minister Lord Woolton, joined forces to devise and promote Woolton Pie – basically carrots and swede (with other veg when available) topped with potatoes or pastry. An editorial in *The Times* noted that 'when Woolton pie was being forced on somewhat reluctant tables, Lord Woolton performed a valuable service by submitting to the flashlight camera at public luncheons while eating, with every sign of enjoyment, the dish named after him.'

The King and Queen did their bit by being seen planting vegetables in the gardens of Windsor Castle and the Royal Parks. The flowers in Kensington Gardens were replaced with rows of cabbages. But attitudes proved hard to shift. As *The New York Times* reported in 1942: 'England has a goodly store of carrots. But carrots are not the staple items of the average British diet. The problem is to sell the carrots to the English public.' It was decided vegetables needed a Hollywood-style makeover, and so ministers approached Walt Disney to see if he could get the nation to go back to its roots. Disney accepted the challenge and devised a family of cartoon carrots including Carroty George, Clara Carrot, Pop Carrot and Dr Carrot. The characters were reproduced in newspaper and poster campaigns, with Carroty George promising to 'tell you what to do with me'.

Another wheeze was to convince the general public that vegetables had magic properties. The Ministry of Food suggested the success of the RAF's most celebrated night-time fighter pilot, John 'Cats Eyes' Cunningham, was down to his love for carrots. Sales apparently improved as people consumed extra helpings following official advice that 'carrots keep you healthy and help you see in the blackout'. But despite Carroty George's help, the country couldn't get to grips with cooking vegetables. Perhaps it was a relic of its pottage past, but Britain seemed hell-bent on boiling all fresh veg to the point of submission, and many consumers actually preferred the tinned variety.

In 1944, nutritionist Frederick (Bill) Le Gros Clark was

commissioned by Hertfordshire County Council to investigate how to get local schoolchildren to eat their vegetables. The Jamie Oliver of his day, Clark was convinced that pupils could be taught to like the detested 'slimy' marrow. A letter to the British Medical Journal entitled 'Children's Food Fads' summed up his conclusion:

> We grow the best vegetables in the world and ruin them in the pot. The bias against greens among these children might easily be accounted for by the sodden tasteless messes put before them, and the indifference to potatoes, especially when boiled, may derive from the same cause. The school canteen can do much to eradicate food dislikes in children, with great advantage to their nutrition, especially if the mothers at home pay more attention to the saucepan and less to the children's whims.

Britain actually emerged from the war a better-fed and healthier nation, but as rationing was removed, a diet class divide emerged. In 1952 the government's National Food Survey studied the effects of social class on food consumption and found that fresh vegetables were 'purchased in decidedly greater amounts by Class A than by the lower income classes'. Poorer families tended to buy large amounts of potatoes, white bread and cheap foods rich in fats and sugar. The report concluded that 'shortage of money induces the purchase of energy-producing foods as distinguished from "protective" foods'.

The second half of the twentieth century saw a transformation in Britain's relationship with food in general and vegetables in particular. Increasing affluence and new technology meant no one needed to go hungry. Diet became a lifestyle choice and for some that meant curries and burgers while for others it was lentils and beans. In 1961, the first Cranks vegetarian restaurant opened up in London's swinging Carnaby Street, a sign that the parsnip might have a role to play in the social revolution. The 1960s hippy counter-culture, guided by the philosophies of the East, helped give vegetables a credibility that would feed the attitudes of generations to come. When Paul McCartney explained that he and his wife Linda 'don't eat anything that has to be killed for us' he was implying that veg eaters occupied the moral high ground.

The carrot and the mung bean were symbols of an earthy alternative to the space-age grub that usually won pride of place on the supermarket shelves. This was the age of fast food – instant coffee, instant whip, instant mash. From boil-in-the-bag to microwave ready meal, domestic eating was increasingly about convenience and speed, enabled by new gadgets and appliances. Nutritionists, who had once enjoyed the ear of government, were sidelined despite increasing scientific evidence of the links between health and diet.

In 1983 Margaret Thatcher was asked 'as leader of the nation and as a housewife' what she intended to do about the assessment of the National Advisory Committee on Nutrition Education that Britain was eating its way to a public health crisis. The groundbreaking report, commissioned by her government, argued it was the job of the state to encourage citizens to eat more vegetables and fruit while cutting down on sugar, fat and alcohol. 'I do not think that those people need advice from me, and I think that it would be presumptuous of me to give it,' the Prime Minister told the House of Commons.

Mrs Thatcher was accused of burying the research to protect her friends in business, but it became increasingly hard to disguise the evidence of a nation with an eating disorder. The administrative arteries of the National Health Service were becoming clogged by consequences of poor diet. The Royal College of Physicians said that so many people were overweight in Britain that a change in the dietary pattern of the whole country was warranted. Health officials warned of a nation indulging in a mock-Tudor diet, consuming far too much red meat and not nearly enough green vegetables. This time, though, it wasn't the wealthiest who were suffering most. It was the poorest.

Researchers working in Norfolk found they were able to predict how many vegetables someone consumed by their job and
their postcode. 'Being in a manual occupational social class, having
no educational qualifications, and living in a deprived area all independently predicted significantly lower consumption of fruit and
vegetables,' they reported.

The Department of Health was bombarded with evidence that
Britain needed to consume more veg, particularly those in the
poorest neighbourhoods. If only the working class could be persuaded to eat their greens, ministers were advised, the health costs
from heart problems, stroke and cancer could be dramatically
reduced. The UK had one of the lowest vegetable intakes in Europe
and one of the worst heart disease records in the world, but many
developed nations were growing anxious about the same problems.
Selling fruit and vegetables to the masses became a global crusade,
with the World Health Organization encouraging governments to
find ways to convince the citizenry of the merits of broccoli and
spinach.

Britain eventually adopted the five-a-day message, suggesting
people eat at least five portions of fruit and vegetables every twenty-
four hours. Teams of officials were hired to count how much veg
the nation was consuming and regularly report progress to ministers. Supermarkets and chefs were recruited to encourage greater
consumption and books appeared on 'the art of hiding vegetables'
and 'sneaky ways' to get your children eating them.

Nutritionists and marketing teams were invited into primary
schools to try and make veg cool. Instead of Carroty George,
twenty-first-century pupils in England and Wales were introduced
to the Food Dudes – cartoon kids who supposedly acted as influential role models. After watching an 'exciting adventure' about
healthy eating, children were then given a portion of fruit and a
portion of vegetable. Those who succeeded in swallowing both won
a prize. Experts hoped such programmes might completely transform the way Britons eat in the future, a prospect that did not enjoy

universal support. Some libertarians argued that 'public health toffs' were waging war on working-class culture and sought to defend the working man's fondness for a Big Mac. At one political meeting held in Westminster in 2010 it was suggested that 'health paternalism is committed to using the mechanisms of social engineering to ease the pleasures of working-class life gradually out of existence.' Shortly afterwards the then Conservative Health Secretary, Andrew Lansley, suggested the Jamie Oliver approach was counter-productive and government should refrain from 'constantly lecturing people and trying to tell them what to do'.

Nevertheless, government-funded campaigning to encourage Britain to the greengrocer's barrow continues. In 2011, ministers instructed the Fruit and Vegetable Taskforce to increase average portions of veg eaten by low-income families and vulnerable older people, with specific targets to increase 'positive potato messages' and 'gardens growing their own'. But the legacy of pottage, soup kitchens and inedible school cabbage means that vegetables remain at the centre of a class battle which slices through British society like Jamie Oliver's cleaver through a turnip.

W IS FOR WWW

One day in 1997, just round the corner from where I lived in north London, the occupants of twenty-six houses on one leafy residential road each took delivery of an identical item: a large cardboard box bearing the black and white markings of a Holstein cow. Inside was a personal computer, the bovine branding a pointer to the parcels' provenance – US technology firm Gateway 2000 (which liked to emphasise its rural Iowa roots). But the cow theme might also have been a clue to the motivation of the sender: the PCs were a gift from Microsoft, which wanted to test whether connecting neighbours to the World Wide Web would see people herd together or drift apart.

The experiment, conducted on what was dubbed 'Internet Street' in Islington, was an early attempt to answer a fundamental question of our age: will computer technology prove to be a force for good in strengthening our communities or will it undermine social ties? It is an issue that still preoccupies British policy advisors.

Back in the late 1990s, the jury was deeply divided on the issue. One research paper on the subject, entitled 'Internet paradox: a social technology that reduces social involvement and psychological well-being?', cannot have made happy reading for the people who funded it, many of Microsoft's Silicon Valley rivals and neighbours. The analysis concluded:

> Greater use of the Internet was associated with small, but statistically significant declines in social involvement as measured by communication within the family and the size of people's local social networks, and with increases in loneliness, a psychological state associated with social involvement. Greater use of the Internet was also associated with increases in depression.

Imagine the executives at Apple, Intel, Hewlett Packard, Bell and others reacting to the news that their own research suggested their products were likely to turn people into sad, stressed loners. The only saving grace was the question mark the researchers had placed at the end of the paper's title. Small wonder that the psychologists were asked to go back and do some follow-ups which, more helpfully, showed that within three years of using the web the negative effects had been replaced by positive results on social relationships and psychological well-being – especially for the highly extroverted. Phew!

The experiment in the Islington district of Barnsbury was part of the same enterprise: the search for scientific evidence that the Internet is good for us. In selecting a side street full of affluent media types and lawyers, Microsoft must have been hoping that north London would come up with the right answer.

After just a fortnight, one national newspaper article suggested that the resident's free access to 'the global Internet, with its 15,000 "newsgroups" and millions of pages of data on the World Wide Web, where they can make airline and hotel reservations and order goods' was already making a difference.

'Maya, a 35-year-old advertising executive who lives at number thirty-six, said: "Now, the first thing I do when I get home is turn on the computer to see if I have been sent any e-mail. I'm almost despondent if there isn't anything there."' (It is a remark from another age: twenty-first-century despondency is not discovering too few emails but far too many.)

A full year after the cow boxes had been unpacked, the BBC popped around to see how the neighbourhood was faring. 'Microsoft's grand experiment at creating a "cyber-street" in north London could, it appears, pull the plug on claims that the Internet makes people antisocial,' it concluded. 'Neighbours have used e-mail and a local electronic bulletin board to co-ordinate opposition to a parking scheme, to try to stop burglars, and just arranging to meet each other at the local pub. Pearson Phillips, a semi-retired journalist and resident of the street, has even started the Barnsbury Bugle, a monthly e-mailed newsletter.' Bill Gates must have smiled at Mr Phillips' encouraging testimony. 'The day I saw somebody put a notice up saying, "We'll be in the pub at eight o'clock – if anyone would like a drink, please come along," I realised that this was going to work.'

The positive noises from Islington would not have impressed two academics at Stanford University, though. In February 2000, Norman Nie and Lutz Erbing published analysis suggesting the more time people spent surfing the web, the more they lost contact with their friends, families and communities. 'Email is a way to stay in touch,' Nie agreed, 'but you can't share a coffee or a beer with somebody on email. Or give them a hug. The Internet could be the ultimate isolating technology that reduces our participation in communities even more than did automobiles and television before it.'

In Britain, where the web was expanding rapidly, it was noted that the dire warnings of social catastrophe were matched by cyber-evangelists proclaiming the reverse. 'The most transforming technological event since the capture of fire' was how John Perry Barlow, lyricist for the Grateful Dead and digital rights activist, described the development of the Internet.

The writer Howard Rheingold, one of the first to log on to an online community in San Francisco in the mid-1980s, claimed to have been 'participating in the self-design of a new kind of culture'. In his book *The Virtual Community: Homesteading on the Electronic Frontier*, Rheingold wrote of how he had plugged his computer into his telephone and made contact with the WELL (Whole Earth 'Lectronic Link), a very early email network. 'The WELL felt like an authentic community to me from the start because it was grounded in my everyday physical world,' he enthused. 'I've attended real-life WELL marriages, WELL births, and even a WELL funeral. (The phrase "in real life" pops up so often in virtual communities that regulars abbreviate it to IRL.)' It all sounded very Californian, but Rheingold had identified the central question for British academics and policy wonks trying to work out the social implications of new technology: would virtual contact translate into physical 'real life' connections? When I interviewed the celebrated social scientist Robert Putnam for a BBC TV series, he presented the issue this way: 'The question is whether the Internet turns out to be a nifty telephone or a nifty television?' In other words, would people cut themselves off from other people by staring at a screen in the same way they watched TV or would it facilitate social communication in the way phones had done?

Putnam was famous for having documented the decline of 'social capital' in the United States, the weakening of the glue that holds neighbourhoods together. His best-selling book *Bowling Alone* suggested the very fabric of American community had been damaged by, among other things, television and the motorcar. 'Years ago,' he wrote, 'thousands of people belonged to bowling leagues. Today, however, they're more likely to bowl alone.' Putnam feared the personal computer might accelerate the process of neighbourhood disintegration still further.

In Britain, there was much debate as to whether the *Bowling Alone* analysis applied here. Although the spirit of the Women's Institute, Cub Scouts and working men's clubs seemed relatively intact, levels of social trust, a key measure of community health, had fallen dramatically. Research showed the proportion of British people who thought 'most people can be trusted', as opposed to 'you can't be too careful in dealing with people', had fallen from 44 per cent to 30 per cent in just five years – a more rapid decline even than in the United States.

Just as these figures were being digested, a government policy team investigating neighbourhood renewal reported how in some areas trust in neighbours has all but disappeared – 'residents described one area as a war zone'. Suddenly social capital was the mantra of Whitehall. The Education Secretary David Blunkett beseeched Britain to 'build up reservoirs' of the stuff. The Chancellor Gordon Brown thought the answer was an era of civic patriotism. The question of whether the rapidly expanding Internet was good or bad for community cohesion took on a new urgency.

In spring 2001, Prime Minister Tony Blair invited Putnam to breakfast in Downing Street. Over coffee and croissants, he listened as the Harvard academic explained how declining social capital was linked to rising crime, chronic illness and early death; how important face-to-face human interaction, community involvement and trust were for social well-being; how critical it was to ensure that developments like the Internet did not further weaken the bonds and bridges that are required for a healthy society.

At the same time, news from Canada was presenting a different picture. Rather than destroying social capital by replacing face-to-face contact, the experience of 'Netville' suggested the Internet might actually strengthen community cohesion and increase neighbourliness. Netville was the nickname of a middle-class Toronto suburb that possessed qualities social network analysts can usually only dream of. All the homes in the development had been offered high-speed Internet access: two thirds of the community had opted to receive the service and a third had declined. The scientists could compare the sociability of those with and without the Internet.

'Wired' residents were soon emailing each other, asking for advice, advertising garage sales and sending invitations to community barbecues. There were echoes of what happened in Islington's Internet Street, but in Netville it was possible to see whether neighbours who weren't linked to the web were more or less involved in the life of the community.

The results were intriguing: on average, wired residents knew the names of twenty-five neighbours, while non-wired residents knew the names of eight; wired residents talked to twice as many local people as non-wired and made 50 per cent more visits to their neighbours' homes. The research team also noticed an unexpected difference in the behaviour of the largely online community of Netville compared with people on housing developments nearby. 'Despite the fact that many homes within Netville were built with spacious patios attached at the rear of the home, the majority of residents had moved a park bench, or a set of inexpensive plastic chairs, to the corner of their driveway or front steps. By contrast, residents of similar nearby developments almost universally chose to sit in their backyards.'

Why had Netvillers acted in this way? When the researchers asked people they explained that by positioning themselves on the front step, they were able to exchange quick greetings with neighbours passing on the street. They could see what was happening in the community, and they were able to keep a watchful eye on their children's activities.

The authors of the Netville study, Barry Wellman and Keith Hampton, dismissed the doom-mongers who feared the web would crush social spirit: 'Warnings of the Internet's impending destruction of community have rarely been encumbered by evidence,' they noted drily. But their report also warned against exaggerating the social implications of computer technology, reminding readers that people interact through atoms and molecules as well as through bits and bytes. Netville was a harbinger of 'glocalization', they said, 'simultaneously globally connected and locally involved.'

Wellman and Hampton concluded that the Internet wouldn't destroy or transform community, but by offering an additional form of communication, it did have the capability to enrich and empower wired neighbourhoods. Their concern was for people who didn't have access, those people on the wrong side of the digital divide. 'What will the Internet do for community then?' they asked.

The British government was already growing anxious about the significant minority of citizens who were not on the web – less because of concerns over neighbourliness than the risk of missing out on the economic advantages promised by e-government: citizens accessing state services, paying taxes, shopping, banking, finding jobs or training online. For Tony Blair, what he called 'electronic service delivery' was a key plank of his public service reforms. 'I am determined that we should capitalise on these opportunities and that by 2005 at the latest, all government services will be online. Equally important is that by the same time, everyone should have access to the Internet, so that the whole of society can benefit,' he wrote.

Blair had set the clock ticking: within five years, everyone should have access to the wonders of cyberspace, the man had said. But how were they going to do that, especially in places already suffering the consequences of social exclusion? Ten million pounds was assigned for the Wired Up Communities Programme (WuC), in which residents in some of Britain's most run-down and poor neighbourhoods, places with negligible Internet access, would be given free computers and invited to cross the electronic frontier.

Ministers had, perhaps, read about Islington's Internet Street and hoped they could have the same results in an old mining village in South Yorkshire, a Suffolk market town, one of Liverpool's most deprived districts, a sheep-farming community in Cumbria and on tough estates in east London and Greater Manchester. When the results were sent to Whitehall, the evaluation made unhappy reading. The authors reported major implementation slippage and uncertainty in relation to the aims of the programme, as ministers fussed and argued over what the pilot projects were trying to do. The scheme was described as experimental – basically, it seems, people were making it up as they went along. A couple of the deprived neighbourhoods didn't get shiny new computers but were given recycled PCs, second-hand machines that were so unreliable they eventually had to be junked.

Plans for local community websites to improve social cohesion proved problematic, with three neighbourhoods becoming 'disenchanted with the experience'. When the evaluation team asked locals whether the exercise had improved neighbourliness, their report admitted it was 'difficult to get a sense of connectedness' in the area.

Most troubling of all, though, was the finding that, despite being given free home computers, the local projects were unable to convince a significant minority of residents of the value of using the Internet. More than a quarter of people given the technology never used it to access the web, with many of those simply saying they weren't interested or had better things to do with their time. Even when residents were given personal training, indifference remained at roughly the same level.

This lack of interest was not what ministers had expected. As the evaluation put it: 'Much of the literature assumes that once people have access to, and have used the technologies, they will embrace them wholeheartedly.' Tony Blair's ambition to get everyone surfing away within five years was based on a belief that the meteoric growth of the Internet would continue, and the job of government was simply to help people aboard. The evidence, however, pointed to a problem: with quite a lot of British citizens apparently happy to be on the wrong side of the digital divide, new technology might serve to increase inequality and social isolation.

Another study into Internet access in London reported the

same difficulty: 'A lack of interest amongst those not connected is probably the most significant problem facing policymakers.' The capital's politicians were warned that the number of non-users with 'no interest' remained stubbornly high and, with a slightly desperate tone, the report added, 'Non-users must be convinced.'

The relationship between new technologies and established communities has often proved unpredictable. The telephone was developed as a business tool but transformed social relations. Radio was designed for the military but inspired a youth revolution. For half a century, mass-produced cars were the playthings of the wealthy, widening the social advantage of the rich over the poor. But with ownership suddenly spreading across the social strata in the 1960s, its impact eroded traditional community life. When televisions were first plugged into people's homes, the expectation was that they might bind nations together through shared events like the Coronation. Later, the TV would be blamed for seeing us staring at *Friends* and *Neighbours* rather than talking to real friends and neighbours.

Perhaps the development of the railway network in the mid-nineteenth century offers the closest analogy to the growth of the Internet. As trains began steaming into public view, there was considerable opposition to using them – particularly from the 'common people'. In 1837, for example, the architect and journalist George Godwin published a pamphlet entitled 'An Appeal to the Public on the Subject of Railways', in which he quoted one common person, a parish clerk who had just seen a locomotive for the first time: 'That was a sight to have seen; but one I never care to see again! How much longer shall knowledge be allowed to go on increasing?'

Godwin, in a lament echoed by those attempting to encourage acceptance of the Internet today, implored the working classes to be open-minded and positive towards technological changes. 'We would strongly and sincerely urge every individual of the society to lend his utmost aid in establishing and increasing their effectiveness,' he wrote, 'not merely to maintain the prosperity of the country, but greatly to increase it.'

Tony Blair's ambition to get everyone on the Internet by 2005 came and went. Seven years later there were still 7.8 million adults who had never been online in Britain. A fifth of UK households had no access to the web, with 54 per cent of those saying they either didn't want or didn't need it.

The digital divide is partly a generation gap, with older people more reluctant to engage with new technology. But it is also a feature of a profoundly worrying aspect of British society: the sizeable minority of citizens who are increasingly disconnected from the mainstream. While just 3 per cent of graduates have never used the Internet, for those without any formal qualifications the figure rises to 55 per cent. There is a clear link between social exclusion and digital exclusion, and government advisors have warned that people they label as 'resistors' risk cutting themselves off still further.

Reading official documents on the subject, one is struck by the frustration of those charged with getting Britain online: they bemoan the negative knee-jerk reaction of some groups to the potential benefits of technology. 'These people,' the government's key Digital Britain report advised, 'need to be clearly shown how digital services could benefit them.' But when resistors were shown a five-minute video designed to do just that, most people still said no – even if offered access for free.

Ministers were warned that those deeply socially excluded, with no meaningful Internet engagement, accounted for 10 per cent of the population and that Britain was at a tipping point in its relation to the online world. 'It is moving from conferring advantage on those who are in it to conferring active disadvantage on those who are without.'

The early dramatic claims for the Internet, that it would either create a virtual utopia or destroy physical community, forgot the importance that people give to real socialising; to sharing a meal or juicy gossip, to handshakes and hugs, to looking people in the eyes and occasionally glimpsing their soul. Emoticons or colon/bracket winks and smiles are no substitute. Facebook, Hotmail and Twitter don't replace conversation and friendship: they build on what is there – just as the railways, the postal service, the telephone and the motorcar have done.

The evidence suggests that a large majority of the social interactions that occur online involve people who know each other offline: the Internet therefore magnifies the connectedness of those who are connected and the exclusion of those who are already excluded. The solution is not simply about access to the web, providing high-speed broadband to remote villages or IT suites in old folks' homes, important though those may be. The challenge is to give the marginalised in Britain – the illiterate, the vulnerable, the desperate – the skills, support and social confidence to cross the electronic frontier.

X IS FOR XXXX

Explaining the alphabetical structure of this book, the question I have been asked more than any other is, of course: 'What are you going to do for X?' In his famous dictionary, Dr Johnson described 'X' as 'a letter which, though found in Saxon words, begins no word in the English language' and, despite every British child being introduced to the xylophone and the X-ray fish at an astonishingly tender age, it is true that the twenty-fourth letter is regarded as an exceptional, perplexing and exotic character.

'X' exerts an emotional force greater than the rest of the alphabet put together: it is a simple kiss and an ancient battlefield; the signature of the illiterate and of democracy itself; it marks the spot of hidden treasure and the source of forbidden pleasure; it symbolises Christ and the unknown. We react to the dramatic crossed strokes of the 'X' because they imply something extraordinary, mysterious or dangerous. 'X' is camouflage for taboos: the X-rated; the X-certificate; the XXXX!

It is that last aspect of Britain's X-factor that I wish to explore: the place of curses, oaths and swear words in British culture; the expletives that tell us far more about our status, our values and our heritage than simply whether we have a foul mouth. How one swears and how often are as indicative of class as top hats and shell suits.

The middle classes (who swear the least) are sometimes prone to cite pervasive working-class coarseness as evidence that Britain is bound for hell in a handcart. The commentator Theodore Dalrymple, a cheerleader for such views, recoils at the way he sees popular culture increasingly pandering to proletarian crudity. 'In Britain we have completely lost sight of the proper place of vulgarity in the moral and cultural economy,' he wrote recently. 'We have made it king when it should be court jester.'

Certainly, the media's access to and search for mass markets has seen the exploitation of the common curse: TV chefs marketed as much on their profanity as their profiterole; the clothing label French Connection selling its wares in Britain cheekily stamped 'FCUK'; beer marketed to lager louts with the boast that Australians 'wouldn't give a XXXX for anything else'; music and video releases so riddled with potentially offensive language that the industry has felt obliged to introduce a Parental Advisory Scheme.

All of this has encouraged new interest in the amount of swearing there really is in British conversation. Linguists recently assembled the wonderfully named Lancaster Corpus of Abuse, a huge collection of expletives filtered from the 100-million-word British National Corpus of written and spoken English. The average Brit, it emerges, uses eighty to ninety expletives every day, but some individuals are measured swearing more than 500 times a day. Ten taboo terms make up 80 per cent of swearing (you can work them out): the words 'bloody' and 'god' are most frequently employed by women, among men the most common expletive is 'f***ing'.

If there is air in cyberspace, it is probably blue: online chat room conversations have been found to include at least one obscenity every minute. The anonymity of the Internet, coupled with its separation from grounded cultural norms, frees consumers to express themselves in terms they would never use in face-to-face conversation.

Swearing has always been an international phenomenon and,

with the spread of global communication, is likely to become more so. There are a handful of places where you are still unlikely to hear expletives: traditionally American Indians don't swear, nor do the Japanese, Malaysians and most Polynesians. But the use of taboo words crosses continents and cultures. Tracking the origin of two of the most offensive English swear words, for example, involves a journey around Europe and back through centuries: the Old Norse *kunta*, the Middle Dutch *conte*, Old Frisian *kunte* and Latin *cunnus* suggest a mongrel parentage for one; the Old Icelandic *fjuka*, Old English *firk*, German *ficken*, and French *foutre* point to similarly cosmopolitan sources for the other.

The British, however, seem to have tapped the power of swearing more enthusiastically than other nations. There are no truly robust international comparisons, but one study looking at the word 'f***' in British and American conversation found it to be much more prevalent in the UK than the US. Analysing tens of millions of spoken words used on both sides of the Atlantic, the research found the f-word being employed twenty-eight times as often in Britain as America. What also emerged from the same study is a difference in the way swear words are utilised: the Americans chuck around expletives more forcefully; when they engage the f-word it tends to be violent. In Britain, we often employ taboo words with gentle insouciance; sprinkling them into our conversations in much the same way we splash vinegar onto our chips.

Swearing is part of British culture, with a rich historical and social back story. Long before there was an America, we were honing our skills. As a young boy, like millions who preceded me, I was caught sniggering at Chaucer's fruity vocabulary, juicy rebellious words that seemed at odds with the chalk-dust desiccation of a strict grammar school classroom. In *The Canterbury Tales*, the Parson reflects upon the widespread nature of medieval swearing in his discourse on the Seven Deadly Sins, upbraiding those who 'holden it a gentrie or a manly dede to swere grete othes' (think it is classy or macho to swear forcefully). Sermons from the period confirm that the clergy were concerned: 'Horible sweryinge, as the most parte of the pepull dose now-adaies' railed one priest.

The English historian Julian Sharman presented a vivid picture of medieval profanity in his book of 1884, *A Cursory History of Swearing*. Britain in the Middle Ages, he suggested, was a country 'inundated with a torrent of the most acrid and rasping blasphemy'. Swearing was the language of religious rebellion, a reaction against the political and juridical power of the church:

> Thus it was that, labouring under the ban of priestly exaction, and confronted on all sides by the ghostly emblems of wrath and condemnation, there descended upon England in the thirteenth and fourteenth centuries, a torrent of the hardest and direst of verbal abuse. Not mere words of intemperate anger came bubbling to the surface, but sullen and defiant blasphemies, execrations that proclaimed open warfare with authority and a lasting separation from everything that was tender in men's faith.

Swearing spanned the social spectrum, with the nobility appearing to take particular pride in a well-chosen expletive. Henry VIII swore regularly and, according to the anthropologist Ashley Montagu, his 10-year-old son Edward VI 'delivered himself of a volley of the most sonorous oaths' when ascending the throne in 1547. His half-sister Elizabeth I apparently swore 'like a man', with the essayist Nathan Drake suggesting that she made the 'shocking practice' fashionable, 'for it is said that she never spared an oath in public speech or private conversation when she thought it added energy to either.'

As with Chaucer, so there has been much schoolboy mirth in discovering rude words in Shakespeare texts. In *Twelfth Night*, for example, Malvolio analyses the handwriting in a letter he believes may have been penned by his mistress Olivia: 'By my life this is my lady's hand. These be her very C's, her U's and her T's and thus makes she her great P's.' Elizabethan audiences were expected to respond the same way as pupils in a modern English class, giggling at the c-word secreted in the text, and the reference to Olivia's 'great pees'.

Hamlet presents the paradox of sixteenth-century swearing. In Act III, the Prince asks Ophelia: 'Lady, shall I lie in your lap?' When rejected, he responds, 'Do you think I meant country matters?' (Cue much schoolboy tittering.) 'That's a fair thought, to lie between maids' legs,' Hamlet adds, Shakespeare determined no dozy student should miss the crude meaning of the Prince's question. But in Act II, Hamlet despairs at the obscenities dropping from his lips, horrified that he 'Must, like a whore, unpack my heart with words, And fall a-cursing like a very drab, A scullion!' Swearing was simultaneously the vice of princes and of prostitutes, kings and kitchen maids.

The lexicographer Eric Partridge once reflected on how the Bard's use of crudity compared with the profanity of class-ridden post-war Britain:

> Sexual dialogue between men is, no less in Shakespeare than in the smoking-room or -compartment, frank and often coarse: between members of the lower classes, both coarse and, often, brutal; between members of the middle class – well, we hear very little of that!; between aristocrats and other members of the upper and leisured class, it is still frank – it is frequently very frank indeed – but it is also witty.

In Shakespeare's day, taboo words were verbal weaponry engaged to display both the sharp wit of noblemen and the rough earthiness of peasants. Status was revealed, not by whether one swore, but how one swore. That was to change, however, with the arrival of the Puritans.

The dawn of the seventeenth century saw strict Protestant values become increasingly influential, a movement that resulted in the 1606 Act to Restrain Abuses of Players. The law made it an offence for any person in an interlude, pageant or stage play to use 'jestingly or profanely' the name of God, Jesus, the Holy Ghost or the Trinity. With a fine of £10 a time (£1,000 in today's money), plays written in the years after this date had little or no obvious profanity, although the legislation is credited with the spread of 'minced oaths' – shortened or altered swear words that could slip past the censor.

The linguistic strictures of the Puritans meant that, when the civil war sliced England in two, swearing became associated with the Royalist cause. The landed gentry would use taboo words, not as a rebellion against the authority of the church, but to put two fingers up to Cromwell and his Puritan Commonwealth. From 1660, with the restoration of the monarchy, England revelled in its freedom to curse once more. 'Odd's fish, I am an ugly fellow,' Charles II pointedly remarked on seeing a portrait of himself. A minced oath for God's face, 'odd's fish' was apparently the king's favourite expletive of many.

Like much of Europe in the late seventeenth and early eighteenth century, Britain was trying to work out how to maintain national stability in the face of bitterly divided religious communities. The general response was a more influential civil domain that introduced a code of secular values around notions of tolerance and restraint.

The shift of power from church to state also saw a shift in swearing habits. Expletives must offend almost by definition, so as blasphemy prosecutions dwindled, so did the use of blasphemous oaths. Instead, swearing became a reaction against the emergence of middle-class gentility. Sexual and excremental obscenities, previously regarded as rather mild profanities, became the most offensive.

The new elite middle class still hit its thumb with a hammer and lost its temper, but exasperation was increasingly met by euphemism, not obscenity. By Jingo! To swear publicly was to reveal oneself as uncivilised as the lower orders. Verbal gentility and self-control were the identification marks of high status, modesty central to the new manners.

Writing in *The Connoisseur* magazine in 1754, the dramatist George Colman revealed the class divide that had emerged.

> The shocking practice of Cursing and Swearing: a practice, which (to say nothing at present of its impiety and pro-faneness) is low and indelicate, and places the man of quality on the same level with the chairman at his door. A gentleman would forfeit all pretensions to that title, who should choose to embellish his discourse with the oratory of Billingsgate, and converse in the style of an oyster-woman.

The fish market at Billingsgate was regarded as the stinking core of British vulgarity. Samuel Johnson's dictionary explained it as 'a place where there is always a crowd of low people, frequent brawls and foul language'. The word 'Billingsgate' had its own definition: 'Ribaldry; foul language', reinforcing the link between swearing and the lower orders.

As the middle-class fashion for modesty spread (see 'T is for Toilet'), so it seems there was an equal and opposite increase in lavatorial crudity among the working classes. The simple word 'shit', which would have raised few eyebrows a century earlier, was scratched into walls of important public buildings by those who resented the power of the bourgeoisie. The word 'piss', which appeared in the authorised King James Bible ('eat their own dung, and drink their own piss': 2 Kings 18:27), gradually became loaded with vulgar association. The c-word, so casually planted in Elizabethan texts, was effectively exorcised from English literature for two hundred years.

With the Victorian era, concern that potentially offensive words might upset sensitive souls led to ludicrous examples of censorship. In *Wuthering Heights*, Emily Brontë makes the point when her character Mr Lockwood relates an encounter with Heathcliff: '"And you, you worthless—" he broke out as I entered, turning to his daughter-in-law, and employing an epithet as harmless as duck, or sheep, but generally represented by a dash.' The c-word on this occasion would appear to be cow.

In fact, *Wuthering Heights* was regarded as quite shocking: the word 'damn' appears twelve times, 'devil' twenty-seven times and on four occasions do characters beseech 'God's sake'. In the Editor's Preface, Emily's sister Charlotte recognises the gamble the novel takes with Victorian sensibilities: 'A large class of readers, likewise, will suffer greatly at the introduction into the pages of this work of words printed with all their letters, which it has become the custom to represent by the initial and final letter only – a blank line filling the interval. I may as well say at once that, for this circumstance, it is out of my power to apologise; deeming it, myself, a rational plan to write words at full length.'

George Bernard Shaw prompted inevitable outrage in 1914 when he highlighted the linguistic social divide in his lampoon on the British class system, *Pygmalion*. The character of flower-girl Eliza Doolittle, whose Cockney accent is transformed to that of a duchess, shocked middle-class theatre audiences by announcing in cut-glass tones: 'Walk! Not bloody likely. I am going in a taxi.' It was reported how, on the first night, the utterance of 'the word' was greeted by 'a few seconds of stunned disbelieving silence, and then hysterical laughter for at least a minute and a quarter'. Headlines suggested 'Threats by Decency League' and 'Theatre to be Boycotted'. The Bishop of Woolwich was apparently horrified.

Shaw's provocative tweaking of bourgeois verbal propriety heralded a period in which the coarse vocabulary of the working man became an international political issue. In 1923 Leon Trotsky wrote in *Pravda* of 'The Struggle for Cultured Speech': 'Swearing in our lower classes was the result of despair, embitterment, and above all, of slavery without hope and escape. The swearing of our upper classes, the swearing that came out of the throat of the gentry and of those in office, was the outcome of class rule, of slave-owners' pride, and of unshakeable power.' He encouraged Russian workers to 'do away radically with abusive speech'.

In France, the philosopher Pierre Bourdieu argued that, since French lower classes had neither the time nor the money to acquire refined speech, verbal gentility was used by the bourgeoisie to maintain the social hierarchy. But he also suggested that the working classes were, in a sense, complicit. 'Groups invest themselves totally, with everything that opposes them to other groups, in the common words which express their social identity, i.e. their difference.'

In pre-war Britain, the same things were happening. The middle classes were using their educational and financial advantage to clip their accent and vocabulary to shape their status. The working classes were asserting their identity by proudly demonstrating rich and often fruity vernacular. Swearing was recruited to the class struggle.

Key battles would be fought in the 1960s. The uncensored edition of D. H. Lawrence's explicit novel *Lady Chatterley's Lover*, published in 1960, three decades after it was written, included repeated examples of the f-word and the c-word. The obscenity trial that followed saw the jury return a 'not guilty' verdict.

In 1965, on a late night television arts show called *BBC-3*, the critic and literary manager of the National Theatre, Kenneth Tynan, was asked if he would allow a play in which sexual intercourse took place. 'Oh I think so certainly,' Tynan replied nonchalantly. 'I doubt if there are very many rational people in this world to whom the word "f***" is particularly diabolical or revolting or totally forbidden.' He was wrong. The BBC's switchboard was jammed with indignant callers and, as Tynan's widow Kathleen noted later, 'the episode for a few days eclipsed all other news, including the Unilateral Declaration of Independence in Rhodesia and the war in

Vietnam.' There were motions in the House of Commons demanding Tynan be prosecuted for obscenity and calls for the BBC's Director-General Sir Hugh Greene to resign. Despite the vehemence of the outcry, however, no heads rolled and the 1960s carried on swinging. In the *Guardian*, the journalist Stanley Reynolds asked why 'that one simple word of four letters can provoke a greater reaction in us than long and complex words like apartheid, rebellion, illegal, police state and treason'.

Deference to the Establishment and its bourgeois values was disintegrating. The alarm of the conservative middle classes was personified in the redoubtable Mary Whitehouse, a Shropshire schoolmistress who founded the National Viewers' and Listeners' Association and accused the BBC's Sir Hugh of being, more than anyone else, responsible for the 'moral collapse in this country'. But the wave of liberalism sweeping over Britain ultimately washed such protests aside. The taboos of the old order became the freedoms of the new; obscenity was, once again, employed as a weapon in the battle for social change.

In the February 1970 edition of the subversive *Oz* magazine, Germaine Greer described the fight for women's rights in deliberately provocative terms: 'The c*** must take the steel out of the cock and make it flesh again.' Feminist groups employed what were called 'semantic shock tactics', using acronyms like SCUM (Society for Cutting Up Men) and advocating revolution by 'f***ing up the system'.

In his *Anatomy of Swearing*, the anthropologist Ashley Montagu noted:

> Until recently swearing in women was negatively sanctioned as unfeminine and bypassed by the resort to emotional expression through weeping. With the growing emancipation of woman from her inferior status she has now altogether abandoned the privilege of swooning and has reduced the potential oceans of tears to mere rivulets.

Today, instead of swooning or breaking into tears, she will
often swear. It is, in our view, a great advance upon the old
style.

Swearing had become the argot of political and intellectual defiance, employed by a wave of British poets and writers including
Philip Larkin, Martin Amis and Jeanette Winterson. As well as
being stockpiled in the armoury of the liberals, expletives also
became ammunition in a generational struggle.

The 1960s had given a voice to teenagers and from their young
mouths poured some ancient oaths. When the Sex Pistols appeared
on television in 1976, the band was encouraged to demonstrate
their 'punk' credentials by presenter Bill Grundy. 'Go on,' he said,
'say something outrageous.' When guitarist Steve Jones replied by
calling him a 'dirty bastard', Grundy urged him to go further. 'Go
on, again,' he goaded.

'You dirty f***er,' Jones duly responded.

It was a sign of how the balance of power had shifted that Bill
Grundy's career was effectively destroyed by the incident while the
Sex Pistols went on to have a string of hits and a number one
album, *Never Mind the Bollocks*. Vulgarity was in vogue, an easy way
for those who made money from the teenage market to connect
with rebellious youth.

In the United States, where the language of the ghetto had a
more aggressive tone, taboo words were increasingly exploited by
the rap and hip hop groups of the 1980s and 90s. Members of the
Miami-based band 2 Live Crew were arrested by a Florida sheriff on
charges of obscenity after performing songs from their album *As
Nasty as They Wanna Be*. Among the tracks were 'Get The F*** Out
Of My House (Bitch)' and 'The F*** Shop', the lyrics of which were
defended at the trial by the prominent literary critic and black
intellectual Henry Louis Gates. He argued the profanity had important roots in African-American vernacular speech and should be
protected. The band was acquitted.

The assertive use of explicit American street vocabulary in the music charts pushed the boundaries in the UK. The f-word was losing its power to shock: when the mainstream romantic comedy *Four Weddings and a Funeral* opened in 1994 with Hugh Grant using eleven 'f***s' and a 'bugger' in the first few minutes, it was given a 15 certificate. Instead, the most potent taboo words were those which challenged the values of tolerance and liberalism that had licensed them.

When broadcasters and watchdog groups looked at British attitudes to swearing in a 2000 report entitled 'Delete Expletives', they noted 'an ever-increasing, but grudging, acceptance of the use of swearing and offensive language in daily life', but increasing concern at words used against minorities. 'Abuse – and especially racial abuse – is at the very top of the scale of severity and was felt to be unacceptable in today's society,' the report found. The c-word remained at the pinnacle of the offensiveness table, but the terms which had moved up the ranking were 'n****r' and 'P**i', 'whore' and 'slag'. Racist and sexist words were assuming the potency once found in excremental and religious obscenities.

Recently, the broadcasting regulator Ofcom conducted further research into public attitudes. 'There were mixed views on the use of the word "f***", which was considered more acceptable by some participants (e.g. younger people and male participants) but less acceptable by others (e.g. participants aged 55–75).' However, abusive discriminatory language was only seen as valid in an educational context and by some of the participants as 'unacceptable in any context'.

With that exception, cursing has become almost conventional, a quality that diminishes its strength like kryptonite on Superman. All but the most offensive terms may now be heard at a country house shoot, suburban dinner party or East End knees-up. The aristocracy and the working classes never gave up swearing – it is the middle class that appears to be changing its mind about profanity. Partly that is because sensibilities have changed, but perhaps it is also a reaction against the idea of being bourgeois. Casually dropping the odd f-word is thought by some to indicate street cred or classless cool.

As that expert on middle-class manners Charlotte Brontë put it: 'The practice of hinting by single letters those expletives with which profane and violent persons are wont to garnish their discourse, strikes me as a proceeding which, however well meant, is weak and futile.'

While I have felt compelled, with respect to the age and sensitivity of those who might stumble across this book, to disguise those words regarded as most offensive, the fashion is for exposure, to discard the camouflage granted by XXXX. To some that merely reflects the times, to others it is further proof that Britain is bound for hell in a handcart.

Y IS FOR YOUTH

When the angry young man kicked me, I couldn't help but think of the irony. His mate was busy punching my cameraman as others stamped on and smashed up his equipment. But despite the panic and the pain, the situation felt otherworldly: a curious, dramatic postscript on the story I was writing – how we have become frightened of our children.

This extract from a post on my BBC blog in 2008 prompted some, shall we say, less than sympathetic responses. The attack happened at the scene of a fatal teenage stabbing in north London, where I had gone to illustrate a television report about young people. *Time* magazine had just printed a front cover which read: 'Unhappy, Unloved and Out of Control – an epidemic of violence, crime and drunkenness has made Britain scared of its young'.

As the flashing fury in my assailant's face exploded in spittle-laden expletives, I understood the fear. I had inadvertently trespassed into a gang's private mourning. One of the 'crew' had died from a blade less than twenty-four hours before. Tearful young women comforted each other beside fresh

flowers laid at the spot. Brooding men sat on a wall, shock and
bewilderment in their eyes. I should have realised before
stumbling in. I was alien. From another world. And like the
immune system fighting infection, they rose up to defend
themselves.

The article attempted to unpick the often dysfunctional relationship between youth and adult society in the UK, a tension illustrated by some of the comments posted beneath it. 'Your blog reveals you as a far too tolerant person,' one contributor wrote. 'What they and nearly all adolescent males need is a healthy dose of fear of retribution.' Another concurred: 'I was a bad kid, I was naughty, but when I got caught I got the crap beated out of me and I never did it again, oh no. Kids just have no respect because parents these days are pathetic, I mean utterly and woefully pathetic.' One post, bemoaning the 'bloody liberals' who only want to 'mollycoddle' young people, demanded a return to caning and spanking, arguing 'that's what it'll take to check today's feral youth.'

Then, a little further down the list of comments, a response from a younger reader. 'I'm a teenager (don't be scared). I am sitting in my room, quietly, revising for tomorrow's Biology AS exam,' he wrote. 'By all means talk about the minority of bad adolescents, but remember the majority who are kind and polite. You may say you never see them, but it's because they are in their bedrooms, revising for the Biology exam tomorrow.'

Over the past twenty years, Britain's generation gap has been widened and deepened by the seismic forces released when prejudice meets panic. Outsiders find our relationship with young people oddly cruel, as I discovered when I went to see how one of our European neighbours responds to delinquency and youth crime.

Standing next to a teenager who is holding a large kitchen
knife, and knowing that she had previously stabbed her

sister, is as good a place as any to consider Britain's relationship with children who commit crime. I am in Finland, a country travelling down a very different philosophical road from Britain. While the UK locks up around 3,000 juvenile offenders, Finland's criminal justice system incarcerates just three. And the girl with the kitchen knife is not one of them.

My research had led me to a 'reform school' just outside Helsinki where troubled young people are helped through to adulthood. The girl with the knife was cutting onions in a cookery class. 'We do not think the proper way to take care of a child is by punishing the child,' the school director Kurt Kylloinen told me. 'You must believe in childhood and not let the child's misbehaviour deceive you. You must believe in the child and that's what we try to do in Finland, whatever the child does.'

Young people cannot be prosecuted until they are at least fifteen in Finland, although in practice very few youngsters under the age of twenty-one are dealt with by the justice system. In England, Wales and Northern Ireland the age of criminal responsibility is ten, among the lowest in the world. Scotland recently raised its minimum age from eight to twelve. When I explained that 10-year-olds are dealt with under the penal code in Britain, the reform school's psychologist Merja Ikalainen looked aghast.

MI: I don't have words for that. It sounds so horrible.

ME: You think it's immoral?

MI: It is.

ME: Why, if a young person knowingly commits a crime?

MI: That's not a young person. That's a child. They need care.

ME: But shouldn't a child have to suffer the consequences of their actions?

> MI: Suffer! You use words that sound really horrible. A
>   child shouldn't be suffering. The word 'suffer' sounds
>   really sad.

Over 60 per cent of the roughly 3,000 young people locked up at
any one time in the UK are known to have mental health problems.
In Finland such youngsters are more likely to be patients in well-
funded psychiatric units. Children who break the law are seen
primarily as welfare cases. When I went to Helsinki's main mall, I
could not find a single shopper who thought the state was 'too soft'
on juvenile offenders. One man, unshaven and heavily tattooed,
gave me this response to the idea that badly behaved teenagers need
punishment: 'That would be useless,' he said, shrugging.

It is not just the Finns with their tradition of pedagogy (from
the ancient Greek *paidagogeo*, 'to lead the child') who find British
attitudes to young people irrational and disturbing. The United
Nations Committee on the Rights of the Child has expressed its
concern at 'the general climate of intolerance and negative public
attitudes towards children, especially adolescents, which appears
to exist in the UK, including in the media, and may be often the
underlying cause of further infringements of their rights'.

The international criticism came after a period in which alarm
at the depiction of teenagers had led some influential British voices
to speak out. Senior police chiefs in England and Wales warned
that the demonisation of young people had become a national
problem. One chief constable said his force received hundreds of
thousands of complaints about young people every year, most of
whom were doing nothing more than 'simply existing or walking
down the street'. The man in charge of Scotland Yard's youth crime
division, Deputy Assistant Commissioner Brian Paddick, told the
press that activity that would have been called youthful exuber-
ance twenty years earlier was increasingly being described as
antisocial behaviour. A generational divide was opening up, driven
by fear.

In the spring of 2005, the giant Bluewater shopping centre in Kent announced it would evict young people wearing hooded tops and baseball caps because 'some of our guests don't feel at all comfortable'. A few months later, an inventor from Merthyr Tydfil in South Wales unveiled his 'mosquito', a sonic weapon which could be used by shops to repel 'rowdy teenage ne'er-do-wells' without being heard by 'law-abiding forty-somethings and septuagenarian war heroes'. Howard Stapleton came up with the device after his daughter had apparently been harassed by youths at the local shopping parade. He tested it in a grocery store in Barry; the screeching noise, unbearable to adolescent ears, could not be heard by mature adults. Sales of the mosquito flourished.

Newspapers were stuffed with stories illustrating the apparent threat from 'hooded gangs of teenage yobs'. The *Daily Express* advised its readers that 'gun-toting 8-year-olds are roaming the streets of Britain' and that 'Britain faces raising a generation of "urban child soldiers"'. Research found that in other European countries most citizens said they would intervene if they saw youngsters vandalising a bus shelter. In Britain barely a third agreed.

Britain was exhibiting all the symptoms of paedophobia, the irrational fear of children, routinely describing young people as feral animals or vermin. When the Conservative leader David Cameron suggested the problem might be more complicated, he was ridiculed. 'Cameron faces backlash for hoodie love-in,' screamed one tabloid. 'Extraordinary defence of hoodie-wearing yob teenagers,' said another. It is worth reminding ourselves what the Tory leader actually said.

Imagine a housing estate with a little park next to it. The estate has 'no ballgames' and 'no skateboarding' notices all over it. The park is just an empty space. And then imagine you are fourteen years old, and you live in a flat four storeys up. It's the summer holidays and you don't have any pocket money. That's your life. What will you get up to today? Take in a concert, perhaps? Go to a football game? Go to the seaside? No – you're talking £30 or £50 to do any of that. You can't kick a ball around on your own doorstep. So what do you do? You hang around in the streets, and you are bored, bored, bored. And you look around you. Who isn't bored? Who isn't hanging around because they don't have any money? Who has the cars, the clothes, the power?

It was a thoughtful and sympathetic view of the teenager, suggesting that the 'hoodie' was not the aggressive uniform of a rebel army of young gangsters but, for many youngsters, a way to stay invisible in the hostile environment of the street. Labour politicians, sensing that Cameron had taken the political risk of challenging widespread prejudice, branded his speech a 'hug-a-hoodie' plan. The *Daily Mail* noted that this 'breath-taking Tory u-turn on law and order' made no mention of punishing children and instead 'stresses the role of "compassion and kindness"'.

One might imagine that all this animosity was a consequence of an increase in teenage delinquency or youth crime. Certainly, there were plenty of press reports claiming there had been a steep rise in juvenile offending after 2003. But, as so often, the stories were based on questionable use of statistics – assuming that because police were arresting more young people, they must be committing more crimes.

When experts looked at what was really happening they uncovered 'net widening': children drawn into the youth justice system in circumstances that would previously have been dealt with outside it. Police, under public and political pressure to respond more aggressively to the perceived youth problem, had been set targets to make more arrests. Surprise, surprise, that is exactly what they did; handcuffing kids for activities that would once have prompted no more than a bit of avuncular advice from the local constable.

Up until the point that police forces in England and Wales were told to improve their 'offenders brought to justice' rate, recorded youth crime had been falling rapidly – down a quarter between 1992 and 2003. As soon as officers were told their performance would be measured by how many children they nicked, it started rising again. Official surveys of people's experience of crime did not suggest any increase – in fact, they showed the chances of being a victim falling throughout this period. It wasn't youth crime that was rising, but the criminalisation of the young.

The incidents of rioting that flared up like bush fires across England's inner cities in the summer of 2011 were swiftly blamed on gangs of youths, even though official records would show 73 per cent of those prosecuted were over eighteen and only 13 per cent were members of gangs. The government found itself under pressure to deal aggressively with what the press had characterised as juvenile anarchy and responded with a promise to 'name and shame' children found guilty of involvement. Of those youngsters dealt with by the courts, two thirds were classed as having special educational needs. The chief constable of the West Midlands, Chris Sims, was so concerned at the vilification of Britain's youth that he took the politically risky step of arguing, 'We must not at this time abandon all compassion for some of our very damaged young people who have been caught up in these incidents.'

How had twenty-first-century Britain reached this point, so hostile to its young that it had won an international reputation for callousness and cruelty? The answers are buried across the previous two centuries – the period in which the phrases 'juvenile delinquent', 'troubled adolescent' and 'problem teenager' were first coined.

In 1659, Samuel Pepys recorded how soldiers and a 'meeting of the youth', apprentices wishing to present a petition, squared up in the City of London. 'The boys flung stones, tiles, turnips etc. at [them] with all the affronts they could give them,' he wrote to a friend. A number of the young protestors were shot dead.

Despite such incidents, it wasn't until the early 1800s that youth came to be regarded as a distinctively threatening or subversive problem in Britain. With urbanisation and industrialisation, the job prospects for working-class boys had worsened: traditional craft apprenticeships disappeared while domestic service increasingly became the province of women. The end of the Napoleonic Wars saw demobilisation of thousands of soldiers, adding to the army of bored and troubled young men wandering city streets.

Britain suffered its first moral panic about youth crime at around this time. In London in 1815, the Society for Investigating the Causes of the Alarming Increase of Juvenile Delinquency in the Metropolis was set up. The committee identified 'the improper conduct of parents, the want of education, the want of suitable employment, the violation of the sabbath and habits of gambling in the public streets' as explanations for the youth problem, 'causes of crime' that in revised form are still trotted out today. Amid the social turmoil of the early nineteenth century, young men came to be associated with the anxieties of rapid change. British youth was to blame for drunkenness, vice, insubordination and rising crime.

It was the American psychologist G. Stanley Hall who introduced the concept of 'adolescence' in the 1900s, arguing that the biological changes associated with puberty drove problematic behaviour that was different from younger children and adults. He described it as a period of 'storm and stress', when young people demanded freedom but needed discipline. In Britain, Hall's theories were embraced as a scientific justification for an ever tougher line against the juveniles who threatened the established order. As it was, two world wars removed and then decimated the adolescent population, delaying the next round of moral panics until the 1950s.

Battered, bruised and broke, Britain surveyed the rubble-strewn post-war landscape and worried. There was particular concern that the damage had exposed national identity to contamination from foreign, particularly American, influence. Along with exotic clothes and loud music, a new word had crossed the Atlantic – teenager. It was a term that reawakened Establishment fears of the juvenile threat but, with the economy expanding, also inspired the development of a new financially independent subculture: simultaneously exciting and terrifying.

Over the next four decades, Teddy Boys, Bikers, Mods, Rockers, Hippies, Punks, Ravers and Grungers put two pubescent fingers up at authority in their own fashion and took delight in watching the staid grown-ups flinch and frown. Young people could cock a snook at their elders, confident that their consumer spending power gave them licence. Adults fretted at the collapse of deference and looked to the criminal justice system to restore order without damaging economic growth.

Wave after wave of youthful rebellion confirmed the cultural idea that teenagers equal trouble. Since younger people were either unable or unwilling to vote, getting tough with out-of-control juveniles was an easy political promise to make. Other countries were facing similar challenges, but in Britain the generational battle lines were scored into the social landscape as deeply as anywhere, and a storm was gathering.

On 12 February 1993, 2-year-old James Bulger wandered off from his mother in a Liverpool shopping mall. In the minutes that followed, security cameras captured him being led by the hand out of the New Strand Shopping Centre by two 'youths' as his mother frantically searched for him. Forty-eight hours later, the badly beaten body of the toddler was found on a railway line two miles away.

The *Daily Star* newspaper offered a £20,000 reward 'to trap the beasts who killed little James'. In the *Sun*, one commentator wrote: 'This is no time for calm. It is a time for rage, for blood-boiling anger, for furious venting of spleen.' The Prime Minister John Major, emphasising his tough stance on crime, told one tabloid that 'society needs to condemn a little more and understand a little less.' Within days his government announced plans to incarcerate children as young as twelve.

When police charged two 10-year-olds for the murder, Britain's anxiety over its relationship with its young boiled over. 'We will never be able to look at our children in the same way again,' said *The Sunday Times.* 'Parents everywhere are asking themselves and their friends if the Mark of the Beast might not also be imprinted on their offspring.'

The circumstances of James Bulger's death were highly unusual, but the crime prompted a political sea change in the treatment of children by the state – not only of those who offended but of those who simply misbehaved. Conservative toughness was matched every step of the way by Labour, a response later characterised as an arms race to control the nation's youth. Among Tony Blair's first acts upon entering Downing Street was to give adults access to legal sanctions for dealing with local children who didn't do what they were told.

The Crime and Disorder Act 1998 meant that any person over the age of ten in England and Wales who acted in a way likely to cause 'harassment, alarm or distress' could be subject to an ASBO – an antisocial behaviour order that, if breached, might see that youngster locked up. Tony Blair's enthusiasm for a zero-tolerance approach to youth nuisance saw the introduction of electronic tagging of 10-year-olds, dispersal orders, exclusion orders, referral orders and penalty notices.

A campaign demanding that young people show more respect to their elders and betters saw the Labour leader refer to what he saw as a pre-war golden age. 'My father, growing up,' Mr Blair said, 'didn't have as much money as we have, he didn't have the same opportunities, he didn't have travel or communications, but people behaved more respectfully to one another and people are trying to get back to that and most people want it.'

At around the same time, a UNICEF report found that

Britain's young people were the unhappiest in any of the world's rich nations. One of the authors blamed the UK's 'dog-eat-dog' society. The Archbishop of Canterbury described a nation gripped by panic, 'tone-deaf to the real requirements of children'.

The last few years have seen much hand-wringing as to how Britain has allowed the relationship between adult and adolescent to become so dysfunctional. In 2009 an independent inquiry panel made up of academics and child experts published a 'Good Childhood' report arguing for a significant change of heart in our society. It railed against the unkindness shown towards teenagers and of the need for 'a more caring ethic and for less aggression, a society more based upon the law of love'.

In government, David Cameron dismantled some of the legal architecture around antisocial behaviour in the hope that communities might re-engage with their young people, but I don't think it fanciful to suggest that generational segregation in Britain may actually have become a greater risk to the fabric of our nation than segregation by race, religion or class. A recent Whitehall report warned ministers that inter-generational prejudice and discrimination could become 'more directly hostile'. The little old lady shuffling to pick up her pension at the post office is intimidated by the group of youths 'hanging around' because she doesn't know any of them. Her grandchildren live miles away and the sinister teenagers in their caps and hooded tops look just like the 'gangs of yobs' her newspaper has been warning about.

I went to Burnley in Lancashire a few years ago to talk to the groups of young men loitering in barren shopping arcades. What emerged was a story of teenagers and adults living separate lives.

At a youth club where he does voluntary work, I asked 17-year-old Steven Jones how much time he spent with his parents. 'None,' he replied with a shrug. In the evening, he was

*out with his mates, returning home after his parents had gone
to bed. And in the morning?* 'No, because I just get up and go
out.'

British teenagers spend more time hanging around with their mates
than almost anywhere else in Europe. A survey of 15-year-old boys
found that in France and Switzerland just one in six said they spent
most evenings out with their peers. In Italy and Germany it was
roughly one in four. In England and Scotland it was about one in
two. Perhaps it should not be a surprise that the teenage pregnancy
rate is so high here. British adolescents often don't seem welcome in
their own homes. While one in ten Italian and French teenagers said
they rarely had a meal with their parents, in the UK the figure was
one in three.

I would understand all of this more if British youth were
going through a particularly defiant and unruly phase. But a recent
government-commissioned report found that standards of behaviour in English secondary schools were at their highest level for
thirty years; teenagers apparently do more charity work than any
other age group – ten times more likely to volunteer in their community than behave antisocially; the chance of being a victim of
youth crime is put at its lowest level since records began in the
early eighties. Where are the modern-day equivalents of rebellious
Mods or Hippies or Punks? In their bedroom, apparently, revising
for the Biology exam.

On a British question and answer site on the Internet, 13-year-
old Ellen asked: 'Why do people hate teenagers ...?' When you're
twelve everyone likes you but then the minute you turn thirteen
everyone hates you. I want people to like me, I'm nice!' Below,
Bethanne answered: 'This is because ages ago teens were smoking
and vandalising things (i.e. in the 1990s perhaps) and it has just
carried on through the years. I couldn't care less if the occasional
ignorant adult hated me: their loss. ☺'

It is 'their loss'. Britain has looked for someone to blame for the breakdown in its community life and, frightened to look in the mirror, has consistently pointed its accusatory finger at 'youth'. It should not be a surprise that sometimes 'youth' hits back.

> As the young man's swinging foot connected with my leg, I winced. He had hurt me. But not nearly as much as our society hurts some of its children.

Z IS FOR ZZZZ

And so to bed, as Pepys would have put it. My alphabet concludes with the soft hypnotic hum of sleep – the song of the winged god Hypnos, its notation a string of zeds.

The British have a paradoxical and troubled relationship with sleep. We spend probably twenty-five years in the Land of Nod, a third of our lives, and yet we are suspicious of the territory, anxious that others might think us indulgent for spending too long strolling its quiet bye-ways, afraid to admit we fancy a snooze. The work ethic of our Protestant heritage associates sleep with sloth.

Simultaneously, we fret that we don't get enough. A survey by pollsters MORI recently found that four out of ten Brits thought they suffered from too little rest, a figure that rose to more than half of those aged between thirty-five and forty-four. The results pointed to a frenzied subset of British society, desperately trying to keep functioning amid fears they were suffering severe sleep deprivation. The kind of person most likely to be trapped by this sleep paradox, it turns out, is a female executive juggling family life with a full-time career in London: 'superwoman', it appears, is constantly knackered.

Other nationalities and cultures don't share our hang-up about sleep. The Spanish *siesta*, the German *mittagspause*, the

Chinese *wujiao*, the Indian *bhat-ghum* – rest has a revered place within the daily routine of millions. Often it is about avoiding the hottest part of the day, but by embracing and celebrating slumber, sleep loses its association with idleness or indolence. For the British, however, there is shame in being caught napping.

The association between sleep and sloth was cemented in the furnace of nineteenth-century industrial expansion. The Scottish surgeon and philosopher Robert Macnish noted in his book of 1830, *The Philosophy of Sleep*, how 'the sluggard wastes the most beautiful period of life in pernicious slumber.' He identified a class divide, contrasting the 'rich, lazy and gormandizing citizen who will sleep twelve or thirteen hours at a time' with 'the hard-working peasant' who was content with seven or eight.

Macnish's Protestant Glasgow upbringing infused his passionate patronage of the early riser. 'The husbandman is up at his labour, the forest leaves sparkle with drops of crystal dew, the flowers raise their rejoicing heads towards the sun, the birds pour forth their anthems of gladness; and the wide face of creation itself seems as if awakened and refreshed from a mighty slumber.'

Compare that with his description of the sluggard:

> He yawns, stretches himself, and stalks into the breakfast parlour, to partake in solitude, and without appetite, of his unrefreshing meal – while his eyes are red and gummy, his beard unshorn, his face unwashed, and his clothes disorderly, and ill put on. Uncleanliness and sluggishness generally go hand in hand; for the obtuseness of mind which disposes a man to waste the most precious hours of existence in debasing sleep, will naturally make him neglect his person.

Victorian Britain, eagerly building an empire, endorsed the idea that sleep was the potential enemy of industry. The bedroom, previously a domestic showpiece into which visitors would be invited, became a private retreat for the seven or eight hours of rest required to prepare for the morrow. The bed itself, once an opportunity for the wealthy to exhibit their status with magnificent drapes, luxurious feather-filled pillows and decorative frames, shrunk down to a modest and functional object. To this day, UK bed sizes reflect nineteenth-century attitudes. A standard double is an inch narrower than most European equivalents, and the width of a British king-size bed is a full fifteen inches less regal than its continental cousin. The bed was stripped of anything that could be regarded as indulgent: a practical solution to the inconvenient necessity of sleep.

The shift from a rural to urban lifestyle, coupled with a culture that imbued sleep with a moral dubiety, meant Britain found it increasingly difficult to nod off. Charles Dickens would observe the nocturnal fretfulness of city inhabitants as he wandered the streets of London suffering from his own insomnia. Dickens' personal remedy was a bed that pointed northwards, in which he would sleep exactly in the middle, his arms outstretched and with each hand equidistant from the edge. More conventional Victorian insomnia cures included quantities of gin, laudanum (opium mixed with alcohol) and cannabis, prescribed for the Queen herself by the Royal Physician to assist sleep.

In 1894 the British Medical Journal worried at the nation's sleeplessness.

> The hurry and excitement of modern life is held to be responsible for much of the insomnia of which we hear; and most of the articles and letters full of good advice to live more quietly and of platitudes concerning the harmfulness or rush and worry. The pity of it is that so many people are unable to follow this good advice and are obliged to lead a life of anxiety and high tension.

As if to emphasise the point, the following year the Prime Minister, the Earl of Rosebery, resigned, blaming chronic insomnia as the main reason. 'I cannot forget 1895,' he would write later. 'To lie, night after night, staring wide awake, hopeless of sleep, tormented in nerves . . . is an experience which no sane man with a conscience would repeat.'

It is often suggested that contemporary Britain is suffering a similar waking nightmare, that the rigours of our 24/7 culture have left us bleary-eyed victims of sleep deprivation. As on so many issues, newspapers are prone to argue that if only we were to return to the habits of the days of empire, when British adults spent a healthy nine hours a night between the sheets, all would be well. And as so often, it is nostalgia for a myth.

It turns out that the key piece of research, trotted out again and again as proof that our recent ancestors slept much more, was actually published in 1913 by two psychologists at Stanford University in California, Lewis Terman and Adeline Hocking. The clue to why their paper might not provide a complete picture of early twentieth-century sleeping habits is in its main title: 'The Sleep of School Children'. Yes, this was a piece of work trying to find the optimum amount of shut-eye for kids. It measured the sleep of American 6-year-olds (average 11 hours 14 minutes) and college students (average 7 hours 47 minutes), figures that match up pretty closely with the amount of sleep children and young healthy adults get in Britain today.

The belief that we are a nation reeling from an increasing epidemic of sleep disorders is too widely held to be undermined by mere evidence. The results of a survey published by the Mental Health Foundation in 2010 were held up as further proof in the papers: 'Sleep-deprived Britain: Two thirds of us suffer from debilitating insomnia'; 'How worn-out Britain finally woke up to its chronic sleep problem'. The poll appeared to confirm the accepted wisdom that our twenty-first-century lifestyle was destroying our slumber. More than a cursory glance at the research, however, revealed that the headlines were nonsense.

'Some caution should be used when discussing the results of

this survey,' the researchers themselves advised, adding that the sample 'cannot be truly representative of the UK population'. The reason for extreme circumspection was that the poll had been conducted on the website of Sleepio, an online resource specifically aimed at people with sleep problems. 'Take just five minutes to answer our survey and you'll get a free tailored report on the state of your sleep,' worried readers were informed. What seems surprising (given the likely users of the site) is not that two thirds of those who filled out Sleepio's questionnaire thought they had a problem sleeping, but that a third did not!

The evidence that Britain's sleep patterns are much worse than they were a century ago is thin. The bulk of research shows that, on average, UK adults get a healthy seven-and-a-half to eight hours a night. Middle-aged, middle-class professionals juggling stressful jobs and demanding children probably manage a bit less, and that, of course, is the demographic of the people who edit national newspapers.

There are plenty of people out to convince us we should feel guilty about not getting enough sleep, just as two centuries ago there were plenty of people out to convince Britain it should feel guilty about getting too much. Our relationship with slumber has been turned on its head.

When the economy was primarily agricultural and ruled by the sun, the rhythm of sleep was in simple time – two beats in the bar, up at dawn and down at dusk. Variation was orchestrated by the four seasons. As Robert Macnish explained, 'some of the circumstances which induce us to sit up late and rise early in summer, are wanting during winter; and we consequently feel disposed to lie longer in bed during the latter season of the year.'

With the birth of the metropolis, the rhythm became more complex, a syncopated beat that drifted away from the natural tempo of the rising and setting sun. On 28 January 1807, the world's first street lighting with gas was illuminated in London's Pall Mall. Three years later, Humphry Davy demonstrated the first arc lamp to the Royal Institution, as British inventors competed to achieve the light bulb moment.

We can argue whether it was Scotsman James Lindsay's electrical device demonstrated to a public meeting in Dundee in 1835 that constituted the first incandescent light bulb, or if Sunderland inventor Joseph Swan should get the credit for developing the first successful 'filament electric lamp' publicly demonstrated on Tyneside in 1878. History books will tell you it was American Thomas Edison who patented the first practical and commercial design in 1879, but most overlook the fact that the world's first light bulb factory was established by Swan at Benwell in Newcastle. In the late nineteenth century, it was Britain that was doing its best to disrupt the sleep patterns of the world.

The United States, however, can legitimately claim to have invented '24-hour convenience', an oxymoronic concept which would soon cross the Atlantic to meddle with British body clocks. Its origins can be traced to Austin, Texas in the autumn of 1962, when the local college football team, the Longhorns, was having a successful season. One Saturday night after the game, a 7-Eleven store nearby found itself so busy with jubilant young fans that it never closed. The manager spotted a gap in the market and began opening the shop twenty-four hours a day, an idea that quickly spread to other outlets in Dallas, Fort Worth and Las Vegas, before sweeping the planet.

Defying the conventions of sleep became part of the youth revolution of the 1960s. Californian teenager Randy Gardner made the point by staying awake for eleven days in 1964, the longest anyone has been recorded going without sleep. 'Mind over matter,' he told reporters as he shrugged off to bed. In Britain the same year, the Beatles sang of 'working like a dog' when they should have been 'sleeping like a log' – 'A Hard Day's Night' was the flip side of rocking around the clock.

Teenagers sought to overcome the demands of sleep; the Mod drug of choice was amphetamine, used to fuel all-night dances at clubs like The Twisted Wheel in Manchester. But they still had to go to work on Monday morning so, along with the uppers, were the downers, as a generation attempted to recalibrate their body clocks.

In the consumer revolution that followed, sleep came to be regarded as a commodity like any other. Science had begun to unlock its secrets: in 1971 the *New Scientist* magazine reported on the 'trendy' research being conducted by Ian Oswald at Edinburgh University – 'sweeping away a lot of myths which for a long time surrounded sleep and dreaming'. The man who would become known as a founding father of sleep research had spent much of the 1960s unravelling the mysteries of dreams and the effects of sleeping tablets, slimming pills and recreational drugs.

Money soon began to pour into what was dubbed a new clinical discipline, much of it from pharmaceutical companies who were wide awake to the potential profits from sleep. Products promising users the power to defy nature, to control their sleeping and waking, became big business in a world encouraged to feel anxious about its hectic lifestyle. The scientific community, though, was torn: some believed the new designer drugs were an answer to the suffering associated with 24/7 demands; others feared corporate greed was driving a dishonest and dangerous pill-pushing racket.

Ian Oswald and colleagues of mine at the BBC's *Panorama* programme found themselves caught up in the row amid reports that the sleeping pill Halcyon, made by the American pharmaceutical firm Upjohn, was addictive and linked to memory lapses. They suggested the drugs company had covered up and lied about evidence of side effects, accusations vigorously denied by the executives at Upjohn's headquarters in Kalamazoo, Michigan.

It all ended in London's High Court in May 1994, the culmination of a long-running libel trial. Justice Sir Anthony May ruled in favour of Upjohn but, illustrating the passions generated by the issue, both Ian Oswald and Upjohn physician Royston Drucker were also obliged to pay damages to each other for libellous remarks. The case exemplified the furious debate that had begun to rage over humankind's quest to become the master rather than the servant of sleep.

There are now an estimated 13 million prescriptions for sleeping pills issued each year in Britain, as the nation looks to the medicine cabinet for help in dropping off. At the same time, sales of 'energy drinks' to keep people awake have been soaring. Analysts reckon Britain spends a billion pounds a year on cans and bottles fizzing with stimulants. Coffee is also a billion-pound-a-year product, with corporate cafe chains barging their way on to every high street for a slice of the action.

It has become relatively normal to begin the day with a jolting Americano and to close it with a dose of Zopiclone: from A to Z where once it was simply dawn 'til dusk. This cocktail of tranquilisers and stimulants, however, has left Britain a restless place, nervous about messing up the balance between alertness and tiredness. To the rescue have come an army of sleep consultants, experts to advise us on 'fatigue management solutions'.

The MetroNaps EnergyPod, for example, is marketed as the answer for stressed-out city executives who currently 'seek rest in places not intended for it: at their desk, in a conference room, a parked car or even a bathroom'. Instead, they could rejuvenate with a power nap in a machine apparently based on years of research and thousands of design hours. Lie back on what looks like a dentist's chair, your head enveloped by a huge dome, and let the soft lights and music guide you on a short round-trip to the unconscious world. The brainchild of a banker who said he kept finding colleagues asleep in lavatory cubicles and store cupboards, the pods have apparently been installed in a number of London city firms, bosses persuaded that the monthly rental is less than the increased productivity.

The phrase 'power nap' reinforces the idea that success comes with the ability to control sleep. Winston Churchill, John F. Kennedy, Margaret Thatcher, Ronald Reagan, Bill Clinton and Tony

Blair were all power-nappers, we are told, insisting on a short and intense rest period in the afternoon that recharged their batteries and invigorated their minds. I once sat on a train with Pierre-Yves Gerbeau, the French businessman who had been asked by Tony Blair to rescue the Millennium Dome project. As the Eurostar sped through the Pas-de-Calais, his aides informed me that PY would now take a nap. With that, M. Gerbeau closed his eyes and sat trance-like in his seat. After precisely ten minutes he opened his eyes once more and continued the conversation, apparently refreshed. It was hard not to be impressed.

The French have had quite an influence on our thinking about sleep. The geophysicist Jean-Jacques d'Ortous de Mairan was the first to discover circadian rhythms in 1729. In the 1950s and 60s, the neurobiologist Michel Jouvet led the way on sleep research, organising the first international symposium on the subject in France in 1963. He is likely to be remembered, though, for events twenty-five years later when he was the director of a laboratory at the pharmaceutical firm Group Lafon. There he made a break-through hailed as a great French discovery, a drug that promised to give us greater mastery over sleep than ever before.

Professor Jouvet had adapted an anti-depressant to make a pill, he said, which did away with the need for rest. He took it him-self to test its properties and claimed it made him super-productive without any apparent side effects. His baccalaureate students also tried the new drug and were said to have seen a marked improve-ment in their capacity for revision, able to stay awake for sixty hours at a stretch with little or no decline in their cognitive per-formance. What made Modafinil such an advance on previous stimulants, though, was that it caused virtually no noticeable rebound. Users didn't need to make up for lost sleep.

The potential of the drug was quickly recognised, not least by the military. At an international defence meeting in Paris, Professor Jouvet told generals that Modafinil could keep an army on its feet and fighting for three days and nights with no major side effects.

The Pentagon was all ears. A $3 billion programme to develop a 'Metabolically Dominant Soldier' was already investigating how to keep US troops in combat for long periods without sleep. It had, for instance, been researching how dolphins manage to send half of their brain to sleep at a time with the hope, presumably, that soldiers might learn to do the same. Now, it was suggested, the answer wasn't in Flipper. It was in France.

British forces were equally intrigued. The Ministry of Defence paid the military technology company Qinetiq to investigate the potential of Modafinil, sold in the UK under the name Provigil. Large orders were placed for tablets just before the invasions of Afghanistan and Iraq in 2001 and 2002. The MoD denied the drugs were being tested on soldiers, but Qinetiq scientist Dr Anna Casey told a committee of MPs in 2005 that 'one is always looking for something that would give military personnel an extra edge.' Modafinil, she confirmed, had been 'shown to enhance physical and mental performance'.

The official line from British defence chiefs was that the pills were purchased for legitimate clinical reasons, prescribed to soldiers suffering from narcolepsy or sleep apnoea, but word was spreading that scientists had come up with a wonder drug. High-powered city traders were among the first to bring supplies to the UK, eager to exploit a product that meant they could operate at full throttle on just a couple of hours' sleep a night.

Students too were quick to spot the potential benefits. The University of York student website ran interviews with Modafinil users in 2009. 'In a typical Modafinil-fuelled night, I take the drug with dinner, go to the pub with my friends and maybe watch a film, before getting in at around 1am and working for another eight hours. It's a productive way of living; it lets me be sociable and academic at the same time,' said Tim. Charles explained the effects. 'People talk about the Modafinil buzz, but there's no high in the traditional sense. I was able to concentrate more easily, like my memory was improved. I could stay awake all night and do nothing but work without getting bored. I wasn't "high" so much as "enhanced".

There were side effects, of course: fever, sore throat and nausea. A few users developed potentially fatal skin diseases and the manufacturers were obliged to update the label to include warnings of the possibility of developing Stevens-Johnson Syndrome or toxic epidermal necrolysis. No one could yet know the long-term effects of use. But it did appear that science had stumbled upon a relatively safe answer to an ancient puzzle. Modafinil, though, also posed a new question: how will humanity use its power over sleep?

My guess is that, in this country at least, a sleepless world would sound too much like a restless world – a relentless environment in which 'Metabolically Dominant Citizens' forget the guilty pleasure of a quiet doze in a deckchair or forty winks while pretending to watch the cricket. Britain may worry about being seen to have too much or too little of the stuff, but we have got enough to keep us awake at night without taking on the responsibilities of the great god Hypnos. And so to bed. Zzzz.

FURTHER READING

A is for Alcohol

1. C. MacAndrew and R. B. Edgerton, *Drunken Comportment: A Social Explanation* (Aldine, 1969)
2. R. Martínez and L. Martín, 'Patrones de consume de alcohol en la comunidad de Madrid', *Comunidad y Drogas*, 5–6 (1987)
3. Social Issues Research Group, *Social and Cultural Aspects of Drinking: A Report to the Amsterdam Group* (SIRC, 1998)
4. G. A. Marlatt, B. Demming and J. B. Reid, 'Loss of control drinking in alcoholics: an experimental analogue', *Journal of Abnormal Psychology*, 81 (1973)
5. M. Hough, *Drugs Misuse and the Criminal Justice System: A Review of the Literature*, (Home Office, 1996)
6. D. B. Heath, 'Flawed policies from flawed premises: pseudo-science about alcohol and drugs', in R. C. Engs (ed.), *Controversies in the Addictions Field* (Kendall-Hunt, 1990)

B is for Bobbies

1. History of the Metropolitan Police, www.met.police.uk
2. R. V. G. Clarke and M. Hough, *Crime and Police Effectiveness* (HMSO, 1984)

3. M. Davis, 'Fortress Los Angeles: The Militarization of Urban Space' in M. Sorkin (ed.), *Variations on a Theme Park: The New American City and the End of Public Space* (Hill and Wang, 1992)

4. G. Kelling, A. Pate, D. Dieckman and C. Brown, *The Kansas City Preventive Patrol Experiment* (Police Foundation, 1972)

C is for Cheese

1. M. Thatcher, Speech at Franco-British Council Dinner, 16 May 1982, www.margaretthatcher.org

2. D. B. Grigg, *The Agricultural Systems of the World: An Evolutionary Approach* (Cambridge University Press, 1974)

3. Anthony Woodward, 'Design Dinosaurs: 11: Lymeswold', *Independent on Sunday*, 10 April 1994

4. Sir Stephen Roberts obituary, *Daily Telegraph*, 19 July 2002

5. *Authenticity in Food and Drinks: New Insights into Consumer Attitudes and Behaviors* (Datamonitor, 2006), www.datamonitor.com

6. British Cheese Board, www.britishcheese.com

7. Capricorn Goats Cheese, www.capricorngoatscheese.co.uk

D is for Dogs

1. A. C. Swinburne, *Mary Stuart: A Tragedy* (Chatto & Windus, 1881)

2. E. Kienzle, 'A comparison of the feeding behavior and the human–animal relationship in owners of normal and obese dogs', *The Journal of Nutrition*, 128 (1998)

3. Canine obesity, www.csp.org.uk

4. Medical and legal implications of veterinary cosmetic surgical procedures, www.animalmedcenter.com

5. Pet Food Manufacturers Association statistics, www.pfma.org.uk

6. R. B. Lee, *A History and Description of the Modern Dogs of Great Britain and Ireland* (Horace Cox, 1893)

7. J. H. Walsh, *The Dog, in Health and Disease, by Stonehenge* (Longman, 1859)
8. A. Manning and J. A. Serpell, *Animals and Human Society: Changing Perspectives* (Routledge, 1994)
9. W. Secord, *A Social History of the Dog in Art* (Antique Collectors' Club, 1992)
10. *Report from the Select Committee of the House of Lords on Rabies in Dogs* (Parliamentary Papers, 1887)
11. N. Pemberton and M. Worboys, *Mad Dogs and Englishmen: Rabies in Britain, 1830–2000* (Palgrave Macmillan, 2007)

E is for Error

1. PRCA membership statistics, www.prca.org.uk
2. B. Engel, *The Power of Apology* (John Wiley & Sons, 2001)
3. A. Massie, 'The art of saying sorry', *Independent*, 30 September 2004
4. A. Boin, P. Hart, E. Stern and B. Sundelius, *The Politics of Crisis Management: Public Leadership under Pressure* (Cambridge University Press, 2005)
5. J. Grout and L. Fisher, *What Do Leaders Really Do?* (John Wiley & Sons, 2007)
6. A. Barry, *Political Events* (University of London, 2002)
7. C. Hood, *The Blame Game: Spin, Bureaucracy and Self-preservation in Government* (Princeton University Press, 2011)

F is for Family

1. *Social Justice Policy Group, Breakthrough Britain: Ending the Costs of Social Breakdown* (Centre for Social Justice, 2007), www.centreforsocialjustice.org.uk
2. *The UK Family: In Statistics* (BBC/ICM, 2007)
3. J. Bowlby, *Forty-four Juvenile Thieves: Their Characters and Home-life* (Baillière, Tindall & Cox, 1946)
4. R. Berthoud, 'Family formation in multi-cultural Britain: diversity and change', in G. Lowry, T. Modood and S. Teles (eds.),

Ethnicity, Social Mobility and Public Policy (Cambridge University Press, 2005)

5. L. Platt, *Ethnicity and family: Relationships within and between ethnic groups: an analysis using the Labour Force Survey* (Institute for Social & Economic Research, 2009)

6. A. Giddens, 'Family', *Runaway World* (BBC Reith Lectures, 1999)

7. P. Thane, *Happy Families? History and Family Policy* (British Academy, 2010)

8. *Doing Better for Children* (OECD, 2009), www.oecd.org

G is for Grass

1. F. L. Olmsted, *Walks and Talks of an American Farmer in England* (Harvard University, 1852)

2. *Report of the Select Committee on Public Walks* (Parliamentary Papers, 1833)

3. J. C. Loudon, *The Utility of Agricultural Knowledge to the Sons of the Landed Proprietors of Great Britain, &c., by a Scotch Farmer and Land-Agent* (1809)

4. J. C. Loudon, *Hints for Breathing Places for Metropolis, and for Country Towns and Villages, on Fixed Principles* (Longman, Rees, Orome, Brown and Green, 1829)

5. A. F. Prévost, *Mémoires et aventures d'un homme de qualité qui s'est retiré du monde* (M.G. Merville & J. Vander Kloot, 1728)

6. *Down with the Fences: Battles for the Commons in South London* (Past Tense Publications, 2004)

7. Urban Task Force, *Green Spaces, Better Places* (DTLR, 2002)

8. D. Tibbatts, *Your Parks: The Benefits of Parks and Greenspace* (Urban Parks Forum, 2002)

9. M. L. Gothein, *History of Garden Art* (J. M. Dent & Son, 1913)

10. A. Bottomley and N. Moore, 'From walls to membranes: fortress polis and the governance of urban public space in twenty-first-century Britain', *Law and Critique*, 18 (2007)

11. Select Committee on Environment, Transport and Regional

Affairs, *Town and Country Parks* (TSO, 1999), www.publications. parliament.uk

H is for Happiness

1. J. Stiglitz, A. Sen and J.P. Fitoussi, *Report by the Commission on the Measurement of Economic Performance and Social Progress* (2009)

2. *The Istanbul Declaration* (OECD, 2007), http://www.oecd.org

3. D. Cameron, 'The next age of government', TED conference, 16 February 2010, www.ted.com

4. P. Noonan, 'There is no time, there will be time', *Forbes ASAP*, 30 November 1998

5. *Declaration on Social Progress and Development* (United Nations, 1969), www.un.org

6. D. Kahneman, E. Diener and N. Schwarz, *Well-Being: The Foundations of Hedonic Psychology* (Russell Sage Foundation, 1999)

7. Strategy Unit, *Life Satisfaction: The State of Knowledge and Implications for Government* (Cabinet Office, 2002), www.nationalarchives.gov.uk

8. R. Layard, *Happiness: Lessons from a New Science* (Penguin, 2005)

I is for Immigration

1. R. Brown, 'Racism and immigration in Britain', *International Socialism Journal*, 68 (1995)

2. 'Citizenship: A History of People, Rights and Power in Britain', The National Archives, www.nationalarchives.gov.uk

3. G. Clayton, *Textbook on Immigration and Asylum Law* (Oxford University Press, 2010)

4. I. R. G. Spencer, *British Immigration Policy since 1939: The Making of Multi-racial Britain* (Routledge, 1997)

5. B. Carter, C. Harris and S. Joshi, 'The 1951–55 Conservative Government and the racialisation of black immigration', *Policy Papers in Ethnic Relations*, 11 (1987)

6. Home Office, *Secure Borders, Safe Haven: Integration With Diversity in Modern Britain* (TSO, 2002)

7. M. Prestwich, *Edward I* (University of California Press, 1988)

8. *Cabinet Papers 1946–68*, The National Archives, www.nationalarchives.gov.uk

9. Andrew Neather, 'Don't listen to the whingers – London needs immigrants', *London Evening Standard*, 23 October 09

J is for Justice

1. P. Colquhoun, *A Treatise on the Police of the Metropolis* (H. Fry for C. Dilly, 1795)

2. W. Allen and Y. Barzel, 'The evolution of criminal law and police during the industrial revolution', *Working Papers* (Simon Fraser University, 2007)

3. Justice Committee, *The Crown Prosecution Service: Gatekeeper of the Criminal Justice System* (House of Commons, 2009)

4. R. Reiner, 'Media-made criminality: the representation of crime in the mass media', in M. Maguire, R. Morgan and R. Reiner (eds.), *The Oxford Handbook of Criminology* (Oxford University Press, 2007)

5. P. Murray, *Signal Crimes: Risk Perception and Behaviour* (ODPM, 2004), www.communities.gov.uk

K is for Knives

1. 'Tackling Knives Action Programme (TKAP) Fact Sheet', The National Archives (2008) www.nationalarchives.gov.uk

2. No to Knives campaign launch, The National Archives (2008) www.nationalarchives.gov.uk

3. M. Easton, 'Knife "fact sheet": the e-mail trail', BBC, 5 March 2009, www.bbc.co.uk

L is for Learning

1. A. Wolf, *Does Education Matter? Myths about Education and Economic Growth* (Penguin, 2002)

2. *Leitch Review of Skills* (HM Treasury, 2006), www.nation-alarchives.gov.uk
3. Table A3.3, *Education at a Glance* (OECD, 2011), www.oecd.org
4. B. Bloom, *Taxonomy of Educational Objectives, Handbook 1: Cognitive Domain* (David O. McKay, 1956)
5. Antonio Di Vittorio, *An Economic History of Europe: From Expansion to Development* (Routledge, 2006)
6. D. S. Landes, *The Unbound Prometheus: Technological Change and Industrial Development in Western Europe from 1750 to the Present* (Cambridge University Press, 2003)
7. I. Brinkley, *The Knowledge Economy: How Knowledge Is Reshaping the Economic Life of Nations* (The Work Foundation, 2008)
8. R. B. Freeman, 'The great doubling: the challenge of the new global labor market' in J. Edwards (ed.) *Ending Poverty in America: How to Restore the American Dream* (The New York Press, 2007)
9. D. Tapscott and A. D. Williams, *Wikinomics: How Mass Collaboration Changes Everything* (Atlantic Books, 2007)

M is for Murder

1. C. Dexter, *Last Bus to Woodstock* (Macmillan, 1975)
2. F. Brookman and M. Maguire, *Reducing Homicide: A Review of the Possibilities* (Home Office, 2003)
3. *Homicides, Firearms and Intimate Violence* (Home Office, 2011)
4. D. Sethi, K. Hughes, M. Bellis *et al.* (eds.), *European Report on Preventing Violence and Knife Crime Among Young People* (World Health Organization, 2010)
5. P. Spierenburg, *A History of Murder: Personal Violence in Europe from the Middle Ages to the Present* (Polity, 2008)
6. F. Brookman, *Understanding Homicide* (SAGE Publications, 2005)
7. D. Freedman and D. Hemenway, 'Precursors of lethal violence: a death row sample' *Social Science and Medicine*, 50 (2000)

8. J. Gilligan, *Violence: Reflections on our Deadliest Epidemic* (Jessica Kinsley, 1999)

9. C. Lombroso, *L'Uomo delinquente* (Hoepli, 1876)

10. C. Goring (ed.), *The English Convict: A Statistical Study* (HMSO, 1913)

11. J. Blau and P. Blau, 'The cost of inequality: metropolitan structure and violent crime', *American Sociological Review*, 47 (1982)

12. M. Gottfredson and T. Hirschi, *A General Theory of Crime* (Stanford University Press, 1990)

N is for Numbers

1. J. Best, *Damned Lies and Statistics: Untangling Numbers from the Media, Politicians and Activists* (University of California Press, 2001)

2. J. Straw, Speech to Royal Statistical Society, 25 April 1995, www.rss.org.uk

3. *Statistics: A Matter of Trust* (TSO, 1998)

4. *Fundamental Principles of Official Statistics* (United Nations, 1994), www.un.org/en

5. *Report of the Rayner Review* (HMSO, 1981)

6. *Statistics Commission Annual Report 2007–08* (TSO, 2008), www.official-documents.gov.uk

7. History of the UK Statistical System, www.statisticsauthority.gov.uk

8. E. Pickles, 'Townhall Waste and Duplication', speech at Hammersmith & Fulham Townhall, 13 October 2010, www.communities.gov.uk/speeches

O is for Opium

1. R. Lart, 'British medical perception from Rolleston to Brain: changing images of the addict and addiction', *International Journal on Drug Policy*, 3 (1992)

2. R. Coomber, *The Control of Drugs and Drug Users* (Harwood Academic, 1998)

3. D. Bewley-Taylor, *The United States and International Drug Control, 1909–1997* (Continuum International Publishing Group, 2001)

4. H. G. Levine, 'The secret of worldwide drug prohibition: the varieties and uses of drug prohibition', *Independent Review*, 7 (2002)

5. W. B. McAllister, *Drug Diplomacy in the Twentieth Century: An International History* (Routledge, 2000)

6. J. Strang and M. Gossop, *Heroin Addiction and the British System: Treatment and Policy Responses* (Routledge, 2005)

7. *Departmental Committee on Morphine and Heroin Addiction: The Report of the Rolleston Committee* (HMSO, 1926)

8. R. Scott, K. Grime and V. Wilmer, *Jazz at Ronnie Scott's* (Hale, 1979)

9. R. Yates, 'A Brief History of British Drug Policy; 1950–2001', *Drugs: Education, Prevention & Policy*, 9 (2002)

10. *After the War on Drugs: Options for Control* (Transform Drug Policy Foundation, 2004)

11. United Nations Office on Drugs and Crime, *World Drug Report 2011* (United Nations, 2011), www.unodc.org

12. Home Affairs Select Committee, *The Government's Drugs Policy: Is it Working?* (TSO, 2002), www.publications.parliament. uk

P is for Poverty

1. T. Hanley, *Engaging Public Support for Eradicating UK Poverty* (Joseph Rowntree Foundation, 2009), www.jrf.org.uk

2. Society of Editors, *Reporting Poverty in the UK: A Practical Guide for Journalists* (2009, Joseph Rowntree Foundation), www.mediatrust.org

3. Pew Global Attitudes Project, *The Global Middle Class* (The Pew Research Center, 2009), www.pewglobal.org

4. L. Bamfield and T. Horton, *Understanding Attitudes to Tackling Economic Inequality* (Joseph Rowntree Foundation, 2009)

5. Work and Pensions Select Committee *Second Report* (TSO, 2008), www.publications.parliament.uk

6. S. Castell and J. Thompson, *Understanding Attitudes to Poverty in the UK: Getting the Public's Attention* (Joseph Rowntree Foundation and Ipsos MORI, 2007)

7. M. J. Lerner, *The Belief In a Just World: A Fundamental Delusion* (Plenum Press, 1980)

8. L. D. Applebaum, M. C. Lennon and J. L. Aber, *Public Attitudes Toward Low-income Families and Children* (National Center for Children in Poverty, 2003), www.nccp.org

9. A. Furnham, *The Psychology of Behaviour at Work* (Psychology Press, 2005)

10. J. T. Jost and O. Hunyady, 'The Psychology of System Justification and the Palliative Function of Ideology', *European Review of Social Psychology*, 13 (2002)

11. A. Furnham, 'The Protestant Work Ethic and Attitudes towards Unemployment', *Journal of Occupational Psychology*, 55 (1982)

12. M. E. Rose, *The English Poor Law: 1780–1930* (Barnes & Noble, 1971)

13. D. Gordon and C. Pantazis (eds.), *Breadline Britain in the 1990s* (Ashgate, 1997)

14. I. Townshend and S. Kennedy, *Poverty: Measures and Targets* (House of Commons Library, 2004), www.parliament.uk

Q is for Queen

1. K. Martin, *The Magic of Monarchy* (Knopf, 1937)

2. T. Nairn, *The Enchanted Glass: Britain and Its Monarchy* (Radius, 1988)

3. P. Smith, *Cultural Theory: An Introduction* (Wiley-Blackwell, 2001)

4. P. Barker, E. Bauer, B. Brown, *et al.*, *The Meaning of the Jubilee* (Institute of Community Studies, 2002), www.youngfoundation.org

5. E. Shils and M. Young, 'The Meaning of the Coronation', *The Sociological Review*, 1 (1953)

6. J. M. T. Balmer, *Comprehending the Constitutional Monarchies of Britain and Sweden: Issues of Trust and Corporate Brand Management* (Bradford School of Management, 2005), www.bradford.ac.uk

7. T. Paine, *Common Sense; Addressed to the Inhabitants of America* (1776)

8. W. Bagehot, *The English Constitution* (Chapman and Hall, 1867)

9. *No Royal Rollercoaster* (Ipsos MORI, 2002), www.ipsos-mori.com

10. D. Cannadine and S. Price (eds.), *Rituals of Royalty: Power and Ceremonial in Traditional Societies* (Cambridge University Press, 1992)

R is for Regions

1. C. Tacitus, *The Life of Gnaeus Julius Agricola*, edited by R. M. Ogilvie, I. A. Richmond (*c.* AD 98; Oxford University Press, 1967)

2. D. Shillan, *The Practice of Synthesis in the Works of Patrick Geddes* (New Atlantis Foundation, 1972)

3. *Royal Commission on Local Government in England: The Redcliffe-Maud Report* (The National Archives, Cmnd 4040, 1969), www.nationalarchives.gov.uk

4. J. Prescott, *Alternative Regional Strategy: A Framework for Discussion* (Labour Party, 1982)

5. J. Bradbury, *Devolution, Regionalism and Regional Development: The UK Experience* (Routledge, 2008)

6. K. Meagher, 'The real battle for the future of the English regions is just beginning', Labour Uncut, 4 November 2010, www.labour-uncut.co.uk

7. H. Elcock, *Is English Regionalism Dead? Lessons after the North-East Referendum* (University of Glamorgan, 2009)

8. The Association of British Counties, www.abcounties.co.uk

S is for Silly Hats

1. J. Timbs, *English Eccentrics and Eccentricities* (R. Bentley, 1866)
2. E. Hobsbawm and T. Ranger (eds.) *The Invention of Tradition* (Cambridge University Press, 1983)
3. K. Grenier, *Tourism and Identity in Scotland, 1770–1914: Creating Caledonia* (Ashgate, 2005)
4. D. Willetts, *Modern Conservatism* (Penguin, 1992)
5. J. Dunleavy and G. Dunleavy, *Douglas Hyde: A Maker of Modern Ireland* (University of California Press, 1991)
6. J. T. Church, 'Confabulations of community: the Hamefarins and political discourse on Shetland', *Anthropological Quarterly*, 63 (1990)

T is for Toilet

1. L. Lambton, *Temples of Convenience and Chambers of Delight* (Pavilion, 1998)
2. R. Middlemist, E. Knowles and C. Matter, 'Personal space invasions in the lavatory: suggestive evidence for arousal', *Journal of Personality and Social Psychology*, 35 (1976)
3. S. Žižek, 'Knee deep', *London Review of Books*, 26 (2004)
4. C. Greed, *Inclusive Urban Design: Public Toilets* (Architectural Press, 2003)
5. G. Jones, *Social Hygiene in Twentieth Century Britain* (Taylor & Francis, 1986)
6. S. Feldman, 'Going to the ladies', *New Humanist*, 125 (2010)
7. M. Douglas, *Purity and Danger: An Analysis of Concepts of Pollution and Taboo* (Routledge and K. Paul, 1966)
8. N. Elias, *The Civilizing Process: Sociogenetic and Psychogenetic Investigations* (Wiley-Blackwell, 2000)
9. D. Erasmus, *De Civilitate Morum Puerilium Libellus* (1530)
10. G. Della Casa, *Galateo* (1609)
11. R. Weste, *The Booke of Demeanour and the Allowance and Disallowance of Certaine Misdemeanors in Companie* (1619)
12. M. Allen, 'From cesspool to sewer: sanitary reform and the

rhetoric of resistance, 1848–1880', *Victorian Literature and Culture*, 30 (2002)

13. E. Chadwick, *Report on the Sanitary Conditions of the Labouring Population of Great Britain* (1842; Edinburgh University Press, 1965)

14. *The SCA Hygiene Report 2011* (SCA, 2011), www.sca.com

15. A brief history of the toilet, www.victoriaplumb.com

16. British Toilet Association, www.britloos.co.uk

U is for Umbrellas

1. J. Golinski, *British Weather and the Climate of Enlightenment* (The University of Chicago Press, 2007)

2. M. Hulme, 'Geographical work at the boundaries of climate change', *Transactions of the Institute of British Geographers*, 33 (2008)

3. L. Boia, *The Weather in the Imagination* (Reaktion Books, 2005)

4. H. L. Jones, *The Geography of Strabo, Volume 1* (Loeb Classical Library, 1923)

5. J. Arbuthnot, *An Essay Concerning the Effects of the Air on Human Bodies* (J. and R. Tonson, 1733), www.archive.org

6. D. Hume, *The Philosophical Works, Volume 3* (Black and Tait, 1826; Little, Brown, 1954)

7. G. Manley, 'Bad summers', *New Scientist*, 16 October 1958

8. V. Janković, *Reading the Skies: A Cultural History of English Weather, 1650–1820* (University of Chicago Press, 2001)

9. E. Howarth and M. S. Hoffman, 'A Multidimensional approach to the relationship between mood and weather', *British Journal of Psychology*, 75 (1984)

10. J. J. A. Denissen, L. Butalid, L. Penke et al. 'The effects of weather on daily mood: a multilevel approach', *Emotion*, 8 (2008)

11. R. Bechtel and A. Churchman (eds.), *Handbook of Environmental Psychology* (John Wiley & Sons, 2002)

12. W. Sangster, *Umbrellas and their History* (Oxford University Press, 1855; Kessinger Publishing, 2010)

V is for Vegetables

1. World Carrot Museum, www.carrotmuseum.co.uk
2. D. Hollingsworth, 'Changing patterns of food consumption in Britain', *Nutrition Bulletin*, 2 (1974; 2007)
3. G. Markham, *The English Huswife* (1615; McGill-Queen's University Press, 1986)
4. R. Semba and M. Bloem (eds.), *Nutrition and Health in Developing Countries* (Humana Press, 2008)
5. M. Bufton, D. F. Smith and V. Berridge, 'Conflict and compromise in the BMA Nutrition Committee 1947–1950', *Medical History*, 47(2003), www.ncbi.nlm.nih.gov
6. *Report of the Inter-Departmental Committee on Physical Deterioration* (The National Archives Cmnd 2175, 1904), www.nationalarchives.gov.uk
7. J. Burnett, *Plenty and Want: A Social History of Food in England from 1815 to the Present Day* (Routledge, 1989)
8. F. Le Gros Clark, *The School Child and the Canteen* (Hertfordshire County Council, 1942)
9. *Ministry of Food, Annual Report of the National Food Survey Committee* (HMSO, 1952)
10. B. Fine, *The Political Economy of Diet, Health and Food Policy* (Routledge, 1998)

W is for www

1. R. Kraut, M. Patterson, V. Lundmark, et al., 'Internet paradox: a social technology that reduces social involvement and psychological well-being?' *American Psychological Association*, 53 (1998)
2. W. Davies, *You Don't Know Me, but… Social Capital and Social Software* (The Work Foundation, 2003), www.theworkfoundation.com
3. A. Morris, 'E-literacy and the Grey Digital Divide', *Journal of Information Literacy*, 1 (2007) N. Nie and L. Erbring, *Internet and Society* (Stanford University, 2000)

4. H. Rheingold, *The Virtual Community: Homesteading on the Electronic Frontier* (Addison Wesley, 1993)

5. R. D. Putnam, *Bowling Alone: The Collapse and Revival of American Community* (Simon & Schuster, 2000)

6. B. Wellman and K. Hampton, 'The Not So Global Village of Netville', in B. Wellman and C. Haythornthwaite, *The Internet in Everyday Life* (Wiley-Blackwell, 2002)

7. D. Devins, A. Darlow, A. Petrie et al., *Connecting Communities to the Internet: Evaluation of the Wired Up Communities Programme* (TSO, 2003)

8. *Digital Britain, Final Report* (DCMS & DBIS, 2009), www.official-documents.gov.uk

9. Commission of Inquiry into the Future of Civil Society in the UK and Ireland, *Making Good Society* (Carnegie UK Trust, 2010)

X is for XXXX

1. A. Millwood Hargrave, *Delete Expletives?* (ASA, BBC, BSC, ITC, 2000)

2. T. Jay, 'The utility and ubiquity of taboo words', *Perspectives on Psychological Science*, 4 (2009)

3. T. McEnery, *Swearing in English: Bad Language, Purity and Power from 1586 to the Present* (Routledge, 2005)

4. T. Dalrymple, 'Against vulgarity', *Spectator*, 18 May 2011)

5. G. Hughes, *Swearing: A Social History of Foul Language, Oaths and Profanity in English* (Wiley-Blackwell, 1991)

6. J. Sharman, *A Cursory History of Swearing* (J. C. Nimmo and Bain, 1884)

7. G. Hughes, *An Encyclopedia of Swearing* (M. E. Sharpe, 2006)

8. A. Montagu, *The Anatomy of Swearing* (The Macmillan Company, 1967)

9. J. Esbensen, *The Use of F*** as a Rapport Management Strategy in British and American English* (Griffith University, 2009)

10. T. Jay, *Why We Curse: A Neuro-Psycho-Social Theory of Speech* (John Benjamins, 2000)

11. T. Jay, *Cursing in America* (John Benjamins, 1992)

12. E. Partridge, *Shakespeare's Bawdy* (Routledge and Kegan Paul, 1947)

13. G. Colman, 'To Mr Town', *The Connoisseur* (1754)

14. J. Swift, *Polite Conversation* (Joseph Wenman, 1783)

15. R. Jones, *Gender and the Formation of Taste in Eighteenth-century Britain* (Cambridge University Press, 1998)

16. E. Brontë, *Wuthering Heights* (Smith, Elder, 1870)

17. P. Bordieu, *Distinction: A Social Critique of the Judgement of Taste* (Harvard University Press, 1984)

18. L. Trotsky, 'The Struggle of Cultured Speech', *Pravda*, 16 May 1923

19. *Audience Attitudes towards Offensive Language on Television and Radio* (Ofcom, 2010)

Y is for Youth

1. P. Richard, R. Layard and J. Dunn, *A Good Childhood: Searching for Values in a Competitive Age* (Penguin, 2009)

2. M. Easton, 'The year we lost the kids' (BBC, 2008), www.bbc.co.uk

3. M. Easton, 'Thinking about children and crime' (BBC, 2009), www.bbc.co.uk

4. M. Easton, 'Bridging the generation gap' (BBC, 2008), www.bbc.co.uk

5. *An Overview of Child Well-being in Rich Countries* (UNICEF, 2007), www.unicef.org

6. J. Locke, *Some Thoughts Concerning Education* (A. and J. Churchill, 1693)

7. L. DeMause, *The History of Childhood* (Psychohistory Press, 1974)

8. P. Aries, *Centuries of Childhood* (Penguin Books, 1979)

9. L. Pollock, *Forgotten Children: Parent–Child Relations from 1500–1900* (Cambridge University Press, 1983)

10. L. Stone, *The Family, Sex and Marriage in England 1500–1800* (Weidenfeld, 1977)

11. J. Savage, *Teenage: The Creation of Youth 1875–1945* (Random House, 2008)

12. Bill Osgerby, *Youth in Britain since 1945* (Blackwell Publishers, 1998)

13. D. Cameron MP, Speech to CSJ Kids Symposium, 10 June 2006

14. P. Scraton (ed.), *'Childhood' in 'Crisis'?* (UCL Press, 1997)

15. G. S. Hall, *Adolescence* (D. Appleton and Co., 1911)

Z is for Zzzz

1. Sleep Matters: The Impact of Sleep on Health and Wellbeing (Mental Health Foundation, 2011), www.howdidyousleep.org/media/downloads/MHF_Sleep_Matters_Report.pdf

2. C. Leadbeater, Dream On (Demos, 2004), www.demos.co.uk/publications/dreamon

3. R. Macnish, *The Philosophy of Sleep* (D. Appleton, 1834)

4. L. Terman and A. Hocking, 'The Sleep of School Children: Its Distribution According to Age, and Its Relation to Physical and Mental Efficiency', *Journal of Educational Psychology*, 4 (1913)

5. I. Oswald, *Sleep* (Penguin Books, 1966)

6. M. Cahill, 'The Ethical Consequences of Modafinil Use', *Penn Bioethics Journal*, 1 (2005), www.bioethicsjournal.com/past/pbj1.1_cahill.pdf

7. I. Sample, 'Wired Awake', *Guardian*, (29/07/2004), www.guardian.co.uk/education/2004/jul/29/research.highereducation

8. J. A. Horne, *Sleepfaring: A Journey through the Science of Sleep* (Oxford University Press, 2006)

9. R. G. Foster and S. W. Lockley, *Sleep: A Very Short Introduction* (Oxford University Press, 2011)

INDEX

Acheson, Dean, 208
acid (drug), 162
Act of Consecration (UK), 185
Act of Union (1707), 207
adolescence, concept of, 274
Advisory Council on the Misuse of Drugs, 168
Age of Reason, 183
agricultural revolution, 233
AIDS, 165
Ajax, 217
alcohol and drinking, 7–16
    and antisocial behaviour, misconception concerning, 9
    Britain's 'intoxication culture' concerning, 13
    and cultural differences, 9–12
    and expected behaviour, 11
    and fighting, 13–14
    and journalism, 7–8
    and links to social problems, 15
    and liver disease, 15
    and murder, 141
    northern European attitude to, 9
    and outdated licensing laws, 8
    pseudo-science about, 15
    and sexual assaults, 13
    southern European attitude to, 13
    UCLA study concerning, 9
    and UK courts, 13
    Washington State University experiment concerning, 11
ale, real, 30
Alfred, King, 193–4
Alternative Regional Strategy, 201
Aliens Act (1905), 92
allotments, 235, 240
American Psychological Association (APA), 221
Amis, Martin, 263
anachronism, and Britishness, 206
Anatomy of Swearing (Montagu), 262–3
Anglo-Saxon Chronicle, 194 [roman in text: OK?]
Anslinger, Harry J., 158, 159–60, 161
anti-Establishment, 188
Anti-Muzzle Association, 39
antisocial behaviour, defining of, 270
Anytown, 205

apartheid, 262
'An Appeal to the Public on the Subject of Railways', (Godwin), 249–50
Apple, 242
Appleby, Mary, 73
AquaClean, 222
Arbuthnot, John, 225
Arctic Circle, 228
Aritama people, drinking culture among, 9
arithmetic, see numbers
Armstrong, Neil, 81
Arnold, Matthew, 133
As Nasty as They Wanna Be (2 Live Crew), 263
ASBOs, 276
aspiration foods, 234
Atlantic City train crash, 46
attachment theory, 56
Attlee, Clement, 93, 94
Auchterarder, 48
Australia, 123, 129

Bacon, Alice, 162–3
Bacon, Sir Francis, 78
bad language, 253–65
    BBC broadcasts, 261–2
    collection of, 254
    and Decency League, 260
    Elizabeth I makes fashionable, 256
    enthusiasm for, 255–7
    examples of, 254, 255, 257, 258, 259, 261, 262, 264, 265
    in film, 264
    in ghetto, 263–4
    on Internet, 254–5
    in literature, 255–7, 259, 260, 261, 263, 265
    medieval, 256
    by monarchs, 256, 258
    in music, 263
    Ofcom research on, 264
    origins of, 255
    in poetry, 263
    and political, 260–1
    in public, 259
    and Puritanism, 258
    racist, 264
    shock value, lack of, 264
    and 1606 Act of Parliament, 258
    2000 report on, 264
    and women's rights, 262

Bagehot, Walter, 183–5
Baker, Chet, 162
Balfour, Arthur, 92
Banham, Sir John, 200
Barmy Army, 207
Barnsbury Bugle, 243 [it's roman in text]
Barrie, J. M., 185
Battersea Home for Lost and Starving Dogs, 37, 39
battles:
  Lyndanisse, 181
  Poitiers, 186
  Rawmarsh School, 231
BBC:
  bad language broadcast by, 261–2
  blogs, 267–8
  consumer programming, 233, 287
  family-life survey by, 54–5
  'God Save The Queen' banned by, 188
  on immigrants, maternity units and translation services, 102
  marital-life lectures on, 57
  murder dominates 1980s news bulletins of, 134
  Reith lectures, 206–7
BBC-3, 261
'beacon of relief', 214
Beatles, 162, 286
Becket, St Thomas à, 48, 186
Beeton, Mrs, 157
Belgium, 144, 223
The Belief in a Just World: A Fundamental Delusion (Lerner), 176–7
Bell, 242
Bentham, Jeremy, 67, 78–9
Beresford, Pamela, 73
Berger, Peter, 188
Berners-Lee, Tim, 126
bhat-ghum, 282
  see also sleep
Bichard, Sir Michael, 51
Billingsgate fish market, 259
Birkenhead Park, 69
Birt, John, 134
Birth of a Flower, The, 4
Black Death, 133
Black Prince, 186
Blackadder, 233
blackout, 236
Blair, Tony, 33, 149, 201
  apologies from, 48
  ASBOs introduced by, 276
  child-poverty promise of, 175
  'drugs tsar' appointed by, 166
  and Internet, 247, 248, 250
  and Iraq invasion, refusal to apologise for, 48
  and licensing hours, 8
  on 'electronic service delivery', 247
  and power-napping, 288–9
  and social capital, 245
  'third way' philosophy of, 60

Blake, William, 208
blasphemy, 256, 258
  see also bad language
Blobby, Mr, 207
blogging, 45, 267–8, 278, 290
Bloom, Dr Benjamin, 130
blue air, 254
  see also bad language
Bluewater shopping centre, 271
Blunkett, David, 50–1, 166, 245
Board of Agriculture, 39
'bodged job' 215
bodily functions, 214, 220
  and bowel cancer, 221
  and constipation, 221
  embarrassment over, 219
  and paruresis, 221
Boer War, 235
Bolivia, Camba people of, drinking culture among, 10
Book of Household Management (Beeton), 156
Bourdieu, Pierre, 261
bourgeoisie, 34
  and hunting, 36
  resentment towards power of, 259, 262, 265
  and social hierarchy, 261–2
  and verbal propriety, 260
  see also class; elitism
bowel cancer, 221
Bowlby, John, 55–6
Bowling Alone (Putnam), 244
boxing, 143
Brain, Lord, 161
Brake, Tom, 156
Breadline Britain, 173–4
'Breakthrough Britain' (Conservative Party), 56–7
Brie, 27, 28
British Academy, 60–1
British Brothers League, 92
British bulldog, 33
British Cheese Board, 29
British Empire, collapse of, 195
British Medical Journal (*BMJ*), 237, 283
British National Corpus, 254
British National Party, 33
British Spirit, 33
Britishness, 205–6
  and anachronism, 206
'broken' Britain, 108, 117, 118
brolly, see umbrella
Brontë, Charlotte, 265
Brontë, Emily, 260
Brookman, Dr Fiona, 141
Brown, Gordon, 117, 118–19, 149, 201
  on civic patriotism, 245
  and official statistics, 151–2
Browning, Elizabeth Barrett, 157
Brunel, Isambard Kingdom, 123
Bryson, Bill, 223

Buchanan, James, 123
Buddha, 78
Bulger, James, 111, 275, 276
Burke, Edmund, 217
Burnham, Andy, 87
Bush, George H. W., 81

Cadbury, 125
calculators, 145
California University (UCLA), 9
Callaghan, James, 98, 99, 163
Camba people, drinking culture among, 10
Cambridge University, 235
Cambuslang, 66
Camembert, 27, 28
Cameron, David, 47, 78, 85, 271–2, 277
    on knife crime, 116–17
    and narcotics, 166
    poverty promise of, 175
    quality-of-life measure announced by,
        87–8
Camillagate, 182
Campbell, Alan, 156
Canadian Supreme Court, 13
cannabis, 160, 165, 166, 167–8
Cannadine, Sir David, 189
Canterbury, Archbishop of, 186, 277
Canterbury Tales, The, (Chaucer), 255–6
capitalism, 68, 73, 81, 106
Capricorn, 30
Caribbean community, 59, 93
    see also immigration
Carnaby Street, London, 237
Caroline, Queen, 65
carrots:
    cartoon, 236, 239
    and night-vision, 236
Carroty George, 236, 239
cars, character of public space changed by, 19
cartoons:
    carrot, 236
    kids, 239
Casey, Dr Anna, 290
CCTV, 20
celebrity culture, 189
cellophane culture, 206
censorship, 253–65
Central Office of Information, 187
Central Park, New York, 69
Central Statistical Office, 147, 148
    see also statistics
Centre for Economic Performance, 84
Chadwick, Edwin, 218
Changing of the Guard, 206
Chapman, Jessica, 50, 110, 111
charitable giving, 170
Charles I, 64
Charles II, 186, 258
Chatsworth, 69
Chaucer, Geoffrey, 255–6
cheese, 25–31, 224

bland, 26, 28–9, 211
Brie, 27, 28
Camembert, 27, 28
Capricorn, 30
centralised manufacture of, 26
Continental, 27
farmhouse, 25–6
goats', 30
Gorau Glas, 30
lost varieties of, 26
Lymeswold, 28–9, 211
National, 26
standardisation of, 26
Chicago, Riverside district of, 69–70
child poverty, 125
Child Poverty Action Group, 173
    see also poverty
children:
    age of criminal responsibility of, 269
    and ASBOs, 276
    Church criticises people's attitude towards,
        277
    and crime, 271–2, 275–6
    and family, 59, 61
    fear of, 271
    Finland's attitude towards, 269–7
    and food, 237
    and good manners, 216
    'naming and shaming' of, 273
    reports on, 277, 284
    sleep patterns of, 284
    special educational needs of, 273
'Children's Food Fads' (Clark), 237
China, 157
    education in, 129
cholera, 218
Christmas Broadcast, 188
Church, Dr Jonathan, 210
church, quasi-religious rituals and, 187
Churchill, Winston, 94, 147, 185, 208
    devolution considered by, 195
    evoking, 33
    and power-napping, 288
Chuter-Ede, James, 94
circadian rhythms, 289
City of London, 273
civic patriotism, 245
civil religion, 187, 188, 210
The Civilizing Process (Elias), 219
Clark, Frederick (Bill) Le Gros, 236–7
Clarke, Kenneth, 108
class, 254
    and bad language, 256, 258–9
    characteristics of, 33
    criminal, 107
    and diet, 231, 234–5, 237, 239–40
    divides, 199, 237, 282
    divides, canine, 35–9
    and employment opportunities, 274, 277
    and excrement, 213, 218, 220, 222
    feral under-, 108

governing, 149
and industrial decline, 124–5
and the Labour Party, 199
middle, emergence of, 258–9
middle, shaping status of, 261
middle, and snobbery, 213
and privilege, 189, 216
professional, 143, 219, 285
and social identity, 211
and soup kitchens, 235, 240
struggle, 65, 70–1, 261
and swearing, 253–65
technocratic, 124
values, 220
'Westminster', 202
see also bourgeoisie; elitism
classless cool, 265
'classroom charity case', 235
Claudius, Emperor, 138
Clicking Act (1723), 107
Cliffe Vale Potteries, 219
Clifford, Max, 46
Clinton, Bill, 49, 288
Club Eleven, 160
cocaine, 158, 160
Cockney slang, 214, 260, 264
coffee, 115, 157, 229, 238, 243, 245
Colman, George, 259
Colombia, 143
    Aritama people of, drinking culture
        among, 9
Colonial Office, 94
Colquhoun, Patrick, 107, 109
Commission on the Measurement of
    Economic Performance and Social
    Progress, 86
Committee for Public Walks, Gardens &
    Playgrounds, Manchester, 69
Common Sense (Paine), 182–3
Commonwealth Immigrants Act (1962), 97–9
community health, 244–5
confabulation, 210
conformity, 205
Confucius, 78
Congo, 143
Connoisseur, 259
Conservative Party:
    Cameron elected leader of, 85
    and devolution, 199
    and family, 54, 56
    fear of Euro-federalism by, 199
    grassroots, 197, 206
    and immigration, 91–2, 94, 98, 101
    and knife crime, 116
    Lieutenancies Act nodded through by, 201
    and 1951 general election, 94
    and 1970 general election, 198
    1998 conference of, 206
    and poverty, 175
    and regional boundaries, 200–1
    and regional regeneration, 196

and 2010 general election, 23, 51, 204, 240
u-turn, 272
Wilson defeats, 196
and young people, 271–2, 276
constipation, 221
consumerism, 115, 189, 284, 286, 287
Corday, Charlotte, 138
Cordingly, Maj. Gen. Patrick, 44
coronations, 185–6
    quasi-religious rituals and, 187
    superstition and religion attached to, 185,
        186
    televised, 185, 186
corporate modernity, 205
Costa, Antonio Maria, 168
Costeker, Mr, 70
CountyWatch, 202–3
Cranks, 237
Crapper, Thomas, 219
'crazy Brits', 208
credit crunch, see global financial crisis
Creme Egg, 125
Cricket St Thomas, 30
crime:
    antisocial behaviour, 9, 14, 23, 61, 74, 113
    and ASBOs, 276
    burglary, 164
    and children, 271–2, 275–6
    daily murder rates, 117
    demand for state to 'do something' about,
        105
    and demonisation of young people, 270–8
    drug-related, see drugs, recreational
    by drunk people, 11–12; see also alcohol
    and electronic tagging, 276
    falling rates of, 273
    and Finnish 'reform schools', 269
    gun, 137
    knife, see knife crime
    lawful industrial gleaning becomes, 107
    low risk of being victim of, 105
    media thrive on stories about, 108
    media's reporting of, change in, 109
    and mental health, 270
    and 'penal populism', 112
    and police, see police
    social capital decline linked to, 245
    statistics, 150
    stories about, leading to fear of, 109
    'tough on', New Labour's rhetoric
        concerning, 111
    and UK penal code, 269
    victims of, 110–12
    violent, as proportion of all crime news
        reported, 109
    youth, 267–79
    see also individual victims; justice; Soham
Crime and Disorder Act (1998), 276
criminal responsibility, age of, 269
Cromwell, Oliver, 64, 258
Crudgington, 25, 28

Crystal Palace, 218
Cub Scouts, 244
Cuba, drinking culture in, 10
Cunningham, John 'Cats Eyes', 236
currency, decimalisation of, 27
A Cursory History of Swearing (Sharman), 256
cyber-evangelists, 243–4
cyberspace, 254
cyber-street, *see* 'Internet Street'
Czech Republic, 100

Daily Express, 7, 271
Daily Mail, 73, 272
Daily Mirror, 7, 109
Daily Record, 91–2
Daily Star, 275
Daily Telegraph, 7
Dalrymple, Theodore, 254
Dando, Jill, 111
Dangerous Dogs Act (1991), 39–40
Darwin, Charles, 36
Davies, Margaret, 30
Davy, Humphry, 285
De Civilitate Morum Puerilium (Erasmus),
    216
Decency League, 260
decimalisation, 27
Deedes, Bill, 7, 16
Defence of the Realm Act (1916), 158
Deiner, Ed, 82
'Delete Expletives' (2000), 264
della Casa, Giovanni, 217
Denissen, Jaap, 227
Denmark, 129
    drinking culture in, 10
Department of the Environment, Transport
    and the Regions (DETR), 201
Department of Health, 239
deprivation, *see* poverty
Derby Arboretum, 68
despondency, twenty-first-century, 243
devolution, 195–7, 201–2
    Churchill considers, 195
Devonshire, Duke of, 69
Dexter, Colin, 133
Diana, Princess of Wales, 190
Dickens, Charles, 283
diet, 231–40
    and class, 231, 234–5, 237
    'five-a-day', 239
    and health, 232–3, 238
    as lifestyle choice, 237
    and NHS, 238
    by postcode, 239
    and soup kitchens, 235, 240
    vegetarian/whole-food, 237
    and vitamins, 235
    see also nutrition
discriminatory language, 264
    see also bad language
Disney, Walt, 236

Disraeli, Benjamin, 146
divorce, 56–7, 58
Divorce Reform Act (1969), 58
Dixon, George (character), 17, 18–19
    see also police
Doctor Who, 208
'Does Living in California Make People
    Happy?' (Schkade & Kahneman), 230
Dog Owners Protection Association, 38–9
dogs, 33–41
    as companions, 40
    current UK numbers of, 39
    designer wear for, 41
    earliest recognised show of, 36
    feral, 37
    feudal fault lines emphasised by, 35
    Fitz, 33
    foreign bloodlines introduced into, 38
    homeopathic remedies for, 41
    hounds, 34, 38
    inbreeding among, 36–7, 38
    in Middle Ages, 38
    more exotic varieties demanded of, 37
    overweight, 40–1
    owners' physical similarity to, 34, 40
    popular names for, 40
    rabies among, 37–9
    snacks sold for, 40
    soaring population of, 37
    as status symbol, 34–5, 39
Domesday Book, 25, 194
Donkin, Sir Bryan, 138
Doulton, 219
Downing Street, 83, 87, 96, 117–19, 149, 151,
    166, 175, 196, 200, 245, 276
Drake, Nathan, 256
dress sense, 205–12
drinking, *see* alcohol
Drucker, Royston, 287
Drugs Prevention Office, 11–12
drugs, recreational, 156–68
    acid, 162
    Advisory Council on Misuse of, 168
    annual cost to Britain of, 167
    Britain's reluctant prohibition of, 157, 158
    'British System' concerning, 159, 161, 162
    cannabis, 160, 165, 166, 167–8
    Carnaby Street raid concerning, 160
    cocaine, 158, 160
    deaths related to, 166
    decriminalisation of, 156
    ecstasy, 165, 168
    and gangs, 157, 161, 164
    government's 'relentless drive' against, 167
    heroin, 160–1, 161–2, 163, 164–5, 167
    marijuana, 162
    morphine, 158
    and needle exchanges, 165
    opium, *see* opium
    purple hearts, 161
    and side-effects, 290–1

and sleep, 286–7, 289–91
from South East Asia, 164
teenagers addicted to, 163
treatment programmes for, 167
'tsar' appointed to deal with, 166
War on, 163, 165, 167
Whitehall committee investigates, 161
see also glue sniffing
Drunken Comportment (MacAndrew, Edgerton), 9–10
duelling, 143
Duggan, Robert, 73
Duncan Smith, Iain, 56–7
Dyke, Greg, 47

East India Company, 157
Easterlin paradox, 85
eccentricity, 208, 223
Economic and Social Research Council, 126
ecstasy (drug), 165, 168
Edgerton, Robert, 9–10
Edict of Expulsion, 90
Edinburgh University, 287
Edison, Thomas, 286
Education Act (1944), 124
education, see learning
Edward I, 89–90
Edward VI, 256
e-government, 247
Einstein, Albert, 44
Eisenhower, President Dwight D., 228
electricity, 285–6
electronic calculators, 145
electronic frontier, see Internet; World Wide Web
Elias, Norbert, 219
elitism, 210, 211
see also bourgeoisie; class
Elizabeth I, 217, 256, 257
Elizabeth II:
    Christmas Broadcasts of, 188
    Coronation of, 185–6
    Diamond Jubilee of, 3
    and modern media, 189–90
    public affection for, 188
    Silver Jubilee of, 188–9
    and social order, 231
    tax affairs of, 190
    see also Royal Family
Elizabeth, Queen (later Queen Mother), 236
Ellen, Barbara, 228
e-mail, 242–3
see also Internet; World Wide Web
Empire Windrush, SS, 92–3
Enclosure Acts, 65
England:
    age of criminal responsibility within, 269, 276
    colonial culture of, 209
    constituency boundary changes within, 191–2, 194
    crime within, 111, 117, 119, 120, 134–5, 143–4, 166, 171–2, 178, 269–71, 273, 276
    education system within, 124
    Regional Economic Planning Boards and, 196
    regions of, 191–204
    unmarried mothers in, 59
    vegetable-eating in, 239
English Civil War, 64
English Constitution (Bagehot), 183–4
English Eccentrics and Eccentricities (Timbs), 208
The English Convict: A Statistical Study (Goring), 138
Englishness, 194, 223
Enlightenment, 183
    pre-, 220
Erasmus, Desiderius, 216
Erbing, Lutz, 243
errors, see mistakes
Essay Concerning the Effects of the Air on Human Bodies (Arbuthnot), 225
Estonia, 100
Ethandun (Edington), 194
ethnic minorities, see immigration
Eugenics Society, 174
Euro-federalism, 199
European Commission, 86
European Community:
    in 1980s, 199
    Structural Funds, 199
European Convention on Human Rights, 99
European Court of Human Rights, 73
European Economic Community (EEC), 27, 169
European Union (EU), 29, 209
Eurostar, 289
Evans-Gordon, Major Sir William, 91, 92
Exchequer, 151, 245
excremental obscenities, 258
    see also bad language
expletives, see bad language

Facebook, 251
Faithfull, Marianne, 162
family, 53–62
    attachment theory concerning, 56
    BBC survey into, 54–5
    break-up of, and children's school attainment, 61
    British Academy's analysis of, 60–1
    and Divorce Reform Act, 58
    Giddens's ideas on, 60
    high levels of breakdown in, 54
    life, work life spilling over into, 82
    and lone parents, 55, 59, 62
    and marriage, see marriage
    OECD's questions concerning, 62
    and work–life balance, 281
fancy dress, 205–12

farmers' markets, 30
fast food, 238, 239
    see also junk food
'father of medicine', 224
'fatigue management solutions', 288
'FCUK', 254
Feed the World, 178–9
feminism, 220, 262, 281
'feral underclass', 108
Fergiegate, 182
Festival of Remembrance, 188
Field, 36
Finland, 129
    age of criminal responsibility within, 269
    'reform schools', 269
First World War, *see* World War One
Fisher, Archbishop Geoffrey, 5
Fitz the Bulldog, 33
Food Dudes, 239
food:
    and affluence, 237
    aspiration, 234
    consumption, 237
    energy-producing, 237
    fads, 237
    'five-a-day', 239
    as fuel, 232
    and Golden Age of Nutrition, 235
    health problems associated with, 232–3, 238
    junk, 231–2, 237, 239
    localism demanded of, 30
    Ministry of, 26
    official guidelines pertaining to, 235
    poor, war and, 235–6, 237
    'protective', 237
    rationing, 235–6, 237
    and social class, 237
    technology, 237, 238
    in Tudor times, 232, 238
    and vitamins, 235
    Woolton Pie, 236
    yearning for authenticity of, 29
    see also cheese; milk; superfoods; vegetables
Foot, Michael, 199
    Alternative Regional Strategy ordered by, 199
Forbes ASAP, 81
'foreign loo' anxiety, 222
Forty-four Juvenile Thieves (Bowlby), 56
foul language, *see* bad language
Founding Fathers, 183
Four Weddings and a Funeral, 264
'A Fragment on Government' (Bentham), 78
France, 86–7, 228
Frankau, Sir Claude, 162
Frankau, Lady (Isabella), 161–2
Freedman, David, 138
Freeman, Prof. Richard, 127
French Connection, 254
Freud, Sigmund, 220
Friends, 249

Fruit and Vegetable Taskforce (2011), 240
fruit, fresh, *see* vegetables
'The F*** Shop' (2 Live Crew), 263
Fundamental Principles of Official Statistics (UN), 148–9
Furnham, Prof. Adrian, 177–8
Fyfe, David Maxwell, 94, 96

Gaelic League, 209
Gainsborough, 5th Earl of, 197
Galleries shopping centre, 72–3
Galton, Sir Francis, 146
Game Act (1671), 35, 39
Game Reform Act (1831), 35–6
Garden City movement, 71
Gardner, Randy, 286
Gateway 2000, 241
Geddes, Sir Patrick, 196
G8, 48
General Elections:
    1900, 91
    1951, 94
    1964, 196
    1970, 198
    1997, 33, 175, 201
    2001, 8
    2005, 101
    2010, 103, 23, 51, 204, 240
A General Theory of Crime (Gottfredson, Hirschi), 141
generation gap, 268–9
    see also young people
George II, 65
George VI, 236
Georgia, drinking culture in, 10
Gerbeau, Pierre-Yves ('PY'), 289
'Get The F*** Out Of My House (Bitch)' (2 Live Crew), 263
ghetto language, 263–4
Giddens, Anthony, 60, 206, 209
Gilligan, James, 139, 142
Girdlestone, Revd Charles, 218
Gladstone, William, 157
global communication, 255
    see also Internet; media; television
global financial crisis, 86–7, 127
globalisation, 89, 115, 127, 222, 205, 209
    WWW powers new period of, 126
    beginnings of, 122
'glocalization', 246
glue sniffing, 163–4
goats' cheese, 30
'God Save The Queen', 188
Godric, St, 215–16
Godwin, George, 249–50
Golden Age of Nutrition, 235
Golinski, Jan, 225
'Good Childhood', 277
Goons, The, 208
Gorau Glas, 30
Gordon, David, 174, 175

Goring, Charles, 138
Gottfredson, Michael, 141
Gowing, Nik, 50
Grant, Hugh, 264
grass, 63–75 *passim*
    country fanatical about, 71
    as open spaces, *see* public open space
    shopping mall appropriates, 72
    state of, in public open spaces, 63
    urban planners convinced of need for, 71
Great Depression, 235
Great Eastern, SS, 123
Great Exhibition (1851), 218
Great House of Easement, 216
Great North Vote, 202
Great Public Demonstration (1902), 92
Greece, 127
    ancient, 78
Green Belt, 66
Greene, Sir Hugh, 262
Greer, Germaine, 262
Gross Domestic Product (GDP), 79–80, 86
Group Lafon, 289
Grundy, Bill, 263
Guardian, 73, 262
Guildford Four, 48
Gulf War, first, 44
Gurría, Angel, 86
guttersludge, 224

Hackney carriages, 224
Hadrian's Wall, 215
Hailsham, Viscount, 196
Halcyon, 287
Hall, G. Stanley, 274
Halpern, David, 83
Hamefarin, 210
Hamlet (Shakespeare), 257
Hampton Court Palace, 216
Hampton, Keith, 246, 247
A Handbook on Good Manners for Children (Erasmus), 216
Hanway, Jonas, 224
happiness, *see* wellbeing and happiness
Happiness: Lessons from a New Science (Layard), 85
'A Hard Day's Night', 286
Harington, Sir John, 217
Harvard, 245
health:
    community, 244–5
    and diet, 232–3, 238
    'five-a-day', 239
    poor, war and, 235–6, 237
    and poverty, 232–3
    public, 218
    and soup kitchens, 235, 240
    and vitamins, 235
    see also World Health Organization
Heath, Prof. Dwight, 14–15

hedonic psychology, 82
Hegel, Georg, 214
Hellawell, Keith, 166
Hemenway, David, 138
Henry II, 48, 186
Henry VIII, 64, 171, 216, 231, 256
heroin, 160–1, 161–2, 163, 164–5, 167
Hertfordshire County Council, 237
Hewlett Packard, 242
Heywood, Jeremy, 151–2
High Court, 178, 200, 287
Highland Society of London, 207
Hints on Breathing Places for the Metropolis (Loudon), 66
Hints to Working People about Personal Cleanliness (LNADSK), 218
hip hop movement, 263
Hippocrates, 224, 230
hippy movement, 73, 81, 237–8, 275, 278
Hirschi, Travis, 141
Historic Counties, Towns and Villages (Traffic Signs and Mapping) Bill, 203
historical tradition, 206
HIV, 165
Hobsbawm, Eric, 206
Hocking, Adeline, 284
Hollywood, 221, 236
Holmes, Sherlock (character), 208
Holy Ampulla, 186
Home Rule, in Ireland, 195, 196
hoodies, 271–2
Hooke, Robert, 225
Hopkins, Sir Frederick Gowland, 235
Hotmail, 251
House of Commons, 185, 191–2, 238, 262
House of Lords, 197, 201
Howard, Ebenezer, 71
Howard, Michael, 101
'hug-a-hoodie', 272
human excreta/waste, 213
    as fertiliser, 220, 232
    Freud on, 220
    see also toilet(s)
humanism, 216
Hume, David, 226
Hungary, 100
Huntley, Ian, 50–1
Hurricane Katrina, 48
Hyde, Douglas, 209
Hyde Park, 64, 65, 218
hydrophobia, *see* rabies
Hypnos, 281, 291

Iceland:
    crime within, 144
    and knowledge, 129
    and SAD, 228
    swearing in, 255
Ideal Home Show (2011), 222
identity, 209
Ikalainen, Merja, 269–70

Il Galateo (della Casa), 217
immigration, 59, 89–104, 209
  and balance between principle and
    prejudice, 104
  black and Asian, Colonial Office's devices
    to discourage, 94
  black and Asian, drastic measures to
    restrict, 95
  Eastern European, 100–1, 102–3
  of Kenyan Asians, 98–9
  Labour's 1968 emergency laws on, 98
  mass, starting point for, 93
  and maternity units and translation
    services, 102
  1961 surge in, 97
  Notting Hill riots concerning, 96
  Powell speech concerning, 98
  of 'right sort', 94
  Royal Commission on, 92
  shift in anxiety over, from colour to scale,
    101
  and Teddy Boys, 95, 96
  and xenophobia, 89; *see also* racism
Imperial College, 128
India, 157
  National Knowledge Commission
    launched by, 128
Industrial Revolution, 106, 123, 126, 195, 234
Infanticide Acts, 135
influenza, 218
information technology, 121–3
  see also Internet; Internet Generation;
    World Wide Web
insomnia, 281, 283, 284–5
  see also sleep
Institute for Social & Economic Research, 59
Intel, 242
Internet, 278
  anonymity of, 254
  Broadband, 251
  community, 247
  cyber-evangelists proclaim, 243–4
  cyber-street, *see* 'Internet Street'
  depression associated with, 242
  dramatic claims for, 250
  'glocalization' created by, 246
  growth of, 249–50
  isolating nature of, 243
  lack of interest in, 248–50
  'newsgroups', 242
  and psychological well-being, 242
  research about, 241–2, 243, 246–9
  and social interaction, 242–6, 250–1
  and swearing, 254–5
  universal access to, 246–9
  and WuC, 247
  see also 'Netville'; WELL; World Wide Web
Internet generation ('NetGen'), 121–2, 130,
    131
  see also information technology
'Internet paradox: a social technology that

  reduces social involvement and
    psychological well-being?', 241–2
'Internet Street', 241–2, 243, 246, 247
  see also Netville
Invisible College, 78
IRA pub bombings, 48
Iraq, 167
  invasion of, Blair's refusal to apologise for, 48
Ireland, Home rule and, 195, 196
Irish potato famine, 48
IRL ('in real life'), 244
Isle of Bute Council, 219
Italy, 14, 127, 170, 178

Jagger, Mick, 162
Jain, Rashmi, 229
Janet and John, 55
Japan, 129
Jennings, George, 218
Jerome, St, 216, 217
Jews, 90, 91, 92
Johnson, Boris, 20
Johnson, Dr Samuel, 226
  Billingsgate definition by, 259
  dictionary of, 253, 259
  letter 'X' described by, 253
Jones, Sir Elwyn, 99
Jones, Steve, 263
Jones, Steven, 277–8
Jouvet, Prof. Michel, 289
junk food, 231–2, 237, 239
  see also fast food
justice, 105–13
  and media, 108
  and 'penal populism', 112
  restorative, 49
  UK's OCD concerning, 105
  and victims of crime, 110–12
  see also crime
Justices of the Peace, 106

Kahneman, Daniel, 82, 83, 229–30
Kansas, policing in, 21
Kennedy, John F., 288
Kennedy, Robert F., 80, 85
Kennel Club, 36
Kensington Gardens, 236
Kensington Palace, 190
kilts, 207
King Edward's chair, 185–6
King James Bible, 259
King and Keys (pub), 7, 16
Kinsella, Ben, 111
knife crime, 111, 116–20, 267–79
  action programme on, 117
  Cameron talks of 'epidemic' proportions
    of, 116–17
  Downing Street 'summit' on, 117
  government statistics concerning, 118–19,
    151
  and 'No to Knives' campaign, 118

nonexistent 'epidemic' of, 116, 120
vigil for victim of, 116
see also murder
Knights of the Garter, 186
knowledge industries, 126–7
Knox, Robert, 111
Kraft, 125
Kuznets, Simon, 79
Kylloinen, Kurt, 269

Labour Party, 33–4, 60, 209,
    and DETR Alternative Regional Strategy,
        201
    and devolution, 199, 201–2
    and immigration, 94, 98
    and 1964 general election, 196
    and 1997 general election, 33, 175, 201
    and poverty, 17
    and regional boundaries, 200
    and statistics, 149–50
    'tough on crime' rhetoric of, 111
    well-being in policy of, 87
    and young people, 272, 276
    see also New Labour
Ladies' National Association for the Diffusion of
    Sanitary Knowledge (LNADSK), 218, 220
Lady Armstrong, 90
Lady Chatterley's Lover (Lawrence), 261
Lancaster Corpus of Abuse, 254
Land of Nod, 281
Landes, David, 125
Lansley, Andrew, 240
Laos, drinking culture in, 10
Larkin, Philip, 263
Last Bus to Woodstock (Dexter), 133
Latry, François, 235–6
Latvia, 100
laudanum, 157, 283
Lymeswold, 28–9, 211
Law Society, 46
Lawrence, D. H., 261
Lawrence, Stephen, 111
laxatives, 220
Layard, Prof. Richard, 82–3, 84–5
League of Nations, 235
learning:
    application, analysis and evaluation of, 130
    and comprehension, 130
    and Education Act, 124
    fees for, 128
    and graduation rates, 129
    inequality in, 124
    and Internet generation ('NetGen'), 121–2,
        130, 131; *see also* information
        technology
    'knowledge' versus, 130
    and knowledge industries, 126–7
    and low skills, 125, 126–7
        and memorising, 130
    'old-fashioned' model of, 130
    and standards of behaviour, 278

and synthesis, 130–1
tripartite system of, 124
and university degrees, proportion of
    young people with, 129
and university degrees, unequal values of,
    128
Lee, Ivy, 46
Lerner, Prof. Melvyn, 176
Lewinsky, Monica, 49
Leyton, Elliott, 139
Liberal Democrats, 156
Liberal Party, 92, 233
liberalism, 262, 264
licensing laws, outdated, 8
Lieutenancies Act, 201
*Life Satisfaction: The State of Knowledge and
    Implications for Government*, 82
light-bulb, first, 286
Lindsay, James, 286
Lithuania, 100
Little Britain, 208
local government, 191, 197, 198
    culture, 203
Local Government Act (1972), 198
    metropolitan counties created by, 198
    opposition to, 198
Locke, John, 225
Lombroso, Cesare, 137–8
London Dock Strike, 91
London Ideal Home Show (2011), 222
London Review of Books, 214
London 2012 Olympics, 3, 223
London Weekend Television, 173–4
Long, Walter, 39
Lord Mayor's Parade, 210
Lord's, 208
    Long Room at, 210
Loudon, John, 66, 68
Louis Gates, Henry Louis, 163
L'Uomo Delinquente (Lombroso), 137–8
Lyndanisse, Battle of, 181

Maastricht Treaty, 200
MacAndrew, Craig, 9–10
McCann, Madeleine, 111
McCartney, Linda, 238
McCartney, Paul, 162–3, 238
Mace, Rev. David, 57
Macmillan, Harold, 196
Macnish, Robert, 282, 285
Maguire Seven, 48
Mail, Glasgow, 91–2
Major, John, 275–6
    Maastricht Treaty signed by, 200
Make Poverty History, 178–9
Manchester:
    Committee for Public Walks, Gardens &
        Playgrounds in, 69
    parks in, 69
Mandelson, Peter, 33–4
mangelwurzel, 233

manufacturing, fall in numbers employed in, 126
Marat, Jean-Paul, 138
Margrethe II, 181–2, 190
marijuana, 162
Marine Police Bill, 108
Marks & Spencer, 30, 148
Marriage Guidance Centres, 57
marriage:
    children born outside, 59
    and divorce, 56–7, 58
    and Divorce Reform Act, 58
    high point in, 58–9
    UK all-time low in levels of, 55
Marxism, 206
Mary, Queen of Scots, 34
Massie, Allan, 49
Matheson, Jil, 152
Matthew, Book of, 170–1
May, Justice Sir Anthony, 287
May, Theresa, 23, 51
Maya, 242–3
'The Meaning of the Coronation' (Shils & Young), 187
media:
    BBC, see BBC
    change in type of crime reported by, 109
    consumerism and, 189
    and courts, 108
    and crime victims, 110
    demonisation of young people by, 144, 268–71
    errors hidden by, 45
    forces of law and order woo, 108
    illegal and immoral methods employed by, 44
    Internet, see Internet generation
    marked rise in crime stories in, 109
    and mass markets, 254
    and rabies, reporting of, 38
    round-the-clock, 115
    Royal Family and, 189
    and 24-hour drinking, 8
    on violent crime, as proportion of all crime news, 109
    see also individual outlets
Mental Health Foundation (MHF), 284
mental health, 270
    problems, young people with, 270
    and sleep, 284–5
    strategy, 87
    weather affects, 227; see also Seasonal Affective Disorder (SAD)
Merron, Gillian, 203
Messalina, Valeria, 138
'Metabolically Dominant Citizens', 291
'Metabolically Dominant Soldier', 290
meteorology, 225
'Method for Making a History of the Weather' (Hooke), 225

MetroNaps EnergyPod, 288
metropolis, birth of, 285
Metropolitan Canine Defence and Benevolent Institute, 37
Mexico, 127, 233
Microsoft, 241, 242, 243
Middle Ages, 34, 142, 215, 232, 256
Middlemist, R. D., 221
Migration Observatory, 103
Milk Marketing Board, 28
milk, plummeting price of, 29
Mill, John Stuart, 64, 67
Millennium Dome, 214, 289
Ministry of Defence, 290
Ministry of Food, 26, 236
Ministry of Justice, 112
'Ministry of Silly Walks', 208
mistakes, 43–52
    candour concerning, 47
    Iraq invasion, Blair's refusal to apologise for, 48
    learning from, 44
    protecting big business from, 46–7
    public, apologies for, 47–9
    risk management to minimise, 44
    sophisticated tactics to deal with, 47
Misuse of Drugs Act (1971), 163
    see also drugs, recreational
mittagspause, 281
    see also sleep
Mitterrand, François, 27
Mizen, Jimmy, 111
Modafinil, 289–91
modesty, 213–22, 258, 259
monarchy:
    Act of Consecration and, 185
    anti-Establishment and, 188
    Bagehot on, 183–4
    coronations and, 185
    critique of, 182–3
    divine right of, 189
    Founding Fathers and, 183–4
    1953 Coronation Committee and, 185
    Paine on, 183, 184
    republicanism and, 182, 183
    Royal Parks of, 236
    stable support for, 188
    status of, 187
    superstition and, 184
    and swearing, 256, 258
    see also individual monarchs
monasteries, dissolution of, 170, 171
Monbiot, George, 73
Monkey Closets, 218
Montagu, Ashley, 256, 262–3
Monty Python, 208
Moore, Jo, 45
Moore, John, 172–3
morphine, 158
MORI, 188, 281

Morse, Ch. Insp. Endeavour (character), 133
    extracts from story concerning, 133, 134,
        136, 137, 139, 140, 142, 144
'mosquito', 271
Mulgan, Geoff, 83, 84
murder, 133–44
    and abusive childhood, 139
    and alcohol, 141
    background of victims of, 136
    by blunt instrument, 137
    Britain's rate of, change in, 142–4
    death-row study concerning, 138–9
    definition of, 134–5
    descriptions of perpetrators of, 137–8
    fascination with, 134
    and gangs, 141–2
    grudge/revenge, 141
    by hitting and/or kicking, 137
    of infants, 135
    mainly male perpetrators of, 137
    mainly male victims of, 136
    male-on-male, 141
    motive for, 140
    in New York, 137
    by shooting, 137
    by stabbing, 136; see also knife crime
    of teenagers and young adults, 136
    times of day, week and year of, 137
    by underclass, 139–40
Muybridge, Eadweard, 4
Muzak, 72
Mytton, Jack, 208

Napoleonic Wars, 274
narcotics, see drugs, recreational; individual
        drugs
National Advisory Committee on Nutrition
        Education (1983), 238
National Cheese, 26
national dress, 207
National Food Survey (1952), 237
National Health Service (NHS), 118–19, 238
National Theatre (NT), 261
National Trust, 71
National Viewers' and Listeners' Association
        (NVLA), 262
Nationality Act (1948), 94
Neather, Andrew, 101
needle exchanges, 165
NEETs (those not in education, employment
        or training), 127
Neighbours, 249
NetGen, 121–2, 130, 131
    see also information technology
Netherlands, 129
'Netville', 245, 246
    see also 'Internet Street'
Never Mind the Bollocks (Sex Pistols), 263
New Atlantis (Bacon), 78
A New Discourse of a Stale Subject, Called the
        Metamorphosis of Ajax (Harington), 217

New Labour, see Labour Party
New Scientist, 287
New Sporting Magazine, 36
New Strand shopping centre, 275
New York terrorist attacks, 45, 81
New York Times, 236
New Zealand, 123, 129
News of the World, 7
Newsnight, 181
NHS, 118–19, 238
Nie, Norman, 243
9/11, 45, 81
1953 Coronation Committee (UK), 185
1960s:
    hippy counter-culture during, 237–8
    regional regeneration in, 196
    social revolution during, 237–8
    teenagers given a voice during, 263
    TV ownership during, 249
    women's rights in, 262
1970s:
    local government during, 198
    politics, 198
    punk emerged in, 263
    weather research during, 227
1980s:
    European Community in, 199
    hip hop movement, 263
    North–South Divide of, 199
    politics, 199
    rap movement, 263
    social turmoil during, 199
    weather research during, 227
1990s:
    hip hop movement, 263
    rap movement, 263
Nixon, Richard, 163
'No to Knives' campaign, 118
No Rest for the Wicked, 12
nonconformity, 208
Noonan, Peggy, 81–2
Northern Ireland:
    age of criminal responsibility within, 269
    cultural diversity within, 209–10
    tradition within, 209
North–South Divide, 199
Norway, 129
NT, 261
Number 11, see Exchequer
Number Ten, 83, 87, 96, 117–19, 149, 151,
        166, 175, 196, 200, 245, 276
numbers:
    as statistics, see statistics; see also Central
            Statistical Office; Royal Statistical
            Society; Statistical Society of
            London; Statistics Commission;
            Statistics and Regulation Service Act;
            United Kingdom Statistics Authority
    technology revolutionises manipulation of,
            145–6
    War of, 146, 148, 152, 153

nurdling, 197
nutrition, 231, 234–7, 238, 239
  see also diet
Nutt, Prof. David, 168
NVLA, 262

obesity, 232
obscenity, see bad language
Observer, 228
O'Donnell, Sir Gus, 84–5, 152
Ofcom, 264
Oliver, Jamie, 231, 237, 240
Olmstead, Frederick, 69–70
On the Origin of Species (Darwin), 36
One Tree Hill, 71
open space, see public open space
opium, 157–8
  in laudanum, 157, 283
  Royal Commission on, 157–8
  Wars, 157
  see also drugs, recreational
Orange Lodge, 209
Organisation for Economic Cooperation and
    Development (OECD), 62, 86, 127, 129
d'Ortous de Mairan, Jean-Jacques, 289
Osbourne, Ozzie, 12
Oswald, Ian, 287
Oxford, murders in, 133–4
Oz, 262

Paddick, Brian, 270
paedophobia, 271
Paine, Thomas, 183, 184, 190
Palmerston, Lord, 157
Panorama, 287
Pantazis, Christina, 174, 175
pantomime, 208, 215
Papago people, drinking culture among, 10
parasol, see umbrella
Parental Advisory Scheme, 254
Parliament:
  Acts of, 35–6, 39–40, 58, 65, 92, 94, 97–9,
      107, 124, 135, 151, 158, 163, 178, 185,
      198, 207, 218, 258, 276
  and agricultural revolution, 233
  and coalition government, 204
  House of Commons, 185, 191–2
  House of Lords, 197, 201
  and Internet, 247–8
  kitsch fancy dress in, 205
  and obscenity, 262
  and public health, 218, 233, 236, 238,
      239–40
  and social capital, 245
  State Opening of, 205
  televised, 205
  see also monarchy
Partridge, Eric, 257
paruresis, 221
Pauper Pedigree Project, 174
Paxton, Joseph, 69

Payne, Sarah, 111
Pearl Harbor, 193
pedagogy, 270
Peel Park, 69
Peel, Sir Robert, 18, 69
penal code, 269
Pennsylvania Railroad, 46
Pentagon, 290
People's Palace, 92
Peplau, Letitia Anne, 177
Pepys, Samuel, 233, 273, 281
Peru, 233
Peter Pan (Barrie), 185
philanthropy, 171, 224
Philips Park, 69
Phillips, Pearson, 243
The Philosophy of Sleep (Macnish), 282
Pickles, Eric, 152
Pitlochry, 102
Plato, 78
Plough Green, 70
Plumstead Common, 70
Poitiers, Battle of, 186
Poland, 100, 129
police:
  affection for, 17
  beat constable, 17–23 passim
  characteristic helmets of, 17
  on demonisation of young people, 270,
      272, 273
  in Kansas, 21
  and neighbourhood policing, 20
  patrol cars adopted by, 19
  targets for, 22
  see also crime; Dixon, George; knife crime;
      Morse, Ch. Insp. Endeavour; young
      people
political arithmetic, 146
Pool of London, 107
poor:
  and diet, 231, 234–9
  and soup kitchens, 235, 240
Poor Laws, 171–2
Pope, Alexander, 44
Popinjay (pub), 7
Portugal, 167
potatoes:
  British love affair with, 23
  and Irish famine, 48
  leprosy thought to be caused by, 233–4
  'positive messages' about, 240
pottage, 232, 234, 236, 240
poverty, 169–79
  academic papers on, 176
  and begging, attitudes to, 178
  and belief in a just world, 176–7
  Columbia University experiment
      concerning, 176–7
  child, 125, 175
  definition of, 173
  doubts of existence of, in UK, 172–3

EEC survey on, 169
fault line in understanding of, 169
health problems associated with, 232–3
and immigration, 90
Ipsos MORI focus groups on, 170, 175
LWT survey on, 173–4
and marriage breakdown, 55
as measure of social exclusion, 173
perceived as families' own fault, 170
politics of, changes in, 175
and Poor Laws, 171–2
Reformation marks shift in attitudes to, 170
and Protestant work ethic (PWE), 177–8
seen as 'sin', 172
and underclass, birth of, 172
Powell, Enoch, 98
power napping, 288
The Power of Soap and Water (LNADSK), 218
Pravda, 260
Prescott, John, 74–5, 199, 201–2
Prévost, Abbé, 65
privacy, 43, 46, 218, 221–2
Problem Families Project, 174
profanity:
    as African-American vernacular speech, 263
    in name of God, banned, 258
    see also bad language
Protestant work ethic (PWE), 258, 177–8
    and sleep, 281, 282–3
Provigil, 290
public conveniences, 214, 218–19
    and privacy, 221–2
    Shy Bladder Syndrome experienced in, 221
    as tourist attraction, 219
    see also toilet(s)
public health, 67, 92, 144, 211, 218, 233, 236,
        238, 240
Public Health Act (1848), 218
public open space, 63–75
    Birkenhead Park, 69
    Central Park, New York, 69
    Derby Arboretum, 68
    and Enclosure Acts, 65
    Green Belt, 66
    Henry VIII appropriates, 64
    Hyde Park, 64
    London parks, 64–5
    One Tree Hill, 71
    Peel Park, 69
    Philips Park, 69
    Plough Green, 70
    Plumstead Common, 70
    postwar local authorities attempt to
            restore, 72
    Queen's Park, 69
    Regent's Park, 64, 67
    royal parks, 64–5, 70
    St James's Park, 64, 65
    shopping mall appropriates, 72
    state of grass in, 63
    Tew Great Park, 66

public relations, staged nature of, 190
Public Relations Consultants Association, 46
public relations industry, 46
    apologies constructed by, 47–8
public space:
    changing character of, 19
    as social 'glue', 20
punk movement, 163, 263, 278
Puritan Commonwealth, 258
Puritanism, 64
    arrival of, 257
    and profanity, 258
Putnam, Robert, 244, 245
Pygmalion (Shaw), 260

Qinetiq, 290
Queen's Park, 69
Queensberry Rules, 143

rabies, 37–9
racism, 89, 264
    and rioting, 96
    see also immigration
RAF, 236
railways, 26, 122, 251, 275
    development of, 249
    early opposition to, 249–50
rain-dancing, 229
Rantzen, Esther, 233
rap movement, 263
rationing, 26, 235–6
    and class divides, 237
Rawmarsh School, Battle of, 231
Rayner, Sir Derek, 148, 152
RCDA, 197
RCP, 238
Reagan, Ronald, 81, 165, 288
real ale, 30
Redcliffe-Maud, Lord, 197
Reformation, 170, 178
Regent's Park, 64, 67
Regional Economic Planning Boards, 196
regions, English, 191–204
    and the Great North Vote, 202
    'regional renaissance' of, 201
    and TAFKAR, 204
Reith lectures, 206–7
Remembrance, Festival of, 188
Renaissance, 78
*Report on the Sanitary Conditions of the
        Labouring Population* (Chadwick), 218
Republic of Ireland, 94, 97
republicanism, 182
restorative justice, 49
Restrain Abuses of Players Act (1606), 258
Retiring Rooms, 218
reverse-SAD, 228
Reynolds, Stanley, 262
Rheingold, Howard, 243–4
Rhodesia, Unilateral Declaration of
        Independence, 261

ribaldry, see bad language
Richard I, 186
Richard the Raker, 216
Richards, Keith, 162
Richmond Palace, 217
riots:
   1870, 70
   1958, 96
   race, 96
   2011, 3, 108, 172, 273
Roberts, Sir Stephen, 28
Rolleston, Sir Humphrey, 159
Rolling Stones, 162
Rose, Denis, 160
Rosebery, Earl of, 283–4
Rosenthal, Norman, 227
Rotherham, Charles, 37
Rousseau, Jean-Jacques, 187
Rowan, Sir Charles, 18
Rowntree, Seebohm, 234
Royal Air Force (RAF), 236
Royal College of Physicians (RCP), 238
Royal Commission on Aliens, 92
Royal Family, 182
   as brand, 190
   and the Lord Lieutenant, 201
   media intrusion of, 189
   Royal Parks of, 236
   'soap opera', 189
   Toilet Duck equated to, 190
   value-for-money debate of, 190
   see also Elizabeth II
Royal Institution (RI), 286
Royal Maundy, 188
royal parks, 64–5, 70
royal ritual:
   Princess Diana's death and, 190
   Queen's coronation and, 185–6
Royal Society, 78, 225
Royal Society for the Prevention of Cruelty to
   Animals (RSPCA), 37, 39
Royal Statistical Society (formerly Statistical
   Society of London), 147, 149
   see also statistics
royalty, 181–90
   critique of, 182–3
   and Puritanism, 258
   and republicanism, 182, 183
   see also individuals by name; Royal Family
Rubin, Zick, 177
Ruddles Brewery, 197
Rural District Councils Association (RCDA),
   197
Russia, 129, 144, 167
Rutland, 197–8
Ryno's Hay Fever and Catarrh Remedy, 158

SAD, 227–8
   see also mental health
Saddam Hussein, 48, 167
St James's Park, 64, 65

Sangster, William, 224
sanitation, 213–22
Sarkozy, Nicolas, 86, 87
Savannah Syndrome, 64
Savoy Hotel, London, 235–6
Schkade, David, 229–30
Scholar, Sir Michael, 151, 152–3
school:
   and family break-up, 61
   meals, 231
   meals, free, 235
   'reform', 269
   standards of behaviour in, 278
   see also learning
Schwartz, Norbert, 82
Scotland, 65
   age of criminal responsibility within, 269,
      278
   character of, 207
   devolution in, 195–6
   historically, 193
   and Scottishness, 206–7
   tartans of, see Scottish tartan
Scotland Yard, 160, 270
Scott, Ronnie, 160
Scottish tartan:
   clan, 207
   Englishman designs, 207
   kilts, 207
SCUM, 262
Seasonal Affective Disorder (SAD), 227–8
   see also mental health
Second World War, see World War Two
secularisation, 187
Select Committee on Public Walks, 66
September 11 attacks, 45, 81
7-Eleven, 286
sewage, 213–22
Sex Pistols, 188, 189, 263
sexism, 58, 210, 264
sexual assaults, 13
sexual obscenities, 258
   see also bad language
sexual politics, 220, 262
sexuality, 34, 39, 59, 62
Shakespeare, William, 256–7
Shapps, Grant, 152
Sharia law, 220
Sharman, Julian, 256
Shaw, George Bernard, 260
Shetland Islands, 100, 210
Shils, Ed, 186–7
Shipman, Dr Harold, 143
shopping malls, 72–3
shopping patterns, 284, 287
Shy Bladder Syndrome (paruresis), 221
siesta, 281
   see also sleep
Silicon Valley, 242
silly hats, 205–12
Sims, Chris, 273

Sims, George, 12
Single Convention on Narcotic Drugs, 161
'sit or squat' debate, 220
sleep, 281–91
    attitudes towards, 281–2
    and bed sizes, 283
    and consumer revolution, 287
    deprivation, 281, 283, 284; see also insomnia
    and drugs, 286–7, 289–91
    and electric lighting, 285–6
    experts on, 288
    going without, record for, 286
    and laudanum, 283
    myths, 284, 287
    philosophy of, 282
    pills, 287, 288
    and power napping, 288
    research, 287, 289
    and sloth, 281, 282–3
    and stimulants, 288, 289–90
    time spent, 281, 284
    'trendy' research on, 287
    Victorian attitudes towards, 282–3
    web-based survey of, 285
sleep deprivation, 281
'The Sleep of School Children' (Terman &
    Hocking), 284
Sleepio, 285
Slovakia, 100
Smalley, Sir Herbert, 138
Smith, Percy, 4
social capital, 244–5
social class, see class
social interaction, and Internet activity, 242–6
Social Issues Research Centre (SIRC), 14, 16
Society for Cutting Up Men (SCUM), 262
Society for Investigating the Causes of the
    Alarming Increase of Juvenile
    Delinquency, 274
Soham murders, 50–1, 110
sonic weapon, 271
soup kitchens, 235, 240
South Asian community, 59
    see also immigration
South East Asia:
    drugs from, 164
    tsunami in, 170
Soviet Union, collapse of, 148
Spain, 14, 167, 170
Spear, Bing, 161
Spencer, David, 110
spin doctors, 44
Squidgygate, 182, 183
SS Empire Windrush, 92–3
SS Great Eastern, 123
standardisation, 205
Stanford University, 243, 284
State Opening of Parliament, 205
Statistical Society of London (later Royal
    Statistical Society), 146–7
    see also statistics

statistics, 145–53
    crime, 150
    and knife crime, 118–19, 151
    'lies, damned lies and', 146
    public view of government manipulation
        of, 152
    societal well-being measure by, 87
    and technology, 145–6
    see also Central Statistical Office; Royal
        Statistical Society; Statistical Society
        of London; Statistics Commission;
        Statistics and Regulation Service Act;
        United Kingdom Statistics Authority
Statistics Commission, 150
    see also statistics
Statistics: A Matter of Trust, 149–50
Statistics and Registration Service Act (2007),
    151
    see also statistics
Statute of Winchester, 106
Stevens-Johnson Syndrome, 291
Stiglitz, Joseph, 86–7
Strabo, 224
Stratton family, 66
Straw, Jack, 149
street cred, 265
street lighting, introduction of, 285–6
'The Struggle for Cultured Speech' (Trotsky),
    260–1
Strutt, Joseph, 68
suicide:
    political, 155
    rates, 228
    and weather, 228
Sun, 183, 275
Sunday Times, 174, 276
superfoods, 231, 234
    see also food
'superwoman', 281
    see also women's rights
Swan, 286
swearing/swear words, see bad language
Sweden, 228

taboo words, see bad language
Tacitus, 192, 223
Tackling Knives Action Programme (TKAP),
    117, 119, 120
TAFKAR, 204
Tapscott, Don, 130
Taxonomy of Educational Objectives,
    Handbook 1: Cognitive Domain
    (Bloom), 130
Taylor, Damilola, 111
Teddy Boys, 95, 96
teenager(s):
    and age of criminal responsibility, 269
    becoming a parent while, 61, 278
    and crime, see crime
    demonisation of, 268–78
    and drugs, 163–5, 286–7

teenager(s) – *continued*
emergence of, 275
hypermedia world of, 122
NEETs, 127
rebellious, 188–9, 263
and sleep, 286–7
and underage sex, 61, 278
violent crime towards, 116, 136, 267
see also young people; youth culture
television:
chefs, 254
consumer programmes, 233
ownership, 185, 186, 249
Queen's Coronation shown on, 185, 186
resistance to, 185
at Westminster, 205
see also broadcasters by name; programmes by name
Terman, Lewis, 284
Test Match cricket, 207, 208
Tew Great Park, 66
Thackeray, William, 219
Thames River Police, 108
Thatcher, Margaret, 27, 148, 151
and drugs, 165
and food–health links, ignored by, 238
'North–South Divide' dismissed by, 199
and power-napping, 288
Tillett, Ben, 91
Timbs, John, 208
time travel, 208
time-lapse photography, 4
The Times, 70, 99, 109, 162, 236
Tipperary (pub), 7
toilet(s), 213–22
Ajax, 217
AquaClean, 222
'beacon of relief', 214
communal, 215–16
first flushing, 217, 219
first public, 218–19
foreign, 214, 220, 222
Freud on, 220
high-tech, 222
in Hollywood films, 221
and laxatives, 220
other names for, 213–14, 220
paper, types of, 220
'pods', 222
and prudery, 213–22, 258, 259
and Sharia law, 220
and 'sit or squat' debate, 220
-training, 213, 220
types of, 214, 215–16, 217, 218, 222
and vitreous china, development of, 219
Toilet Duck, 190
Tolstoy, Count Nikolai, 203
tomatoes, thought to be poisonous, 233
Tomlinson, George, 98
Tomorrow's World, 27
Townsend, Prof. Peter, 173

Townshend, Lord Charles, 233
toxic epidermal necrolysis, 291
Trades Union Congress (TUC), 91
Transmitted Deprivation Programme, 174
travel writing, 223
A Treatise on the Police of the Metropolis (Colquhoun), 107
Trooping the Colour, 188
Trotsky, Leon, 260–1
Tudor times:
menus in, 232
mock-, 238
obesity during, 232–3
Tupperware, 223, 230
Turner, S., 174
Turnip Townshend, 233
TV, *see* television
Twelfth Night (Shakespeare), 256–7
'24-hour convenience', 286
24/7 culture, 284, 286, 287
Twin Towers attack, 45, 81
Twisted Wheel, 287
Twitter, 251
2 Live Crew, 263
Twyfords Ltd, 219
Tynan, Kathleen, 261
Tynan, Kenneth, 261–2
typhoid, 218

UCLA (University of California, Los Angeles), 9
Uffington White Horse, 198
umbrella, 223–30
origins of, 224
UN, *see* United Nations
UNCRC, 270
unemployment, 22, 55, 89, 90, 97, 127
United Kingdom Statistics Authority, 151
see also statistics
United Nations (UN), 79–81, 86, 148–9
Committee on the Rights of the Child (UNCRC), 270
General Assembly, 80
and narcotics, 160, 161, 163, 166, 168
Office on Drugs and Crime (UNODC), 168
on statistics, 148–9
UNICEF, 276–7
United States, 15, 123
and narcotics, 158, 159, 163
University of California, Los Angeles (UCLA), 9
University College London, 177
University of York, 290
UNODC, 168
Upjohn, 287
Urban Green Spaces Taskforce, 74
urbanisation, 106
Urubu people, drinking culture among, 9
utilitarianism, 78–9
new, 82–7

Vagrancy Act (1824), 178
Valdemar II, 181
vegetables and fruit:
    as animal feed, 234
    cartoon, 236, 239
    caution surrounding, 233
    during agricultural revolution, 233
    eating, 231–40
    exotic, 233
    'five-a-day', 239
    in France, 232
    fresh, 235
    'grow your own', 240
    Hollywood-style makeover of, 236
    as lowly ingredients, 234
    'magical properties' of, 236
    misshapen, 233
    myths surrounding, 233
    as objects of ridicule, 233
    official guidelines pertaining to, 235
    overcooked, 235, 236, 237
    poor, war and, 235–6, 237
    rationing, 235–6
    in Tudor times, 232, 238
    types of, 233–4
    Woolton Pie, 236
    see also food
Vetting and Barring Scheme, 50
Victims' Advisory Panel, 111
Victims' Commissioner, 111
Victoria, Queen, 37, 123, 283
Vietnam War, 262
    protests against, 81
Vindolanda, 215
Virgin Mary, 186
The Virtual Community: Homesteading on the
    Electronic Frontier (Rheingold), 244
'virtual utopia', 250
vitreous china, development of, 219
vulgarity, 259, 263
    see also bad language

Wales:
    age of criminal responsibility within, 269,
        276
    Celts of, 193
    crime within, 111, 117, 119, 120, 134–5,
        143–4, 166, 171–2, 178, 269–71, 273,
        276
    devolution in, 195–6
    education system within, 124
    Princess of, 190
    unmarried mothers in, 59
    vegetable-eating in, 239
Walker, Peter, 28
Walpole, Sir Robert, 65
Walsh, John Henry, 36
Warren, Patrick, 110
Wars of the Roses, 192
Washington, England, 72–3
Washington State University, 11

Watt, James, 126
WCs, see toilet(s)
weapons of mass destruction, 48
weather, 223–30
    activity associated with, 225
    apparel, 223–30
    Arctic Circle, 228
    Californian, 230
    diaries, 225
    Icelandic, 228
    mood associated with, 227–9
    obsessives, 225–6
    and SAD, 227–8
    and suicide rates, 228
    Tupperware, 223, 230
    and vitamin D, 228
    and 'winter blues', 227
    see also Seasonal Affective Disorder
web, see World Wide Web
Weber, Max, 177, 178
websites, local community, 248
Wedgwood, 219
WELL, 244
Well-being: The Foundations of Hedonic
    Psychology (Kahneman, Deiner,
    Schwartz), 82
well-being and happiness, 77–88
    Bentham's utilitarian take on, 78–9
    British statisticians work on measure of, 87
    Cameron's announcement on, 87–8
    efforts to define, 78
    and Gross Domestic Product (GDP),
        79–80, 86
    left–right thinking on, 83–4
    money as yardstick for, 79
    psychology aims to measure, 82
    wealth fails to bring about, 81, 85–6
Wellman, Barry, 246, 247
Wells, Holly, 50, 110, 111
West Britonism, 209
Westminster Abbey, 185, 186, 187, 188
'Westminster Class', 202
Westwood, David, 51
white bread, 234
White Hart (pub), 7
White Horse, Uffington, 198
Whitehall, see Parliament
Whitehall Well-being Working Group, 84
Whitehouse, Mary, 262
Whittington, Dick, 215
Whittington's Longhouse, 215
WHO, 139, 140, 144, 228, 239
Whole Earth 'Lectronic Link (WELL), 244
whole-foods, 237
    see also food; diet
WI, 244
Wikinomics (Tapscott), 130
Willetts, David, 206
William the Conqueror, 194
William Wilson & Sons, Bannockburn, 207
Wilson, Harold, 98, 147, 196, 229

Windsor Castle, 236
Windsor, House of, 182
winter blues, 227
Winterson, Jeanette, 263
Wired Up Communities Programme (WuC), 247–8
Wirral, rise in drug addicts in, 164
The Wizard of Oz, 182
Wolfgang, Walter, 48
Women's Institute (WI), 244
women's rights, 220, 262, 281
Woodstock, 81
Woolton Pie, 236
Woolton, Lord, 236
Woolwich, Bishop of, 260
working men's clubs, 244
World Bank, 86, 127
World Health Organization (WHO), 139, 140, 144, 228, 239
World Nurdling Championships, 197
World Trade Center, attack on, 45, 81
World War One, 158
World War Two, 26, 55, 56, 79, 196
    food rationing during, 235–6, 237
    outbreak of, 235
    parks and greens ploughed up during, 72
    post-, 237, 274–5
    pre-, 261
    Royal Parks during, 236
World Wide Web (WWW), 241–51
    birth of, 241
    and information technology, 126
    and social interaction, 242–6
    universal access to, 247
    see also Internet; WELL
Worsted Act (1777), 107
WuC, 247–8
wujiao, 282
    see also sleep
Wuthering Heights (Brontë), 260
WWW, *see* Internet; World Wide Web
Wymeswold, 28

X, 253–65
    emotional force of, 253
    as symbol of something, 253

xenophobia, 89
'XXXX', 254

York University, 290
Yorkshire Evening Post, 199
Young, Lord, 47
Young, Michael, 186–7
young people, 51, 263, 267–79
    and adults, dysfunctional relationship between, 267–8, 270, 277–8
    and antisocial behaviour, defining of, 270
    and ASBOs, 276
    charity work carried out by, 278
    and corporal punishment, 268
    and criminal activity, *see* crime; knife crime
    with degrees, 129
    demonisation of, 144, 270–8
    in Europe, 278
    'feral', 108, 268, 271
    Finland's attitude towards, 269–70
    and generation gap, 268–9
    historically, 273–4
    hoodie-wearing, 271–2
    interpersonal violence involving, 144, 267
    media/public perception of, 144, 268–71
    murder among, *see under* murder
    as NEETs, 127
    and pedagogy, 270
    and 'reform schools', 269
    from Third World, 129
    and UN, *see* United Nations
    with mental-health problems, 270
    and youthful rebellion, 275
    zero-tolerance approach towards, 276
    see also teenager(s)
youth culture, 73, 81, 163, 237–8, 263, 275, 278, 286
    see also teenager(s); young people
YouTube, 122, 231

Žižek, Slavoj, 214
Zopiclone, 288